WITHDR~

FROM
UNIVERSITY OF PLYMOUTH
LIBRARY SERVICES

KW-269-645

This book is to be returned on
or before the date stamped below

CANCELLED

16. JUN. 1999

- 5 JUN 2000

UNIVERSITY OF PLYMOUTH

PLYMOUTH LIBRARY

Tel: (01752) 232323

This book is subject to recall if required by another reader
Books may be renewed by phone
CHARGES WILL BE MADE FOR OVERDUE BOOKS

POLICY ADVICE AND ORGANIZATIONAL SURVIVAL

This book has been published with the help of a grant from the Social Science Federation of Canada, using funds provided by the Social Sciences and Humanities Research Council of Canada.

For Karen

Policy Advice and Organizational Survival

Policy planning and research units in British government

MICHAEL J. PRINCE
School of Public Administration
Carleton University, Ottawa

Gower

© Michael J. Prince 1983

All rights reserved. No part of this publication may be reproduced, stored in a retrieval system or transmitted in any form or by any means, electronic, mechanical, photocopying, recording or otherwise without the prior permission of Gower Publishing Co. Ltd.

PLYMOUTH POLYTECHNIC
LIBRARY

Accn No	157638
Class. No.	352.34 PRI
Contl	0566004577

Published by
Gower Publishing Co. Ltd
Gower House
Croft Road
Aldershot
Hampshire GU11.3HR

British Library Cataloguing Publication Data

Prince, Michael J.
    Policy advice and organisational structure.
    1. Public administration
    I. Title
    350   JF1351

ISBN 0 566 00457 7

Printed and bound in Great Britain by
Robert Hartnoll Ltd Bodmin Cornwall

Contents

Figures

Introduction

In public administrative systems around the world the 1960s and early 1970s appeared to be a new age of reason in governing, a period of tremendous faith and optimism in rationality and reform in governmental policies, structures and processes. Systems analysis, corporate management and planning became international catchwords as well as administrative techniques. The blind faith and bold optimism are gone. In many jurisdictions the age of reform already seems over, replaced by a period of retrenchment. This belief has recently been expressed by John Garrett who has drawn attention to the apparently dismal record of administrative reform in Britain. 'Most of the management technology we thought really would modernize British public administration – unified grading, a powerful Civil Service College, corporate management, programme budgeting, programme analysis review, policy planning units, accountable management, performance review, efficiency audits, management by objectives – now lies rusting and forgotten'.[1]

This book is about one of these reforms: policy planning and research units. *Policy Advice and Organizational Survival* provides the first in depth analysis of planning and research units in British local and central government. It brings together a theoretical, historical and practical understanding of this new type of British public organization in action.

The major focus throughout the study is on policy planning and research units as organizations – their origins, functions, staffing, structure and members' attitudes. More specifically, the study is an examination of the establishment and performance of policy planning and policy research organizations in the British system of government. As a study of government planning the book examines the nature of policy advice and research, some operational issues of the planning and research processes and the organizational context of policy advice. Hence the focus considers the organizational and interorganizational setting of policy analysis, the use of research in government, and the integration of a new reform into the public administrative process. The book highlights four aspects of reforms in general and policy planning and research units in particular: the structural, procedural, personnel and philosophical.

This volume should be of considerable interest to policy planners and researchers in central and local government in Britain and in other countries, professional advisers in private research institutes, students and teachers of public policy and administration, politics and sociology, and the main clients of planning and research units, that is, administrators and politicians.

The approach adopted for this study is not a rigorous application of a single model, but rather an attempt to examine policy units from several perspectives in public policy and administration. An organizational behaviour perspective is employed to examine the functions and performance of planning units, the behaviour of individuals in and around them, intergroup relations, the role of perceptions and the mobilization of support. Accordingly, the study is a description and analysis of what actually happens in units. This analysis is based on an investigation of thirty-two policy planning and policy research organizations in central government departments and local authorities, and interviews with more than eighty officials who generously took time to discuss policy advice in government.

Management and organizational theory is used in considering the creation of planning and research bodies, and in examining recent administrative ideas on structural design, staff—line and staff—executive relations and the size of policy planning units. Another perspective adopted is the sociology of professions. The study explores the nascent professionalization of policy advisers and its implications for advisers and their clients. The study also draws on the policy studies literature and considers the work processes of advisers and their contributions to policy formulation, corporate management and decision making. Hence, the book evaluates the planning and research unit from the perspective of policy structure, procedure, personnel and administrative philosophy.

The central theme of this book is that the experience of planning and research units has been the product of a conflict between organizational survival and rational policy advice. This book shows how the tension between these two forces has been handled by policy advisers. The combination of policy advising and organizational surviving creates conflicts between the aims of analytical rationality and structural continuity. Some forms of policy advice designed to rationalize government threaten the very survival of planning and research units. A trade-off therefore emerges between advising and surviving. Rationality and security do not always conflict but there are many situations where these two goals clash and pose problems of choice. Indeed, policy units have adopted an evolutionary approach to developing their role in British government. Considerations of organizational survival and legitimacy have inhibited the development of rational policy analysis. Planners and researchers in these units have been preoccupied with intelligence projects and short term results at the expense of programme evaluation and long term planning.

In addition a number of specific propositions and conclusions arise from the analysis in this study. The policy unit is a distinct and novel type of public organization in Britain. A planning and research unit is a permanent government organization which performs policy oriented staff functions. It is usually small in size, recently established and has an informal bureaucratic style. The reasons for the emergence of policy units in British public administration are numerous both in general and as they apply to specific units, and reflect business management and public administration values. Planning and research units were given ambitious and ambiguous mandates leaving policy advisers to define their objectives in relation to environmental factors. The result is that policy units have undergone a process of goal abridgement, performing only some of their intended functions

Policy unit personnel are generally full time and in permanent positions, relatively young and well educated. As an occupational group they are exhibiting some early signs of professionalism. Policy units tend to be located in the upper hierarchy, and resistance in accepting units as equal partners continues to exist. Advisers are advocates. They emphasize administrative and political feasibility plus other concerns in formulating their projects, and they actively promote acceptance of their work. In terms of impact policy units have strengthened the advisory and learning capacity of governments, improved the status of research officials in government and influenced relations between politicians, administrators and outside groups in various ways.

Many people have contributed to this study. Those who were interviewed provided much information and their co-operation is gratefully acknowledged. Several colleagues and friends offered valuable comments and suggestions: Ed Black, John Chenier, Bruce Doern, Bill Jenkins, Jim Rice, Brian Smith and Jeff Stanyer. A doctoral fellowship during 1976–78 from the Canada Council enabled me to conduct the original research for the study. This book has been published with the financial help of a grant from the Social Science Federation of Canada using funds provided by the Social Sciences and Humanities Research Council of Canada. Carleton University provided funds to assist typing and editorial work. In particular, I wish to thank Trish Donnelly and Monica Wright for their assistance. Finally, and most importantly, I should like to thank Karen, my wife, whose encouragement and efforts were vital to the research, writing and completion of this study.

Michael J. Prince

Note

1   John Garrett, 'Book Review', p.105.

1 Policy planning and research units

Policy research organizations are a fascinating subject, much neglected in organizational theory, political science and democratic theory alike.

Yehezkel Dror

One of the more striking developments in British government in recent decades — but least studied — has been the establishment of policy planning and research units. Whether called branches, divisions or sections, these organizations have been specially established to provide a range of policy and programme advice to policy makers and administrators. The widespread use of policy planning and research units is a relatively recent development in British government. While a few central government departments and local authorities have had such units for a considerable period, it is only in the last ten years that they have proliferated. It seems an opportune time, therefore, to look at some units and assess their impact. There are now sufficient units with substantial experience to provide an important and fruitful area for research. An examination of their success or otherwise, should provide some insights into the efforts of governments to enshrine planning and research into the policy process.

Policy analysis has become a major growth industry in modern administrative systems around the world. The importance of this trend is clear. 'The more pervasive the influence of governments and the larger their investment in research', says David Donnison, 'the more urgent becomes our need to understand the contribution which research can make to policy'.[1] In Britain considerable resources are being devoted to new planning and research structures, processes, techniques and personnel at both levels of government.[2] More than 130 central research and intelligence, and corporate planning units are present in local government. Nearly all social services departments employ their own research staff and other departments in local authorities also frequently have researchers and policy planners. In fact there are over 1,000 officers carrying out various kinds of research and planning activities in British local government. This could represent an annual investment of several million pounds. In general, all the major central government departments and public corporations as well as many other government bodies have a policy planning or research capability. The number of specialist civil servants who are economists, statisticians or research officers has grown to over 1,300 in the central government service. The annual research programme for the Home Office Research Unit alone, for example, involves an expenditure of about one million pounds sterling.

Such investments in policy planning and research units and personnel deserve systematic assessment. Indeed the head of the Home Office Research Unit has said: 'It is legitimate to enquire by what considerations, in terms of practical and ideological aims, the planning of this social research programme is informed'.[3] Furthermore policy units are important to study because an understanding of their present uses may lead to future improvements. To understand these organizations, we must examine their origins, organizational goals, staffing, internal organization, interorganizational relations and various types of effects.

A focus on these units within British government can shed some light on several key issues of public administration. What is the policy planning and research unit in Britain — simply another American fad sweeping past or a meaningful advance in public organization? How do these units actually operate? What kinds of people are in them? What is it like to work in one? How do policy advisers interact with other officials and politicians? What, if any, influence and impacts do units have upon the British political system? Some reliable answers to questions like these can be of value not simply to the appointed and elected public officials who work in and around such units, but to students of organizational behaviour, British government and politics.

For planning and research units the politics of policy advice are the politics of organizational survival. Policy units are a new and distinct pattern of public organization generally characterized by an unclear mandate, low degree of professionalism and hostile environment. While some have great prestige, others have great nuisance value for many public servants, and few can yet be shown to the public or their critics to work as their supporters claim they can. The general thesis of this study is that the exigencies of organizational survival have limited policy units in providing planning and advice. For new advisory units in government, organizational acceptability and policy rationality are somewhat inconsistent. The response of policy planners and researchers has been a compromise in which both organizational continuity and policy rationality are valued and neither takes absolute priority over the other. This compromise occurs primarily through the administrative processes and relations of policy units. An understanding of policy units requires that they be examined in the political and administrative setting of which they are a part, and in the context of the pioneering work on units which provides a foundation for this study.

Foundations of the study

Many writers on British government and politics have drawn attention to the existence of policy planning and research units, but there has been little systematic and comprehensive study of them. The early literature on policy planning and research in British government has been largely concerned with promoting and prescribing the creation of policy units. After diagnosing what is wrong with British government, this type of work strongly recommends a greater capacity to conduct research and planning and usually urges the formation of policy or corporate planning and research units (Grey 1972, James 1973, Robertson 1971, Stewart 1969 and 1971).*

While a prescriptive literature is necessary and understandable for a fairly new type of organization, it lacks a basis of empirical research and a sense of political and administrative considerations. For instance, in arguing for financial planning units in local authorities, A.H. Marshall says the unit staff should be 'able, skilled in their professions, far-seeing, imaginative, sympathetic to the services, precise but not over-meticulous and able to work together and with other departments'.[4] Such writing advances more a view of what should be rather than what can be achieved in introducing administrative reforms. Better diagnosis before prescription is needed on items like the internal structure of units, relations between advisers and other officials, and the reaction of officials to the establishment of policy units. Moreover, there is very little published material which assesses the work of units or their impacts (Leigh 1977).

In the 1960s and 1970s a series of government reports appeared which argued for policy planning and research, and set out the machinery and functions of policy units (Herbert 1960, Fulton 1968, Seebohm 1968, Sharp 1970, Bains 1972, and Greenwell 1973). Despite the numerous critiques of these reports (Grey and Simon 1970, Brown 1971, Garrett 1969 and 1972, Smith 1973, Garrett and Sheldon 1973, and Richards 1974), few writers have examined the actual operation of policy units. Some have, it is acknowledged, documented the extent to which central government departments or local authorities have set up

*References in brackets refer to works cited in the Bibliography.

policy units along the lines of various report proposals (Fry 1972, Stewart 1973, Hinings et al. 1974, Greenwood et al. 1977, and Midwinter 1978a).

The literature on policy planning and research units divides along types of public organization: central government departments, publicly owned enterprises, local authorities and other government bodies. Most of what empirical research there is takes the form of single case studies; a few studies compare a number of units at one level of government or the other. Comparative studies of policy units between levels of government are not examined in Britain, probably because comparative analysis has not been a major thrust in the study of British public administration.

The focus of the published material on policy units in local government has been on the research and intelligence unit of the Greater London Council (GLC). The GLC's Intelligence Unit was established in 1966 and was the first permanent organization for the provision of a comprehensive range of research and information services in a British local authority. In a pioneering article in 1965, L.J. Sharpe examined some of the implications of a research and intelligence unit for the GLC and London boroughs, as well as the more general question of the role of research in local government.[5] Sharpe reviewed the origins of the proposal to establish the Intelligence Unit, discussed how it might operate in practice, and investigated the relationship between research findings and policy making. Subsequent works have described the origins and development, functions and work of the GLC's unit (Carr 1967, Fry 1968, Fry and Martin 1968, Little 1968, Firth 1968 and 1971, Benjamin 1969 and 1970, Self 1971, Watts and Peacock 1971, Foley 1972, Rhodes 1972, Russell 1972 and Kennington 1972). Since 1967, the GLC has published a *Quarterly Bulletin* which provides information on the work and activities of the unit, research memorandum and research reports.

The first head of the GLC unit, Bernard Benjamin, has written a thoughtful and comprehensive book on the research and statistical machinery of local government in Britain (Benjamin 1976). The book is concerned with the problems of organization and organizational behaviour in and around research and statistics units. Benjamin describes the way in which administrators and statisticians should come to terms with the expanded role of research and statistical machinery and advice in policy making. Benjamin stresses that to survive, research and statistics units must endeavour to win the confidence of policy makers and managers. Survival is based on credibility. To establish credibility, in Benjamin's view, involves recruiting a staff of at least three, and consulting with politicians and public servants about the objectives of the unit. Officials need to be assured that the unit will try to improve management and the use of information, but will not attempt to dictate policy.

As units were formed in other local authorities in the late 1960s and early 1970s, published studies appeared on the role of the corporate planning units and research and intelligence units in Kent (Rugman 1973), Cheshire (Lee et al. 1974), Greater London, Birmingham, Cheshire, Kent and Sheffield (Smith 1974), Avon and West Glamorgan (Taylor 1976), a north-western local authority (Kakabadse 1977), researchers in social services departments (Leigh 1975 and 1977, Benjamin 1973, and Booth 1970), and in Scottish local government (Midwinter 1978b).

A recent survey conducted by the Institute of Local Government at the University of Birmingham has produced a descriptive outline of central research functions in local authorities in England, Wales and Scotland (Davies 1979a and 1980). The survey provides basic information on several aspects of the central research capability but unfortunately does not offer a critical investigation nor an analysis of research units as organizations.

There is also a growing body of literature written by policy and research unit personnel which describes their projects and methodologies (for example, Pinkham 1976 and Bentley 1978). This material is of interest for two reasons. Much of it is highly technical and illustrates specialized administrative and policy techniques in action within public agencies. Moreover, some of this literature describes the political and management issues linked to policy analysis and shows how such issues affect the provision of advice.

The seminal work on policy planning and research units in British central government departments is an article by Geoffrey K. Fry published in 1972.[6] Fry described how policy units in ten central government departments were arranged in terms of historical origin, staff size and composition and main tasks. Policy units were found to be relatively small, almost wholly composed of career civil servants, and the unit heads generally of assistant or under secretary status. At the same time, he concluded, the various government departments differ considerably in their approach to policy planning and to the need to have a permanent unit or units formally engaged in such activity. More recent surveys (Razzell 1976 and 1980, and Macdonald and Fry 1980) of the planning units in thirteen central government departments have made similar observations. In particular, Macdonald and Fry state that no planning units of the type proposed by the 1968 Fulton Report on the Civil Service have emerged. Moreover, they assert that the attention paid to policy planning since 1968 has actually consolidated and extended the established procedures of British public administration. The obstacles to administrative reform they identify include the principles of ministerial responsibility, civil servant neutrality, and unity of departmental command, along with wider political and cultural factors in

British society. It is clear from their analysis that the giving of policy advice, especially of a long term kind, is very much a political activity and that to survive and be effective, policy units have had to adjust to their organizational environment.

A small, multi-disciplinary Central Policy Review Staff (CPRS) was set up in the Cabinet Office in 1970–71. The CPRS or Think Tank as it has become popularly known, has attracted more interest than any other policy unit in government due to its proximity to the cabinet and prime minister, and its concern with topical matters. Pieces on the CPRS have been written by journalists (for example, Jay 1972, Fox 1973, and Nicholson-Lord 1978), academics (Heclo and Wildavsky 1974, Pollitt 1974, and Beloff 1977), a politician (Bruce-Gardyne 1974) and CPRS members themselves (Plowden 1973, 1974 and 1976, and Berrill 1978). This published material provides information and opinions on the main tasks of the CPRS, its work programme and methods, staff composition, relations with other policy actors and organizations and some speculations on the impact of the CPRS on the policy process.

There is also a handful of case studies, normally written by civil servants, dealing with individual policy planning and research units in central government departments. The Home Office Research Unit, set up in 1957, has been examined in terms of the factors leading to its creation and development (P. Hall et al. 1974, Lodge 1974) and the content and formulation of its research programme (Clarke 1977, Croft 1978). The crime policy planning organization in the Home Office, established in 1974, has been examined by a former head of the Crime Policy Planning Unit (Train 1977). The analysis identifies factors within the organizational context of the Home Office which influence crime policy planning, and considers the problems of how to relate a planning unit to the rest of a department, what the unit should do, and how the unit should be staffed. In addition, a planning system for the Home Office's Prison Department has been investigated (Garrett and Home 1972). The planning machinery in the Department of Education and Science, and the functions and problems of planning for education have been described by the then permanent secretary (Pile 1974). An administrative history on the development of the planning system in the health and personal social services side of the Department of Health and Social Security (Razzell 1978) illustrates some of the problems faced in established policy advisory units in government. It is clear from these studies that the problems of security and survival are never far away.

Similarly, a recent article on central policy planning and co-ordination efforts in the Department of the Environment (Painter 1980) highlights the ambitious scope and intentions of administrative reforms in the past decade. The article focuses on the central management structures created in DOE to help integrate departmental activities, including a strategic planning directorate. This directorate faced difficulties in defining and relating departmental objectives and was generally frustrated in performing a comprehensive planning role. In contrast, a brief study on the work research unit of the Department of Employment by two officials in that department (Pleasance and Saldanha 1979) basically describes the origins and objectives of the unit, and outlines the different ways it pursues these objectives. The organizational politics of planning and research units is ignored.

A final area of studies on central government policy planning and research units has been the field of foreign policy planning (Bloomfield 1977 and 1978). Policy planners in the CPRS and the Foreign and Commonwealth Office's planning staff have been described and compared with foreign policy planners and planning staffs in several other countries mainly in terms of their own views on policy planning and whether planning foreign policy can actually be done.

Useful information on strategic and policy planning in British government is also contained in some articles by practitioners on public industrial enterprises. Studies have been done on the National Coal Board (Ezra 1973 and 1974, and Sedgwick 1978), the British Gas Corporation (Mills 1974), the British Steel Corporation (Kingshott 1975), British Airways (Wheatcroft 1973–74), and, the British Airports Authority (Turner 1976). Attention has been given to the objectives of planning in a given enterprise, the planning organization, the procedures and techniques used. Finally some literature examines policy research and planning structures and processes in other government bodies such as area health authorities (Brody 1979) or with particular reference to specific policy fields such as housing (Tinker and Brian 1979).

To sum up, the existing material on policy planning and research units in Britain is scattered and reflects an uneven emphasis. There is a dearth of empirical research by students of public administration on the organizational dynamics of policy units and their implications. Aspects of organizational structure and behaviour not satisfactorily considered in the literature which are particularly important for an understanding of policy units include the role perceptions of policy advisers, the organizational setting in which units are located, relations between advisers and other officials and considerations of feasibility in the work of policy units. Furthermore, an overview is needed of the many specialized policy units which have been established throughout British government.

The study of policy planning and research organizations in British government lacks a consistent and coherent vocabulary. This reflects the prescriptive nature of much of the literature, the relative novelty of these organizations, and the absence of a framework for studying these organizations. What we do know of such organizations is fragmentary, non-comparative and unsystematically organized. Avoidance of these faults will be sought, in part, through precise definition of each of the three concepts on which the organizational type is based — policy, planning and research.

Key definitions

A British student of public administration, Brian Smith, has provided the definition of policy found most useful for this study: 'a deliberate course of action or inaction taken by those in office under the influence of values and pressures on the way resources (expenditure and coercion) are to be used in pursuit of objectives or in support of other policies'.[7]

This definition contains a number of important ideas. Policy involves deliberate behaviour to pursue certain objectives. The distinction between action and inaction properly emphasizes that policies can initiate change or resist change. These choices of action are made by those in office, that is, offices of the state or public authority at all levels of government in the political system. 'Public policy', adds Smith, 'is the outcome of decisions about the political allocation of resources and is therefore characterised by the use of legal and coercive sanctions; by being of general concern; and by the application of political values to problem solving'.[8] Moreover, at each level of government, policy can be made at any but the lowest levels of the public service depending on the importance of the issue.[9] There are different kinds of public policy. Policy may involve the authoritative expression of values and intentions, the raising and allocation of resources, the provision of goods and services, and the regulation of behaviour. Policies can vary in terms of value preferences, amount and type of resources, degree of legitimate coercion, and scope of application. Policy is intended to affect all or selected parts of the external and internal environment of the political system. This suggests that 'policy is not a final product but an aspect of an ongoing interaction among the various elements of the social situation', government and private organizations, social groups and individuals.[10]

A policy consists of a series of actions and decisions. A policy is not a single act or decision although one of the more visible aspects of a policy is the formal or official decision selecting one course of action or inaction among various options. This decision is referred to as the policy decision, or policy output, and may be contained in legislation, regulations, memoranda, circulars, policy statements and the like. As a process, the interrelated events leading up to a policy decision can be called policy formulation or policy making. The series of events and activities following a policy decision undertaken to pursue that decision is called policy implementation or execution.

Policy and administration become closely intertwined through formulation as well as implementation and programmes. A programme is a subset of a policy and is often more specific and detailed than the policy decision. In this context, a programme is a concrete course of action intended to put into operation and pursue a policy decision. The actual effects of a policy output or decision when implemented, whether intended or not, are policy outcomes. The determination of the actual effects of a policy is referred to as policy evaluation. The policy process then refers to the overall sequence of interrelated activities which make up and shape the formulation, decision, programme, implementation, outcome and evaluation of policy.

Planning as a government activity is one part of the policy process and is usually a method of policy formulation. In general, planning is the attempt to control or determine the future through present actions. The definition of planning used here is by William Plowden, a past member of CPRS. Plowden defines planning as: 'a flexible and tentative process, in which assumptions are explicit and challengeable, in which alternative responses to a range of possible contingencies are explored and their wider implications examined, as a first-step for decisions'.[11]

Planning is a purposive activity. Planning activities are intended to lead to a pattern of distribution of resources closer to that desired by the government in question than will result in their absence. Often, planning is a continuous and flexible activity done by officials within government organizations on public policy and programme. Planning is a process comprising several related steps such as definition of goals, data collection, analysis and formulation of alternatives. As a public administrative process, planning is important for developing new policies, relating new policies to existing ones and changing existing commitments. Planning is an advisory process of preparing a set of choices for policy decisions to be made and implemented by other elected and appointed officials and organizations. Planning is aimed at achieving more or less specified goals including suggestions on the means for achieving goals. Planning is primarily action oriented and may be seen as applied policy analysis. 'The task of planning is not merely one of visualizing brave new worlds. It is a task of constructing sequences of behaviour that can be carried out and that will bring these brave new worlds into actual being'.[12]

Planning is directed toward the future which introduces varying degrees of uncertainty and involves the use of quantitative and qualitative techniques to predict future events and reduce the uncertainty. Because planning is a tentative and iterative process it can mean different things to different people. Indeed, it can mean different things to the same people at different times. That this dynamic nature of planning has implications for policy unit personnel and organizational survival will be evident in later chapters. Finally, planning is the co-ordination or accommodation of these intended goals with existing policies, interests and available resources. The planning process consists of the whole set of these related activities. A plan is the product of the planning process and may be a formal written document or verbal recommendations and informal advice.

The notion of planning is a kaleidoscopic concept; it is an extremely varied and continually changing group of ideas, techniques and processes. There are many different types of planning and in the last few decades new kinds have appeared. The result is a long and bewildering list: economic planning, social planning, resource planning, connective planning, development planning, town and country planning, military planning, community planning, transport planning, structure planning, regional planning, metropolitan planning, normative planning, comprehensive planning and so on. It seems everything is subject to planning, so how can we begin to evaluate the process?

Planning can be distinguished on at least four grounds which help to highlight its scope and nature.[13] One is the 'organizational space' the planning activity is to apply to and the consequent level of control over the subject of the activity. For instance, the planning process may focus on administrative structures and operations internal to the organization, on the total organization and its external environment. Second is the managerial level that the planning occurs; for example, strategic or directive at the top level in organizations, divisional or project planning at the middle levels, and operational planning at the lower levels. Third is the time perspective over which the planning objectives are to be achieved, such as short term (up to one year), medium term (the next five years or so), long range (usually ten years or more) and futures (perhaps several decades or more). Fourth is the policy field or fields subject to planning which may be a specific policy field like health, several related policy fields subject to a sectoral approach like social policy or a more comprehensive national plan.

While there are many types of planning the main focus here is on two recent reforms in government, namely policy planning and corporate planning.

The term policy planning became popular in central government after the Fulton Committee on the Civil Service devoted a section of its 1968 report to policy planning and policy planning units. The Fulton concept of policy planning was a shorthand expression for long term policy planning and research. Fulton emphasized that research is the indispensible basis of proper planning and that policy planning refers to the assembly and analysis of information required for policy planning, as well as forward thinking, long term planning and expert advice.[14]

The Fulton Committee saw policy planning as largely occurring at the upper levels in government organizations and being applied in all the policy fields of the major central government departments. The time perspective of policy planning was clearly in the medium and long range. They also recognized that some policy planning activities would have implications extending beyond the boundaries of a single department and may need central direction.[15] Nonetheless, the committee emphasized policy planning as an activity within individual departments.

The Fulton concept of policy planning entails a number of elements. The first is the anticipation and identification of the future problems and long term policy objectives of government departments. The second is the study of these problems and objectives. This involves the assembly of information and the use of analytic techniques to evaluate alternative methods of achieving long term objectives. The third is to see that day-to-day policy decisions are taken with as full a recognition as possible of their likely implications for the future and the long term objectives of the central government department.[16]

The writings by J.D. Stewart and others used the term during the late 1960s in the context of local authority policy planning. However, as Stewart notes, corporate planning became generally accepted in the early 1970s as the term to describe planning for the affairs of a local authority as a whole in light of the needs of the environment in which it is situated.[17] A corporate planning approach has also been introduced into central government organizations like the Department of Education and Science, the Department of Energy and the British Gas Corporation.[18] Unless otherwise stated, corporate planning will be used in this study to refer to local authorities.

Corporate planning has been developed at various organizational levels in local authorities.[19] Most of the attention, however, appears to be on senior officer and elected member structures and processes. The time perspective of corporate planning includes the medium and long term, and is often directly involved in the short term, through the annual budgetary process.

While policy planning can frequently apply to only one or a few organizational units, corporate planning represents a deliberate attempt to encompass all local authority activities. Thus, corporate planning tries to secure unity of purpose in the affairs of the local authority by taking an overall view. This form of planning necessarily cuts across all the policy areas and organizational units of the authority and may relate to other public and private agencies in the area. Corporate planning concentrates upon the adjustment of all the activities and available resources (human, physical, informational and financial) of the authority to take account of the needs, problems and opportunities of the people in its area.

11

Like policy planning, corporate planning consists of several elements or stages:

> setting objectives for the authority in the light of problems and needs known and anticipated; and proceeds through

> consideration of alternative ways of achieving those objectives;

> evaluation of those alternatives in the light of the objectives;

> decisions on the alternatives;

> setting targets for managerial action in the light of the alternative selected;

> taking necessary action;

> the review of the results in the light of the targets set; to

> feedback of the results of that review to modify action taken, targets set, alternatives adopted, or objectives set, thus continuing the process.[20]

The concept of research used in this study is influenced by the suggestions of Roger Bennett regarding the relationships between basic and applied research.[21] Bennett emphasizes three aspects of research as an activity in the policy process: basic research, applied research and the translation of basic research findings into practical applications. Figure 1.1 illustrates the relationship between the three aspects.

The two types of research are represented along the vertical axis and the horizontal axis shows their main uses. Point A demonstrates that the major aim of basic research is to generate new knowledge and develop concepts to explain the world we live in and to further our understanding of it. Point B indicates that basic research can also aim towards predicting and controlling events, at least at a theoretical level. The process A–B is called 'inventive' since it is concerned with producing new ideas and theories, and testing their validity.

Applied research can also aim at developing understanding of everyday problems (point C) as well as controlling and predicting their outcomes (point D). The process C–D is called 'reactive' since it is essentially concerned with reactions to problems arising in ongoing situations.

The 'adaptive' process (points B–C) involves the translation of basic research findings into practical applications. New ideas or methods developed in the inventive process A–B are translated into 'useful working principles' to be used in the reactive process C–D.

Bennett's scheme of research types and their uses and relationships illuminates our later inquiries into organization goals and impacts of policy units. It is useful in pointing out that both basic and applied forms of research are necessary and are used in the public policy pro-

FIGURE 1-1
TYPES OF RESEARCH AND THEIR USE

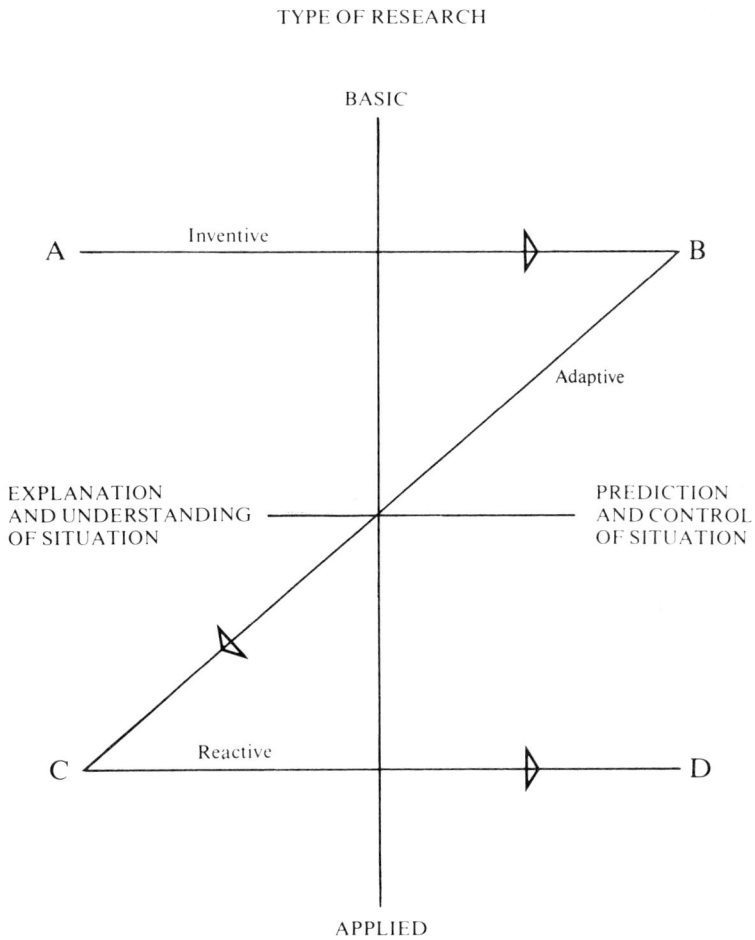

TYPE OF RESEARCH

BASIC

A ——— Inventive ——————▷——————— B

Adaptive

EXPLANATION
AND UNDERSTANDING ———————————————— PREDICTION
OF SITUATION   AND CONTROL
                                    OF SITUATION

C ——— Reactive ——————▷——————— D

APPLIED

source: Roger Bennett, "The Role of Research
in Management Decision Making",
Management Decision, Vol. 12, no. 3
(1974), p. 193.

cess. Another important feature is that a key part of much research activity is the translation of concepts, theories and principles into relevant and practical applications for policy and programmes. Thus, both basic and applied research can have policy and administrative implications. Bennett correctly points out that it is this translation of basic research into practice which many observers overlook in discussions of research.

As we shall see, the words policy, planning and research are subject to wide differences in definition among policy advisers, administrators and politicians, and even among policy advisers themselves. For some, research is concerned mainly with description while for others it is evaluation; corporate planning has been described as a set of techniques and as a philosophy. These differing perceptions constitute part of the reality of public policy advice. In this context then policy, planning, and research are all government activities and processes as well as the outputs of these activities. Individually, of course, policy, planning and research are not new to government. Collectively, however, there is something novel associated with the term 'policy planning and research' — the establishment and proliferation in recent years of government organizations especially to perform these activities.

A new type of organization

So varied are the directorates, branches, divisions, units and, sometimes, local authority departments which have been set up to provide policy planning and research services to politicians and public servants, that formidable problems of classification confront the organization analyst. It seems there is no clear pattern among the officially styled policy planning units nor is it always clear what distinguishes them from some of the other bodies that are called research units.[22] In part, the apparent lack of a clear pattern among these bodies is because there does not exist a framework for defining and classifying policy planning and research organizations in British government. Given the complexity and variety of activities in central government departments and local authorities, it is not surprising that policy planning organizations display diversity.

Official names differ considerably. Local authorities call these bodies, among other things, research and intelligence unit (and variations thereof, for example, intelligence, research and development unit, or central research and intelligence unit), corporate planning unit, programme planning department, central research and evaluation unit, and policy analysis group. The central government uses titles such as long term planning unit, research and planning division, corporate planning and finance division, departmental planning unit, and central policy review staff.

Besides their nomenclature, these organizations differ in terms of their organizational location and context, functions, and the policy and personality context in which they work. Some observers believe that all policy research organizations are different from one another and cannot be compared. While every organization is unique, to some extent, the differences between policy research units are not so considerable as to prevent treating them as a new and distinct type of organization in British government. Differences between policy planning and research organizations are differences in degree, not in kind.

Simon, Smithburg and Thompson, a group of American public administration scholars, once wrote that 'almost any governmental agency that is entrusted with a goal and with very few and ineffective means for achieving that goal is likely to be called a "planning" agency'.[23] To be sure, planning and research agencies are very often small and modestly endowed organizations.

The definition of the policy planning and research unit as a distinct organizational type can be fruitfully approached by distinguishing component characteristics. A distinction can be made between those features that all organizations in this category exhibit, and those features that are, in varying degrees, common to these organizations. The definition attempts to describe the features characteristic to all the organizations under study here as well as to identify the less common features which are influenced by particular circumstances. Such a distinction between 'primary' and 'secondary' characteristics leads to a more detailed and realistic classification and permits a comparison of structures across levels of government. The definition of policy planning and research unit in this study is an empirical, classificational type. The definition is a type in that it is intended to represent a typical or average policy unit in contemporary British government. It is a classificational type in that a number of common and specific characteristics are used to determine which organizations fall within the classification and those which do not. The definition is empirical in that the classification characteristics were derived inductively and refined by the author from the accumulation of data on thirty-two organizations and are intended to correspond as closely as possible to organizational reality. The data were complemented with information from other theoretical and empirical studies of policy units in Britain as well as similar organizations in the United States and Canada.[24]

A policy planning and research unit is an organization that exhibits every one of five primary characteristics and some or perhaps (but not necessarily) all of a number of secondary characteristics.[25] An organization is a policy planning and research unit if and only if it exhibits the following primary features. First, it is a formal and permanent organization. Distinct from nearly all royal commissions, task forces and other ad hoc advisory bodies, policy planning and research units are engaged in the policy process on a more or less continuous basis. Second, it is located within government. A policy unit can be at various levels in government often at a senior and or central position, and can be situated in a department, a central agency or as a separate administrative entity. Third, it is a staff organization. Policy units do not undertake line functions such as administering programmes. A unit provides a paper pure service and transforms the raw materials of information and ideas into analysis and advice as its main output.[26] Fourth, it is a policy oriented staff organization. Distinct from other staff functions like personnel or public relations, a policy unit performs at least one of the functions of policy and programme planning, research, liaison and co-ordination and, occasionally, evaluation. The general purpose of a unit is to improve the process and content of public policy and programme. Fifth, it is composed of one or more people whose sole or primary employment is in that organization. A policy unit may be a single official or a group of officials within an organization or in a separate department.

On the basis of these five primary characteristics, the preliminary definition of a policy planning and research unit is as follows: a permanent, government organization which performs policy oriented staff functions.

For a more complete understanding of policy units, particularly of the similarities and differences between them, it is useful to identify secondary characteristics that units may exhibit in conjunction with the primary characteristics. Any individual policy unit may exhibit any combination of these secondary characteristics. Thus, the closeness of fit between the secondary features and a given unit can vary. Nonetheless, most policy planning and research organizations display the following secondary characteristics. Probably most important, they are organizational newcomers to government.[27] Very few units existed before 1964 and the large majority were established during the early 1970s. Their young age has implications for size and structure as well as other dimensions like goal clarity and staff—line relations. Another secondary characteristic is that policy units are usually small organizations in terms of number of personnel. Very few units have over twenty members and the most common size of a unit is about six or seven people. Moreover, they generally have an 'organic' organization. In large part due to its small size and staff functions a policy unit often has a fluid internal structure, personalized modes of communication, an easy-going work atmosphere and an emphasis on team work. As a small organization it is possible to have face to face relationships between all unit members and for the unit leader to know all the other members.

Thus, a comprehensive definition is obtained by combining the primary and secondary characteristics. A policy planning and research unit is a permanent, government organization which performs policy oriented staff functions, and is also usually new, small in size and with an organic organizational structure and climate.

In addition to these main characteristics, some policy units have in common other more exclusive characteristics. A unit can be subclassified according to the level of government in which it is located and the kind of department. Hence, we may speak of central or local government policy units and social service or personnel department policy units. A further distinction can be made between central policy units which have a mandate with regard to the whole of the central government or of a local authority (like the CPRS in central government or the Central Research and Intelligence Unit in Tyne and Wear), and departmental policy units whose mandate is limited to one department. Departmental policy units can be divided into two subclasses which can be called corporate and programme. Corporate departmental policy units are usually at a senior level with a jurisdiction which spans the whole department. Programme departmental policy units, in contrast, are often at middle or lower organizational levels and are responsible for only a part of the entire departmental mandate.

This definition permits a number of preliminary observations. While policy planning and research units can be described as staff units they are not always part of the executive level in government nor are they necessarily closer to executive officials than line units. Many policy units are linking pins situated between senior management and operational administrators. Corporate planning units and research and intelligence units in local government are often called integrative structures with responsibilities for authority—wide co-ordination of policy analysis. However, there are several varieties of policy units in British government. Many are not central or corporate units but are departmental or programme oriented. Thus some policy units are structures for horizontal co-ordination while others are structures for vertical integration.

The classification type provides a useful framework with which to organize the information and to study this novel and distinct government organization. A classification and set of definitions, however, say little about why governments should engage in policy planning and research, who should perform these activities, in what organizational setting, and for whom. To answer these and other questions, it is first necessary to examine the origins of policy planning and research units in Britain.

Notes

1 David Donnison, 'Research for Policy', p.518.
2 See E.M. Davies, 'The Role of Research and Intelligence'; J.M. Gillespie, 'Whither Local Government Research and Intelligence'; Andrew Leigh, 'The work of social services researchers and its impact on social policy'; and, Home Office Research Unit, *Programme of Research 1977–78*. The estimated expenditures for 1977–78 were £978,999 which included £650,000 for internal unit research and £328,000 for external research supported by Home Office grant.
3 John Croft, *Research in Criminal Justice*, p.1.
4 A.H. Marshall, *Financial Management in Local Government*, p.326.
5 L.J. Sharpe, 'Research in Local Government – the Role of the Research and Information Unit of the Greater London Council', p.3.
6 Geoffrey K. Fry, 'Policy–Planning Units in British Central Government Departments'.
7 Brian Smith, *Policy Making in British Government*, p.15.
8 Ibid., p.15.
9 Desmond Keeling, *Management in Government*, p.16.
10 David Easton, *The Political System*, p.172.
11 William Plowden, 'The Role and Limits of a Central Planning Staff in Government: A Note on the Central Policy Review Staff', p.22.
12 Herbert Simon et al., *Public Administration*, p.448.
13 There is vast literature on planning. For a review of some commonly used definitions and a multi-dimensional definition similar to the one used here, see Y. Dror, *Ventures in Policy Sciences*; Robert N. Anthony, *Planning and Control Systems: A Framework for Analysis;* Kenneth Kraemer, *Policy Analysis in Local Government*; S.D. Walker, 'Planning in the Civil Service', and Jan Tinbergen, *Development Planning*, chapter 2.
14 *Report* of the Committee on the Civil Service, Cmnd. 3638, 1968, vol. 1, para.173.
15 Ibid., para.177. The committee did not consider this question of central direction as it was a question of machinery of government which was beyond their terms of reference.
16 Ibid., para.173. On policy planning see also John Garrett, *The Management of Government*, chapter 4; Robin Hambleton, *Policy Planning and Local Government*, chapter 2; and the Paterson Report on *The New Scottish Local Authorities*, chapter 5.
17 J.D. Stewart, *The responsive local authority*, p.27, footnote 1.

18   For further details see Sir William Pile, 'Corporate Planning for Education in the Department of Education and Science'; and C.E. Mills, 'Corporate Planning in the British Gas Corporation'.

19   On corporate planning in local government see J.D. Stewart, *Management in local government — a viewpoint*; T. Eddison, *Local Government — management and corporate planning*; J. Skitt (ed.), *Practical Corporate Planning in Local Government*; J.D. Stewart, *The responsive local authority*; and R. Greenwood and J.D. Stewart (eds), *Corporate planning in English local government: an analysis with readings 1967—72*. On the differences and similarities between corporate planning in government and business see J.D. Stewart, *The responsive local authority*, pp.39—42; R.J. East, 'Comparison of Strategic Planning in Large Corporations and Government'; and S.D. Walker, 'Planning in the Civil Service'.

20   J.D. Stewart, *The responsive local authority*, p.15.

21   Roger Bennett, 'The Role of Research in Management Decision Making'.

22   Geoffrey K. Fry, 'Policy—Planning Units in British Central Government Departments', p.153.

23   Herbert Simon et al. *Public Administration*, p.445.

24   For those interested in the methodology and a listing of the organizations in the research sample see Appendix A. For discussions on the salient features of think tanks, task forces and research organizations see, for example, Robert N. Anthony, *Planning and Control Systems*; Lawrence W. Bass, *Management by Task Force*; Guy Benveniste, *The Politics of Expertise*; Paul Dickson, *Think Tanks*; Yehezkel Dror, *Public Policymaking Reexamined*, and *Design for Policy Sciences*; Desmond Keeling, *Management in Government*; Arnold J. Meltsner, *Policy Analysts in the Bureaucracy*; Elisabeth Crawford and Norman Perry (eds) *Demands for Social Knowledge*; Ronald S. Ritchie, *An Institute for Research on Public Policy*; and Paul I. Slee Smith, *Think Tanks and Problem Solving*.

25   This approach has benefited from the ideas of Anthony Downs, *Inside Bureaucracy*, chapter 3.

26   The term 'paper—pure' is from Bruce L.R. Smith, *The RAND Corporation*. For a discussion of the concepts 'staff' and 'line' in government see Peter Self, *Administrative Theories and Politics*, chapter 4.

27   Further discussion of the chronology of units is contained in chapter 2.

2 The origins of an organization

*Much light can be shed on the working of a political
system if we take into account the fact that much of
what happens within a system has its birth in the efforts
of the members of the system to cope with a changing
environment.*

David Easton

Behind the birth of any organization is a history of ideas, issues and
interests. Any inquiry into the creation of public service organizations
raises a number of political and administrative questions. Why were
efforts to rationalize the policy process in British government more
prominent over the 1960s and 1970s than in earlier decades? Why the
deep interest with the structure of government when attempting to
improve policy content? Why was a new type of organization, the
policy planning unit, established? What was the thinking behind its
institution? What were the particular circumstances in which these
units were established in British government?

An examination of the origins of policy units touches upon several
important issues of public administration theory and practice. James
Q. Wilson has noted, 'Theories about how organizations behave abound;
theories about how organizations come into being scarcely exist'.[1]
Although Wilson says it would be premature to formulate a theory of
organizational formation, he does suggest two tentative generalizations.
First, the formation of organizations tends to occur in 'waves' or in
large numbers. Second, organizations become more important when
ideas supporting their formation become more important. Testing the
validity of these propositions in relation to the formation of policy
planning and research units may contribute to a better understanding
of the growth and development of British government, the processes
by which public organizations are formed, and the direction in which
public administrative thought in Britain has developed in recent decades.

The reform of government

When the 'what's wrong with Britain?' debate began in the early 1960s, a part of it focused on the machinery of central and local government. The Civil Service was singled out for much criticism because 'there seemed to be something wrong, fundamentally wrong with British government: its operations lethargic, its policies half-hearted, dilatory, and far too often misconceived'.[2]

The Civil Service and machinery of government became the subject of considerable academic and political scrutiny for a number of reasons: (i) the failure to use new techniques, experts and skills developing in the private sector, (ii) the narrowness of outlook, (iii) the lack of long range planning and formal co-ordination, (iv) the reactive style of policy making and, (v) the structural rigidities in the system such as departmentalism at both levels of government and excessive professionalism in local government.[3]

Much public administrative thought in Britain during this period assumed that structural change was a prerequisite for improved policy making and performance. Organizational rationality was seen as a necessary condition for policy rationality. Structure as a main determinant of policy was emphasized in the systems approach to government decision making popularized during the 1960s and early 1970s.

There are several reasons for this preoccupation with structural reforms to improve policy making and performance. Since policy roles are attached to official positions within institutions, a discussion on how to increase the analytic capability of administrators 'becomes entangled in a discussion of the merits or defects of the structure of government'.[4] Secondly, many of the faults of the Civil Service and local government were seen to stem from organizational structure and arrangements. Some commentators argued that structure more than personnel accounted for the defects of government and that structure had a major influence on administrative behaviour.[5] Furthermore, the Civil Service was seen as an obstacle to policy innovation and implementation by both Conservative and Labour politicians. Discussions on how to introduce innovations in government and improve policy execution invariably involved proposals for structural change. Such change was a means to increase the role of elected political leaders in policy making and co-ordination.

Thirdly, the Conservative Party, concerned over the expansion of state responsibilities and the 'steady bureaucratisation' of life, saw reform of government machinery as an opportunity to transfer state functions and activities to the private sector.[6]

Fourthly, public administrative thought in Britain has traditionally regarded government in terms of machinery. This demonstrates a concern with means and processes rather than ends and a view of government as a passive, reactive entity.[7] A belief strongly expressed in administrative thinking during this period was that new structures were needed for new roles (chief executive officer), new processes (corporate and strategic planning) and to ensure old tasks (research) were adequately performed. In short, the belief was 'get your institutions right and the way ahead will be clear'.[8]

From both a political and administrative perspective, organizational change is not merely a means through which policy is executed but can also be an important end in itself. 'It is frequently the case that a new structure or reorganization *is* the policy, or at least one of the most politically convenient policy outputs that can be produced in the short run in response to policy demands.'[9] The interest with structure may point to attempts to cope with a new substantive policy issue and to relate ongoing programmes in different and usually more integrated ways.

The idea of distinct organizations to undertake policy planning and research functions can be traced back sixty years to the Haldane Committee on the Machinery of Government. The Haldane Committee urged that 'A Minister in charge of an administrative Department must have at his disposal, and under his control, an organization sufficient to provide him with a general survey of existing knowledge on any subject within his sphere', and that responsibility for this research and inquiry should be 'in the hands of persons definitely charged with it'. In addition, the committee proposed 'for some purposes the necessary research and enquiry should be carried out or supervised by a Department of Government specially charged with these duties'. Haldane also urged that special attention be paid to the methods of recruiting the personnel to be used for inquiry, research and reflection before policy is made and implemented.[10]

Similar appeals for special structures to perform policy planning and research were periodically voiced over the next four decades. A few such structures like the Economic Advisory Council, the Joint Staffs, and the Central Economic Section were set up. Until recently, however, policy planning and research were unstructured and non-specialized activities in most government departments and local authorities.

During the 1960s and early 1970s the idea of formalized policy units really came into favour in British administrative thinking. The concept of policy units was closely associated with other developments in public administrative thought during this period. In central government, reports like the Plowden Report on Public Expenditure, the Heyworth Report on Social Studies, and the Trend Report on Civil Science argued for more formal processes of policy planning, research and review, and the need for greater input by specialists to government policy making.[11]

In local government, the Maud Report, the Mallaby Report, the

Redcliffe-Maud Report and the Bains Report all advocated the greater use of management services like research and intelligence, and a corporate view of local government.[12] The idea of corporate management implied that the various services provided by a local authority be examined in relation to the needs and problems of the people in its immediate environment and in relation to one another and the authority as a whole. Policy units were increasingly seen by senior officials in local authorities as one type of reform that could contribute to corporate management.[13]

Reports by management consultants for central government departments and local authorities, and academic work also supported the idea of corporate management and planning and its concomitant techniques, structures and processes. One reform frequently suggested was a planning or research unit.

A number of official inquiries into local and central government made specific recommendations for the establishment of policy units. These reports provided the rationale and a principal impetus to the formation of units. In 1960 the Herbert Commission on Local Government in Greater.London said (para.758):

> The first requirement of all is that the Council for Greater London should set up a first-class Intelligence Department. One of the difficulties of the present system ... is that no one is responsible for continuous research into these interlinked problems of Greater London as a whole. There is a vast amount of information in existence but there is no body responsible for knowledge.

In 1967 the Maud Committee on management in local government recommended the setting up of a local government central office, to carry out or promote research and further intelligence and statistics relating to the range of services which local government provides. In 1968, the Seebohm Committee on Local Authority and Allied Personal Social Services devoted an entire chapter in its report to the question of research and proposed that, 'Within each local authority area there is in our opinion a need for a research and intelligence unit to serve all departments of the authority'.[14] And in 1970, the Sharp Committee on Transport Planning stated that, 'Every local authority needs an intelligence section, to provide both economic and social data ... to all departments and undertake research relevant to all the responsibilities of the authority'.[15]

In central government the Fulton Committee on the Civil Service highlighted the need for, and encouraged the adoption of, policy units. The Fulton Committee paid a good deal of attention to the issue of policy planning and research. As Haldane did fifty years earlier, Fulton argued that 'a department's responsibility for major long-term policy-planning should be clearly allocated to a planning and research unit'.[16]

The rationale for policy units

'We consider the general case for research to be undeniable.' This confident statement expressed by the Seebohm Committee epitomised a central belief, held by many administrative thinkers in the late 1960s, of the clear and pressing need for new planning and research structures. Yet Klein and Lewis remind us, 'In trying to trace the origins of institutional innovations, it is always tempting to rewrite Genesis: to search, in other words, for evidence of some deliberate design and clear sense of purpose'.[17] In the case of policy units in British government their design was more or less deliberate though somewhat vague in detail, and their purpose was complex and multifaceted. The various proposals put forward for establishing policy units contained many different reasons and, in some instances, conflicting reasons.

Probably the fundamental rationale for policy units is what can be called the Gresham's Law argument. Gresham's Law states that when functions like long term planning and research are the responsibility of administrators responsible for routine and operational tasks, the administrator will tend to neglect or give only sporadic attention to planning and other non-routine tasks. This general tendency, believed to exist in all types of organizations, was thought to be aggravated in the British Civil Service. Operating in a political environment, civil servants deal with the operation of existing policies, the preparation of briefs, answers to parliamentary questions and ministers' cases, and the consultations associated with the preparation of legislation. It was felt that these tasks drove out the non-routine ones like planning. The Herbert Committee and the Seebohm Committee both expressed concern over the small amount of research going on in local government.

The Gresham's Law argument figured prominently in both the evidence to, and the final report of, the Fulton Committee: 'At present policy-making, especially long term policy thinking and planning, is the responsibility of officers overburdened with more immediate demands arising from the parliamentary and public responsibilities of Ministers'. In discussing the work of civil servants, particularly members of the administrative class, the report stated, 'Almost invariably there are urgent deadlines to be met in this kind of work. In this press of daily business, long term policy planning and research tend to take second place'.[18]

Many commentators during this period observed that planning, research and co-ordination were being neglected. 'The result', Brian Chapman wrote in 1963, 'is that easily foreseeable problems are not considered dispassionately and rationally well in advance, but are dealt with in an atmosphere of crisis by hasty, and frequently ill-considered, emergency measures when they are too pressing or electorally dangerous to be ignored any longer.'[19] To help overcome such crisis problem solving and to ensure planning is a mainstream function in government, the Fulton Report recommended that each major department's responsibility for long term policy planning and research be clearly allocated to a planning unit which should not carry any responsibility for the day-to-day operations of the department.

A second reason is what can be called the responsiveness argument. For some critics long term planning and research was being ignored because of 'an over-riding passivity and attachment to the status quo, attributable perhaps to bureaucratic inertia, perhaps to the amateurism of civil servants, perhaps to the social class interests of the administrators'.[20] Policy planning units were to be thinking organizations, generally active and sensitive to new issues. Policy units were seen as a means to improve the capacity of government bureaucracies to comprehend and respond to public needs and changes in those needs. The Fulton Report argued that the Civil Service must show initiative in working out what are the needs of the future and how they might be met. The policy planning unit was an institutional device to inform the Civil Service of new ideas and techniques, enabling it to be in touch with experts inside and outside government. This argument in central government was a 'technocratic' view of responsiveness. On the other hand, the Seebohm Committee saw its recommended research and intelligence unit in each local authority as being 'responsible for collecting information about the operation of the local public services, the community they serve, and the needs with which they ought to be concerned'.[21] Effective personal social services required research and planning to identify emerging trends, assess longer term repercussions, and estimate the nature of future needs. A unit for collecting information and co-ordinating research in local authorities could provide an overall picture of present and likely social needs of an area and make plans to meet them. In this context, policy units were a means of improving the services to, and the wellbeing of, clients and citizens. For Seebohm, research represented 'important insurance against complacency and stagnation'. This argument was a societal view of responsiveness. The social responsiveness case for policy units was given greater emphasis in local authorities than central government because of the corporate management movement in local government and the nature of the services administered.

A third argument suggested policy units could provide valuable staff assistance to appointed officials, particularly chief executives and senior civil servants. The notion of establishing an independent planning staff as aid to the chief executive officer goes back to classical organization theory in the early 1900s. Fulton's Management Consultancy Group argued for a high level staff to serve the top management of departments for planning and perhaps other management systems like information control. The Fulton Committee recommended that in most

26

departments there be a senior policy adviser as head of the proposed planning unit. The senior policy adviser was needed to assist the over-burdened permanent secretary and partly assume the permanent secretary's responsibility for forward thinking. A similar rationale for policy units was put forth in local government. For instance, at a seminar of local government officers in 1973 on the subject of re-search and intelligence, there was general agreement on the need for an R & I function in new authorities. It was also agreed that such a unit should be answerable and responsive to the needs of the chief executive officer and/or chief officers' management team.[22]

Closely related is a fourth reason: that policy units could enable politicians to extend their influence over the bureaucracy. The senior policy adviser was to be the minister's main adviser on long term policy questions and their implications for the day-to-day policy decisions. Furthermore, the adviser was to have unrestricted access to his or her minister and be free to determine what problems the unit should tackle subject only to the approval of the minister. The Fulton Com-mittee believed that this arrangement 'should provide Ministers with a wider range of expert advice at the highest level than at present'. Fulton saw its recommended planning unit and senior policy adviser as a means to strengthen ministerial control of departmental policy making. Moreover, the *central* policy unit concept was frequently portrayed as a device to allow for greater political/executive input to the co-ordination of public policy and the setting of priorities.[23]

A fifth justification advanced in some government departments and local authorities was the objectivity argument. According to one commentator, the establishment of the Programme Evaluation Group in the Ministry of Defence in the mid-sixties was 'an attempt to create an impartial body of experts to assess objectively the claims made by the three services, particularly where they were in conflict with each other'.[24] Objective, impartial information was seen as superior to bureaucratic and political interests, and could be applied to making policy decisions and determining priorities. In proposing the establish-ment of the Central Policy Review Staff the 1970 White Paper on Central Government Reorganisation said the CPRS would present to ministers 'information on a basis free from purely departmental con-siderations' and evaluate as objectively as possible 'the underlying implications of alternative courses of actions' that are being considered. A similar argument was made in local government, where officers spoke of the need for a 'think tank' in their local authority.[25]

A sixth reason advanced for policy units was the co-ordination/con-trol argument. The Seebohm Committee partly based their case for research on the need for co-ordination between decisions and services. 'Decisions in one field must also affect the situation in others. Research techniques now exist which allow these interrelationships to be investigated, and in this way they provide an opportunity for developing co-ordinated planning over much wider fields.' A central research unit could help achieve co-ordination among various researchers and policy planners in a public agency, and help remedy or prevent errors of policy co-ordination. Policy units were seen as a means for controlling or co-ordinating policy and resource decisions taken within a single organization or possibly a set of organizations. They were also seen as a vehicle for relating departmental policies to the government's policies as a whole and thereby reinforcing the collective or corporate responsibility of ministers or chief officers. This emphasis on co-ordination is closely linked to the corporate approach which has pervaded administrative thinking at the local level in recent years. The corporate approach generally assumes a single management entity, a unity of purpose and generally accepted criteria by which to control policy execution.[26]

That policy units would secure greater efficiency in policy planning and research activities was another argument. Setting up specific organizations to perform policy planning and research functions was justified on the grounds that the fragmentation of scarce and expensive research resources was wasteful. Such fragmentation of research could lead to the diffusion and potential duplication of effort, inconsistencies in work, and missed opportunities to apply new concepts in various policy fields. Moreover, operational departments often face similar kinds of data and technique problems, and methods developed in one are often applicable in another. The specialization of research and planning was often linked with administrative efficiency and effectiveness. Specialization would permit greater skill and expertise to be developed within policy units in the performance of their functions. It would encourage better use of scarce resources. However, not all students of public administration agreed that policy planning and formulation could become more effective separate from administration. Professor E.N. Gladden has said, 'the widespread current inclination to separate planning from administration is to divorce from a major activity one of its essential ingredients and thus to carry specialization to unrealistic lengths'.[27] Professor Gladden believes planning is so central to government management that it should not be made a separate activity in its own organization. He feels there is a real danger that planning will become widely accepted as a process desirable on its own account rather than as an aid to management.

A less common argument was that separate planning and research organizations would clarify the lines of responsibilities and contribute to accountable management in government. Both the Fulton Report and the Conservative Government of the early 1970s emphasized the idea of accountable management. The creation of a policy unit was a way of linking planning and research with accountability. Policy units were not only needed to ensure that planning and research functions were done but also to permit an assessment of their performance. Policy units would enable the responsibility for these functions to be clearly defined and allocated to officials who could then account for their performance.[28]

A ninth reason advanced for specialized policy units is the career argument. In its investigation of specialists in the Civil Service, the Fulton Committee concluded that the career prospects of the research officer class were 'unduly depressed'. The research class includes officials employed in the collection, analysis and interpretation of information in the social sciences. Four features illustrated the unsatisfactory position of research officers in the Civil Service: they are often poorly used and confined to a back room role far removed from the main stream of policy decisions; the work they are asked to do is frequently of a quality below their capabilities; they are often without routine clerical assistance; their career prospects in their class are far inferior to those of the economist class and also to those of the administrative class.[29]

The Fulton Report argued that research should be recognized as an essential component of their recommended policy planning units and that the introduction of the units would help to provide better career opportunities for research officers. In addition, policy units could offer attractive short term opportunities in government to 'outsiders'.

The career argument was invoked more in local government for justifying the need for policy units because a career structure for research personnel (statisticians, economists, research officers) as existed in central government was completely absent in local government. A report issued by the Society of Town Clerks in 1973 argued for research and intelligence units partly on the grounds that such units, if large enough, could 'offer an attractive career structure to qualified staff who would otherwise have only very limited outlets in the field of Local Government. This will apply particularly to the statistician, the economist, the sociologist, operational research specialist, etc.'[30] Policy units were seen as providing career structures for these skills and permitting local authorities to compete better with central government and industry in attracting specialists.

Related changes

During the 1960s and 1970s there were many reforms in the structures and policy processes of central and local government which contributed to the establishment of policy units. These related changes represent a larger wave of government adaptation and innovation that provided a supportive climate for the introduction of policy units.

The central government's adoption of a public expenditure survey committee (PESC) system in 1961, and the introduction of planning programming budgeting systems (PPBS) in a few central government departments and in some local authorities, was a major stimulus to the development of resource and policy planning systems. These systems were efforts at improving the analytical component in budgeting and thus highlighted the need for a more co-ordinated approach to policy planning and management. A few policy units were established partly as a result of the requirements of these new budgeting procedures.

The trend toward central—local government joint planning of activities was another factor encouraging government to strengthen their planning capabilities. In 1961 local health and welfare authorities were asked by the Ministry of Health to formulate ten year plans for the development of their services. Four years later the Ministry of Housing and Local Government asked local housing authorities to prepare multi-year estimates of housing needs and programmes. This trend toward more comprehensive planning continued into areas like physical planning, education, public transport and social services. Local authorities were increasingly being asked to plan five to ten years ahead for their services. This placed demands on both local authority services and their corresponding central government departments to develop long term policy planning capabilities.

The establishment of the Government Economic Service in 1964 was another factor contributing to the formation of policy units, enabling a number of central government departments to establish 'teams of economists under high-level direction' who can contribute towards policy planning and analysis.[31] Likewise, the Civil Service Department (CSD) played an influential role in the formation of policy units within central government departments. From the CSD's establishment in 1968, a key feature of its work was on planning and research systems. The attention of the CSD's machinery of government division especially in its early years 'concentrated on the planning machinery in departments, the way in which it operates and skills on which it calls, in the light of the Fulton recommendations on planning units and senior policy advisers'.[32]

While the government has not been requiring departments to set up policy planning units, the CSD had been encouraging the formation of administrative arrangements for both planning and research.

Other developments in central government supported or facilitated the formation of policy units. The Civil Service College founded in 1970 started to train civil servants in policy analysis and planning. The policy planning and research machinery in a number of departments has come under scrutiny as part of the programme of management reviews instituted by the CSD in 1972, to improve the efficiency of operations and to assist senior management. A central focus of these reviews centres on planning, resource allocation and control systems. The creation of giant departments like the Department of the Environment has 'made it particularly important for the Prime Minister and members of the Cabinet to have better tools for policy review'.[33]

Some policy units in the Civil Service were established partly as a result of the requirements of the programme analysis and review (PAR) system introduced in 1971. A main objective of PAR was to complement and strengthen the analytic base for public expenditure planning and allocation decisions through a greater emphasis on defining programme objectives, measuring programmes in output terms, and presenting alternative choices of action. PAR was designed to provide ministers with improved information to make decisions about resource allocation across the government as a whole and thereby encourage ministers to assume a more active role at the cabinet committee level in policy fields outside the domain of their departments. This led to new demands being placed on members of cabinet and senior officials in departments. Policy units were set up to help officials meet the demands of the PAR system.

Undoubtedly the development which most facilitated the establishment of policy units in many local authorities was the corporate management and planning movement which swept through local government during the 1960s and early 1970s. One major feature of corporate management was that the clerk to the authority should be recognized as the chief executive of the authority and be responsible for the co-ordination of policy at the officer level and provide leadership in policy formulation and management systems. The chief executive should concentrate on securing a co-ordinated approach to policy advice, planning and authority affairs. As Margaret Lomer has said, 'the new concept of the chief executive as a major policy advisor rather than an administrative co-ordinator meant that a structural change in management was required'.[34] In particular, the chief executive would require a research and intelligence unit and/or corporate planning unit to assist in this policy advisory role.

Hence the introduction of policy units was but part of a larger wave, perhaps a tidal wave, of reform in the British governmental system. Policy units were swept along in the reform current and established in all types of public agencies. This has meant the reputation and success of policy units is linked to the performance of other related changes. In some cases it seems likely units were an unanticipated part of administrative reform. This raises doubts about the commitment behind the origins of such units and suggests an explanation why the initially supportive climate for this new organization form quickly changed.

Where policy units originate

Against the background of administrative thinking and institutional and policy process changes, policy units arose within a number of specific circumstances. Units such as the Housing Analysis and Monitoring Unit (HAMU) in the Department of the Environment (DOE) and the Planning Unit in the Health and Social Services side of DHSS were set up to develop a green paper or conduct a particular policy review. Originally seen as temporary, such units were often formalized into ongoing organizations.

A few units were established as the direct result of demands from the social environment. An example is the Systems Analysis Research Unit (SARU) in DOE. SARU was set up by an interdepartmental committee in response to the publication of *Limits to Growth* projecting world trends in population, resource availability and environmental effects; the resulting public debate; and the Stockholm Conference on the Human Environment held in 1972.[35]

Several units were created due to the efforts of politicians who regarded policy formulation as important and hoped to institute major policy and/or wanted additional support staff assistance to operate their department. In central government Barbara Castle established the Research and Planning Division in the Department of Employment in 1968, and Anthony Crosland set up the Planning Branch in the Department of Education and Science in 1966. Of the policy units in local government examined, only the Central Research Unit at Newcastle City originated from the efforts of councillors. The Newcastle unit was set up by a group of progressive members in the Labour majority who wanted to have a louder voice in decision making and civic administration.

More frequently, the impetus for policy units has come from appointed officials. The Central Research and Evaluation Unit at Avon was initiated by the director of personnel and management services. The Research and Intelligence Unit set up in Kent was largely due to the efforts of an assistant clerk. The units at Exeter, Lambeth, Cheshire, Sunderland and Tyne and Wear were set up as the result of efforts by the clerk or chief executive officer. In many of these cases the officer advocating a unit had come from another local authority, often a London borough, which had a policy unit. The initiative for the establishment of the crime policy planning organization in the Home Office in 1974 came mainly from an assistant secretary and deputy secretary in the criminal department. They felt, as did other officials, that a formal organization was needed to take a broader and longer term look at criminal justice policy. Similarly the impetus for the formation of the Planning Unit in the Ministry of Agriculture, Fisheries and Food (MAFF) in 1970, came from officials within the agriculture and food policy groups, who believed there were some advantages to setting up a separate unit responsible for policy planning.

Some policy units were introduced at the outset or shortly after the establishment of a department. The Economic Planning Staff in the Ministry of Overseas Development in 1964, the Planning Branch in CSD in 1968, and the research sections in many Seebohm social services departments in the early 1970s are examples. Moreover, the reorganization of a department or part of a department, following changes in the structure of government or a management review, has involved the establishment of policy units. An example is the Policy Analysis Division in the Treasury which was set up in 1975 following a management review.

The origin of a few policy units is rooted in administrative politics and functional decentralization within a large department. In the Department of the Environment a strategic planning directorate (later renamed the central policy planning unit) was established to aid the top management of that giant organization. Yet various functional directorates in DOE asserted the right to conduct their own policy planning and review functions in part to offset the central capability and in part because 'they came to be seen as a way of staking a claim for resources and attention, or shifting policy in a new direction'.[36] Thus policy review was effectively delegated to line branches away from the departmental centre. A transport analysis and monitoring unit was set up in 1976 and a similar one in housing the next year.

A number of policy units originated from proposals contained in management consultant reports. A & C Management Consultants Ltd recommended a planning system and unit for the Prison Department of the Home Office. Recommendations from a study by Urwick, Orr and Partners Ltd led to the establishment of the research and intelligence unit at Sheffield. Reports prepared by McKinsey and Co. led to the formation of programme planning departments in Liverpool and Greenwich. Islington set up a planning and programmes office following a recommendation by the consulting firm Booz, Allen and Hamilton International Inc., and the PE Consulting Group investigation of Swindon led to the appointment of a corporate planner as part of the development and corporate planning group.[37]

In several local authorities and a few central departments, it appears that a necessary condition for the establishment of a policy unit was the prior existence of other management services like work study, Organization and Methods and Operations Research. In the cases of Cleveland, Cheshire, Kent, South Hampshire and the DHSS, the existence of management service units paved the way and they were expanded into policy units. Management services like O&M predate corporate planning and research as generally acknowledged government management functions. Thus, if a local authority or central government department did not have these more traditional services, it seems unlikely they would suddenly adopt policy planning and research by themselves. The prior existence of other management services could demonstrate the utility of related services, serve as precedents for the formation of new units, and identify senior officials favourably inclined to the application of management techniques.

Another factor contributing to the establishment of policy units is legislation requiring or enabling a research capability to be set up. A section of the Criminal Justice Act 1948, enables the Home Secretary to spend money on grants for criminological research. This reflected a change in the general attitude toward criminological research which, in turn, partly led to the founding of the Home Office Research Unit in 1957.[38] Other general legislative provisions for research to be undertaken at the central and local levels include the Education Act 1944 (section 82), National Health Service Act 1946 (section 16), Health Visiting and Social Work (Training) Act 1962 (section 2) and the Children and Young Persons Act 1963 (section 45). Kathleen Slack has commented, 'It is clear in these instances that if there is the will there is the way for research, necessary for the formulation or re-formulation of social policy, to be undertaken'.[39] In addition, the recommendations of the Royal Commission on London Government to establish a central fact-finding unit resulted in a section in the 1963 legislation establishing the Greater London Council which required the Council to set up an intelligence department. Similarly, the Local Government Act 1972, enables a county council to carry out research and collect information on any matters concerning the county.[40]

No single factor explains fully the emergence of policy units. They were usually set up as a result of a mixture of different factors and influences. For example, in one local authority examined, the formation of a policy unit was determined by a series of events: in 1968 a new chief executive was appointed with a policy adviser and co-ordinator role based on the Maud and Mallaby Reports; the chief executive brought in a management consultant firm the next year to examine the departmental organization of the authority and among its recommendations the consultants proposed the formation of a research unit. The chief executive and the management consultant's report were important factors in why the authority set up a unit. Contributing factors were that other progressive authorities were setting up such units and that policy units were part of the contemporary wisdom in British administrative thought. In central government as well the formation of policy units has frequently been the result of a combination of influences — thinking within a department, the attitudes of the minister and permanent secretary, the Fulton Committee's recommendations, encouragement from the CSD and the experience of other departments.

Some government agencies have ignored or rejected the call to establish central policy planning units. A 1978 survey sent to all local authorities in England and Wales plus Scottish regions and districts, found a substantial majority, 259 or 68.5 per cent of 378 authorities that replied, do not carry out central research work.[41] Why? Exploring this situation can highlight the factors which determine whether or not a policy unit is established.

In a survey conducted in 1973 of 172 local authority social services departments, nearly half (84 authorities) did not employ research staff.[42] Some interesting patterns were found in those authorities which did not have research personnel. The smaller the population served, the less likely it was that an authority would have a research unit. A similar pattern appeared in the case of expenditures on the social services departments, although the relationship was less marked. Significant differences existed between authorities with no research staff and the type of authority. While about half of county boroughs and county councils did not employ researchers, only a few London boroughs had no research staff. Likewise the 1978 survey earlier mentioned found the highest percentage of authorities with a central research unit to be the metropolitan counties and London boroughs while the lowest rate was in metropolitan and, in particular, non-metropolitan districts. As the Bains Report suggested, it is more likely for a central research or planning unit to be set up at the county level than in district authorities.

In examining the introduction of corporate planning units in the London boroughs, Mike Clegg found that six boroughs had rejected management consultant advice, and decided not to initiate corporate planning or establish a unit.[43] Clegg contends the boroughs rejected the corporate planning system because elected members thought it would reduce their influence. Clegg's analysis points to the importance of member support if a corporate planning unit is to be established.

In the early 1970s the London Borough of Camden, like many other local authorities, introduced a PPB system. As Enid Wistrich documents in a comprehensive study of the reorganization and programme planning reforms in the borough, 'Camden however did not propose to centre this work in a large planning unit within the Chief Executive's department, preferring to draw on the work of officers in various departments coordinated and directed from the centre'. Moreover, Camden did not set up a chief officers group for planning purposes as had most London boroughs. Wistrich suggests two reasons why the idea of establishing a planning unit was discarded in Camden. First, the chief executive's view of his own role and style of work was that it was preferable to act through informal and *ad hoc* discussion rather than by the exercise of authority. Second, the chief executive's role conception was reinforced, at least in his view, by the frequent shifts in party political control of Camden Council. The majority group changed from Labour in 1964–65 to Conservative in 1968–71 and back to Labour in 1971–74. It was thought that in such a situation long term plans could be 'radically altered' by a change in political control.[44]

Coventry was one of the first local authorities to adopt a formal corporate planning approach. However, no central corporate planning or policy analysis unit was set up to support the process. The chief executive wanted to play the role of co-ordinator, retaining direct lines of communication with chief officers, to develop a corporate view of the authority's policies. J. Skitt points out 'the Coventry experiment relied heavily on the personality and determination of the chief executive and his ability to provide effective leadership'. Moreover, 'the alternative of setting up a chief executive's department was considered but discarded because it was felt that such central control would have tended to destroy the role of other chief officers, interfere with departmental management and, therefore, would have failed to provide a corporate spirit among all officers'.[45]

These case studies provide empirical support for the argument made earlier that the main impetus for the establishment of policy units has come from demands and supports generated by officials within the British political system itself. More specifically, these cases demonstrate the importance of personalities, the role conceptions of key policy actors, and organizational relations within government in understanding the emergence of policy units. Other factors, of course, influence decisions to establish or not to establish a policy unit. One important factor is the real or perceived availability of human, financial and technical resources in an organization to carry out policy planning and research. This is arguably the main reason why many local authorities, especially at the district level, have not set up policy units. It would be improper to conclude, however, that public agencies which reject policy units completely reject change. While many authorities have not established a permanent unit they frequently make use of temporary structures, new techniques and new processes of policy review and planning. Instead of pursuing major administrative reforms through the introduction of new organizations and specialists, a reliance largely on existing arrangements may be preferred and can be used to realize policy and administrative changes.

A review of the machinery of British central and local government over the post-1945 period suggests that the emergence of policy units falls into three distinct periods.

In the first, the years 1945–64 were characterized by the formation of only a few units scattered over the period. By the mid-1960s there were just a handful of specialist policy units in central departments and even fewer in local authorities. Examples are the Research Unit set up in the Home Office in 1957 and the Planning Staff in the Foreign and Commonwealth Office in 1964. The Central Statistical Office set up by Birmingham City Council in 1948 was virtually alone in local government.[46]

The second phase, beginning around 1964 and ending in the mid-1970s, can be described as the boom period with the widespread establishment of policy units. This period can be subdivided with respect to the two levels of government. In central government the greatest concentrated growth in policy units occurred over the 1968–72 period. The units set up then were often called Fulton or post-Fulton units, indicating the impact of the Fulton Committee's recommendations on planning units and the encouragement of the Civil Service Department. In local government the greatest concentration of growth in the number of policy units appears to have been over the 1973–75 period, in and around the time of local government reorganization and the setting up of new local authorities.

The third and most recent period, encompassing the later half of the 1970s and into the 1980s, is characterized by a sharp decline in the establishment of new policy units and the disbanding or reorganization of existing units.

The formation of policy units since 1945 clearly indicates a trend or pattern which is not random. In part, the pattern of growth of policy units in British government can be explained by changing fashions and ideas in public administrative thought. While the idea of the policy unit can be traced back to the Haldane Report, it did not really come into favour until the 1960s and early 1970s. The creation of most policy units coincided with this favourable thinking.

Units established before the boom period served as examples of the new fashion. Staff from the older units, especially in local government, went to other authorities to set up new units. Given the concentrated growth of policy units over the last decade in Britain, it seems 'there is an internal dynamic or law of bureaucratic proliferation that operates to generate additional research entities. The appearance of such new research organizations in the past decade is probably to some extent the inevitable concomitant of the growing specialization and complexity of the decision-making process. But also to some degree there has probably been a tendency for the particular organizational form to become 'modish'.'[47]

Several departments and local authorities reacted in a bandwagon fashion in establishing policy units. The rationale behind some units was that the organizational form was modish, other departments and authorities were setting them up, and officials wished to exhibit a progressive, modern image.

Most policy units, therefore, are organizational newcomers to British government. The widespread creation of distinct organizations to undertake policy planning and research functions has been a recent development and has taken place in a concentrated fashion and large scale. The pattern of growth of policy units supports Wilson's hypothesis that the formation of organizations tends to occur in waves and that organizations become more numerous when the ideas supporting their establishment become popular.

Sources of government reform

Numerous writers have attributed the rise in government reforms to the quickening pressures of change in the modern world. The accelerating rate of change has created new and more complex and interrelated policy problems, aggravated old problems, widened the gap between expectations and governments' abilities to satisfy those expectations, made incremental change increasingly irrelevant, placed increased time demands on executive politicians and senior officials and provided new and better ways to solve problems. Changes in the environment of government did encourage reforms of government structures and processes. Both academics and practitioners in public administration acknowledged the influence of the environment on their thinking and actions with respect to government reforms. Public and political dissatisfaction with Britain's performance especially in economic and foreign affairs, led to criticisms of government and considerations of administrative reform and greater planning in the 1960s.[48]

A distinction should be made, however, between the broad environmental trends that provided the general and favourable conditions for calls of reform and organizational change, and the specific factors, usually personal and institutional based, that directly influenced the formation of policy planning and research units. Much of the work on policy reforms speaks only of broad environmental trends, neglecting the more particular factors and situations in which policy units have arisen. By themselves, environmental explanations are too general adequately to account for specific government reforms. They lack an historical context and ignore the role of administrative thought and actors within the political system.

Most policy units are the result of structural withinputs, that is, officials within the political system promoting changes in the machinery of government. Structural withinputs derive only indirectly from the social environment and 'deal mainly with matters of structural reorganization within the political system itself'.[49] Policy units are set up or not largely because of demands and supports generated from within the British political system by politicians, their advisers and civil servants, with supporting roles played by academics, management consultants and business representatives.

The primarily withinput nature of the formation of policy units is evident from a number of observations. The administrative thinking and writings of the 1960s and early 1970s was largely by and for academics and government practitioners. In the main, it was not aimed at the general public nor did it raise much public interest. Richards suggests that reforms of structure and management techniques in government 'may well arouse less public interest because such issues are specialized and arouse far less emotion than attempts to alter a county boundary'.[50]

An important stimulus for the creation of policy units came from a number of government reports calling for a more rational approach to policy making with some of these reports making specific proposals for policy units. Quite often the impetus for these reports came from within the political system rather than inputs from the environment. Examples include the Plowden Committee set up as a result of the efforts of Treasury officials, the Maud and Mallaby Committees set up by the Ministry of Housing and Local Government at the request of four local authority associations, and the Fulton Committee set up as a result of a parliamentary committee report drawing attention to poor recruitment into the Civil Service. Critical writings by academics, politicians and civil servants on British government were also an important stimulus.

Several interrelated institutional and process reforms within government provided an impetus towards the establishment of policy units. Many of these other reforms were also withinputs. PESC, PAR and the CPRS were largely self-induced changes about which the public knows almost nothing. 'No public outcry has created them', Heclo and Wildavsky state, 'these reforms are firmly rooted in insiders' dissatisfactions with the immediate past.'[51] This view is supported by Smith and Stanyer in their general examination of recent administrative reform and change in British government. They offer the provocative conclusion that 'reform arises from political demands or political expediency, and the language of rational discovery is a façade. The political demands need not be simply partisan; they may arise from power struggles within the system of government'.[52] We can add that such demands may also arise from power struggles within the larger political system. In at least a few cases, policy units were set up within government so that government could counteract and be less vulnerable to the criticisms of outside organizations such as political parties and interest groups that had developed the resources and skills to analyse public policies. Thus, units could be partly viewed as a defence mechanism for government.[53]

Individual actors within the political system provided an important impetus toward the adoption of reforms and, more specifically, the establishment of policy units. In his study of reforms in British government, Frank Stacey asks, 'how do we account for the quickening pace of reform in the years from 1966 to 1974?' In part his answer is that the 1950s and the early 1960s was a period of relatively few reforms although many of the reforms in the 1966—74 period originated in those earlier years. Stacey suggests that 'Harold Macmillan, as Conservative Premier from 1957 to 1963, seemed to be largely unconvinced of the need for reform'.[54] J.H. Robertson, a former private secretary to the secretary of the cabinet goes even further and asserts, 'Conservative administrations between 1951 and 1964 had had no coherent philosophy of government reform'.[55]

It is debatable whether the Labour administration between 1964 and 1970 or the Conservative one from 1970 to 1974 had a coherent philosophy of government reform. However, government reform was a popular ideology and both administrations had a relatively more coherent approach towards machinery of government reform than the Macmillan administration. For whatever reasons, both Harold Wilson and Edward Heath as prime minister supported the need for reform, expressed broad reform preferences and sponsored a number of major administrative changes.[56]

The idea for policy planning and research units has its roots in British administrative thinking during the first decades of this century. It was generally argued that policy units in central government were necessary to ensure the long run was not forgotten in the political context of day-to-day administration; to encourage responsiveness to new techniques and ideas; to aid cabinet ministers; to formalize the lines of staff accountability; and to improve the status of research specialists. In the world of local government, policy units were proposed to encourage responsiveness to community needs; to assist senior managers; to promote co-ordination or a corporate approach; and, to create career prospects for various policy specialists. Thus different reasons were put forward for establishing policy units in central and local government. Such reasons as efficiency, control and accountability reflect a business management philosophy. Yet policy units are based not only on private sector managerialism; their rationale also rests upon special problems of public administration, organization theory and an emerging policy studies literature. Whatever the intentions lying behind these organizational innovations, their real nature today was significantly determined by the various processes of translating those ideas and intentions into reality.

Notes

1 James Q. Wilson, *Political Organizations*, p.195.
2 Michael R. Gordon, 'Civil Servants, Politicians and Parties: shortcoming in British policy process', p.35.
3 R.G.S. Brown, *The Administrative Process in Britain,* chapter 2; and Frank Stacey, *British Government 1966–1975*, chapter 7.
4 R. Rose, *People in Politics*, p.106.
5 See Alexander Grey and Andrew Simon, 'People, Structure and Civil Service Reform'; and R.G.S. Brown, 'Organization Theory and Civil Service Reform'.
6 David Howell, *A New Style of Government*. See also Christopher Pollitt, 'Rationalizing the Machinery of Government: The Conservatives, 1970–1974'.
7 See Rosamund Thomas, *The British Philosophy of Administration: A Comparison of British and American Ideas 1900–1939*.
8 N. Johnson, 'Editorial: The Reorganisation of Central Government', p.1.
9 G. Bruce Doern and V. Seymour Wilson (eds), *Issues in Canadian Public Policy*, p.342.
10 *Report* of the Machinery of Government Committee (Haldane) Cd. 9230, 1918, paras. 60, 13 and 14(b).
11 *The Control of Public Expenditure*, Cmnd. 1432 (1961), *Report of The Committee on Civil Science*, Cmnd. 2171 (1963) and *Report of The Committee on Social Studies*, Cmnd. 2660 (1965).
12 *Management of Local Government, Staffing of Local Government*, Royal Commission of Local Government *Report*, vol. 1, Cmnd. 4040, and *The New Local Authorities.*.
13 R. Greenwood (ed.) *Conference Papers on Management and Administration in the Local Government Service: 1969–70.*
14 *Report* of the Committee on Local Authority and Allied Personal Social Services (Seebohm), Cmnd. 3703, para.466.
15 *Transport Planning: The Men for the Job*, para.55.
16 *Report* of the Committee on the Civil Service, 1966–68 (Fulton), Cmnd. 3638, vol. 1, paras. 173 and 149.
17 Rudolf Klein and Janet Lewis, *The Politics of Consumer Representation*, p.11.
18 *Report* of the Committee on the Civil Service, para.172.
19 Brian Chapman, *British Government Observed*, p.19.
20 M.J. Hill, *The Sociology of Public Administration*, p.157.
21 *Report* of the Committee on Local Authority and Allied Personal Social Services, para.466.
22 David L. Smith, 'R & I INLOGOV'.

23 *Report* of the Committee on the Civil Service, paras. 184, 187 and 285. Also see Peter Bowden, 'Structure and Creativity: A Civil Service Hypothesis'.

24 Hugh Hanning, 'Our first defence need is better machinery for taking the big decisions'.

25 *The Reorganisation of Central Government*, Cmnd. 4506, paras. 46 and 47. See also David L. Smith, 'R & I at INLOGOV', and J.M. Gillespie, 'R & I Debate'.

26 E.G. Nelson and D.A. Longbottom, 'Planning for Effectiveness in the Social Services – An Appraisal of the Corporate Approach'.

27 E.N. Gladden, *Central Government Administration*, p.280.

28 *Report* of the Committee on the Civil Service, p.105, para.12 and paras. 145–62. See also *The Reorganisation of Central Government*, paras. 11–12 and John Garrett, *The Management of Government*, chapter 7.

29 *Report* of the Committee on the Civil Service, vol. 1, p.155, para.31.

30 A.J. Greenwell et al., op. cit., p.3.

31 Sir Alec Cairncross, 'Economists in Government', p.2.

32 *CSD Report 1969*, p.45. See also, *CSD Report 1971–73*, pp.10–13.

33 Peter Self, *Administrative Theories and Politics*, p.132.

34 Margaret Lomer, 'The Chief Executive in Local Government 1974–1976', p.21.

35 See the report issued by the Cabinet Office, *Future World Trends*, and Sir Peter Baldwin, 'The Use of Operational Research and Systems Analysis in Government Decision-making', pp.17–18.

36 Martin J. Painter, 'Policy Co-ordination in the Department of the Environment, 1970–1976', pp.144–5.

37 See John Garrett and Norman Home, 'A Planning System for the British Prison Department'; John Garrett, *The Management of Government*; B.C. Smith and J. Stanyer, 'Administrative Developments in 1970: A Survey', p.432; and, R. Greenwood et al., *New Patterns of Local Government Organisation*, pp. 48–51.

38 T.S. Lodge, 'The Founding of the Home Office Research Unit', pp.12–13.

39 Kathleen Slack, *Social Administration and the Citizen*, p.88.

40 See London Government Act 1963, section 71, and the Local Government Act 1972, section 151.

41 E.M. Davies, *The Central Research Function in Local Government*, pp.62–3.

42 Anne Wedgewood-Oppenheim, 'A Look at Research Staff in

Local Authority Social Services Departments'.

43 Mike Clegg, 'Corporate Planning, Corporate Planning Units and Planning Departments'.

44 Enid Wistrich, *Local Government Reorganisation: the first years of Camden*, p.241. The importance of political fragmentation on council and the chief executive's philosophy in explaining the rejection of a planning unit is illustrated in a case study of Cambridgeshire County Council. See John Barratt and Simon Merrington, 'Cambridgeshire: an attempt to improve corporate planning without a unit'.

45 J. Skitt, *Practical Corporate Planning*, pp.228 and 229.

46 See D.L. Smith, 'Research and intelligence in the new local authorities'.

47 Bruce L.R. Smith, *The RAND Corporation*, pp.90—1.

48 See, for example, Donald A. Schon, *Beyond the Stable State; Report* of the Committee on the Civil Service, volumes 1 and 5; R.G.S. Brown, *The Administrative Process in Britain*; R.J. East, 'Comparison of Strategic Planning in Large Corporations and Government'; and Michael R. Gordon, 'Civil Servants, Politicians and Parties'.

49 Richard J. Van Loon and Michael S. Whittington, *The Canadian Political System*, p.368.

50 Peter G. Richards, *The Reformed Local Government System*, p.141.

51 H. Heclo and A. Wildavsky, *The Private Government of Public Money*, p.265.

52 Brian Smith and Jeffrey Stanyer, *Administering Britain*, p.266.

53 Phoebe Hall et al., *Change, Choice and Conflict in Social Policy*, pp.78—9.

54 Frank Stacey, *British Government 1966—1976*, p.2.

55 J.H. Robertson, *Reform of British Central Government*, p.6.

56 See Harold Wilson, *The Labour Government 1964—70*, chapter 1; and George Hutchinson, *Edward Heath*, chapter 13. See also G.K. Fry, *The Administrative 'Revolution' in Whitehall: A Study of the Politics of Administrative Change in British Central Government Since the 1950s*.

3 Organizational goals

Whilst there is merit in starting in a small way with a central unit where the authority has not previously co-ordinated research and intelligence, it will be important at the outset to define the aims and role of a central unit.

Society of County Clerks,
Report on Research and
Intelligence in the New
County Councils

The goals of policy planning and research units serve as a convenient and useful starting point for organizational analysis. Goals help define relations between units and other organizations, provide a source of legitimacy for a unit, and serve as a standard to appraise organizational performance. Goals also provide a standard to compare the fit between the goals advocated in administrative thought and those actually adopted by units, and to compare policy units. Furthermore, the study of goals can highlight the forces affecting organizations.

Official ideals and actual practices

A central feature of all organizations is their orientation toward goals. An organizational goal is a desired future state or condition, a guiding image held by particular individuals which the organization as a whole tries to attain. Organizational goals help define the general purpose and the *raison d'être* of an organization. Two different types of organizational goals can be identified, namely, official goals and actual goals.[1] Official goals are the stated goals and broad purposes of an organization. They are usually contained in annual reports, planning documents, position statements and other official documents, as well as official and/or public statements by members of the organization. Actual or operative goals are the general aims towards which the organization's members actually guide their operating policies and actions. This distinction raises the question, to what extent are the official goals also the actual goals of any given policy unit?

The goals that have been prescribed for policy units in recent British administrative thought can be compared to the official and actual goals of the units under study. A case study of the development of a policy unit's goals is presented to illustrate the interactive process of goal setting. A major reason for presenting the aims and goals of policy units is that much of this information has never been available to a general audience.

Interviews with unit members as well as some unit clients provided valuable information on the perceptions that officials have of the actual organizational goals of units. Various documents of the policy units such as annual reports, internal working papers and organization charts were examined to supplement the interviews. The documents enabled an analysis of unit decisions and unit development. Information on the amount of resources (financial, material and human) available and the allocation of these resources within units was also collected, wherever available, to help determine the degree and direction of effort toward organizational goals.

The Fulton Report recommended the creation of a planning unit or units for each major department in the central government. The units were to be clearly responsible for a department's major long term policy planning and research. More specifically, the report said that planning units should be equipped to assemble and analyse the information required for its planning work. Their main tasks would be to identify and study the problems and needs of the future and the possible means to meet them; it would also be their job to see that day-to-day policy decisions were taken with a recognition of their likely implications for the future. The report added: 'The staff of Planning Units should develop close contacts with the appropriate experts both inside and outside the Service. They should be aware of, and contribute to, new thinking in the field. They should also be trained in, and have the capacity to use, the relevant techniques of quantitative analysis'.[2]

Since the planning unit should not be responsible for the daily operations of a department, the Fulton Report said it would be important for a unit 'to ensure that it does not become too much detached from the main stream of the department's work'. Finally, the units 'should also provide an environment in which those who possess qualities of imagination and foresight can be identified and developed'. While the Fulton Report recognized that in some departments with diverse activities, like the Home Office, it might be necessary to have more than one planning unit, the basic concept and goals of the units were to be the same from department to department.[3]

46

The Bains Report on the management and structure of the new local authorities discussed both the question of research and intelligence units and corporate planning units. It observed that at the county council level, 'a strategic information and research function may well develop which might require the creation of a central Research and Intelligence Unit staffed by suitably qualified officers'. Rather than set out its own general model of an R & I unit, the Bains Report included the goals of an existing unit, in a county council. The objectives of that unit were to provide effective information for managers; miscellaneous intelligence; a consultancy service to departments; and corporate planning.[4]

The Bains Report advocated a corporate approach to local government management and structure to create a sense of unity of purpose within authorities. The report stated: 'there should be a realistic attempt to plan ahead on an authority-wide basis, to formulate objectives, evaluate alternative methods of achieving those objectives and measure the effectiveness of ultimate performance against those objectives'. To facilitate the planning and monitoring aspects of corporate management, Bains supported the idea of a corporate planning unit with a terms of reference something on the following lines: identification, formulation and review of objectives; evaluation of short term programmes aimed at achieving those objectives; consideration of priorities within those programmes as between different services; formulation of proposals for linking presentation of objectives, programmes and budgets; developing longer term plans; monitoring and reviewing progress as against plans.

These terms of reference were taken from an existing interdepartmental Corporate Planning Group comprised of the deputies of all the departments in one county council. Bains believed that such detailed and sophisticated terms of reference would not be justified in some district councils.[5]

In 1973, the Society of County Clerks prepared a report for its members on 'Research and Intelligence in the New County Councils', with particular reference to the Bains Report. The Society of County Clerks' report recommended the establishment of a central research and intelligence unit in each authority. It noted that from the experience of European statistical bureaux, and the beginnings of central units in English local authorities, certain defined needs for research and intelligence services were emerging from which it was possible to recommend the definition of the role for a central unit. The report therefore recommended that a central R & I unit in a new county council should have the following three main tasks: (a) common information and forecasting services, especially for population and census data, (b) research consulting services, and (c) corporate planning support services.[6]

Administrative thinking in Britain during this period articulated an ambitious number of goals for policy planning and research units at both levels of government to pursue. The interested observer must therefore consider to what extent these administrative philosophies were reflected in the official mandates of policy units established in British government.

The Central Policy Review Staff (CPRS) was formed in the Cabinet Office and began work in February 1971. The terms of reference of the CPRS were set out in a White Paper, *The Reorganisation of Central Government*, issued by the government in October 1970. The White Paper set out the role of the CPRS as follows:

> Under the supervision of the Prime Minister, it will work for Ministers collectively; and its task will be to enable them to take better policy decisions by assisting them to work out the implications of their basic strategy in terms of policies in specific areas, to establish the relative priorities to be given to the different sectors of their programme as a whole, to identify those areas of policy in which new choices can be exercised and to ensure that the underlying implications of alternative courses of action are fully analysed and considered.
>
> The new staff will not duplicate or replace the analytical work done by departments in their own areas of responsibility. But it will seek to enlist their co-operation in its task of relating individual departmental policies to the Government's strategy as a whole. It will, therefore, play an important part in the extended public expenditure survey process described below, and it will also be available to promote studies in depth of inter-departmental issues which are of particular importance in relation to the control and development of the Government's strategic objectives.[7]

The Home Office Research Unit, established in 1957, conducts and supports research on criminal policy and social policy like community relations, and on the criminal process, the causes of delinquency, the misuse of drugs and the treatment of offenders. The role of the Research Unit has been officially described recently as follows:

> The Research Unit provides a comprehensive service of research and professional advice in the social sciences, including criminology. It initiates and carries out research for administrative purposes or for formulation of policy. It provides information to the Home Office about research in the social sciences, encourages and assists such research by universities and other organisations, and considers applications for research grants.[8]

The Research and Planning Division of the Department of Employment was formed in 1968. The division is responsible for the following tasks: giving day-to-day professional advice (economics, psychology and statistics) to policy divisions, advising on and co-ordinating the research programme and commissioning external research. In addition, research is undertaken internally by members of the staff.

The purpose of research projects commissioned or undertaken by the Department are fourfold: to meet the research needs of policy divisions; to increase the Department's understanding of basic problems in its area of responsibility; to build up knowledge required for the formulation of policy; to evaluate, monitor and examine the impact of particular measures.[9]

The Systems Analysis Research Unit (SARU), located in the Department of Environment, was set up in 1972. As a central body of research expertise within the Civil Service, the role of SARU is to provide the facility for appraising methodologies in forecasting, modelling and projection construction on the global scale and over the long term, that is, into the 21st century. The terms of reference of SARU fall into three parts: evaluation of global modelling studies carried out by other research groups; investigation of the potential for modelling methods to study interacting global problems; studies of specific resource problems using analytical and simulation methods.[10]

The Department of the Environment also has a Central Policy and Planning Unit (CPPU) which services the Department's Policy and Management Group. The group meets weekly under the chairmanship of the permanent secretary and provides the secretary of state with advice on major policy and management issues relevant to the whole Department. The mandate of CPPU is quite detailed and wide ranging. One role is to service the Policy and Management Group and help it to co-ordinate the policy advice of the various functional directorates and to ensure that such advice is consistent with general departmental policies. Another duty is in consultation with the appropriate directorates, to organize the drafting of submissions, reports and papers on policies which span several directorates and where no other directorate can naturally take the lead. Third, CPPU, where appropriate, and at the request of the group, is to provide the chairman or secretariat, or both, of internal departmental task forces and working parties. Moreover, CPPU is to identify needs for contingency plans, and to plan ahead; to liaise with Central Policy Review Staff; to co-ordinate the Department's contribution to the Programme Analysis and Review (PAR Programme); to ensure information systems are available for selected transdepartmental issues, such as progress of legislation. Finally, the unit is expected to co-ordinate the Department's interests in Energy Conservation.[11]

While the official goals of policy units in local government are equally ambitious in scope they are partially different in emphasis.

In Cleveland, the Research and Intelligence Unit was established and fully operational in April 1974. With about twenty-five permanent staff, the Cleveland R & I unit is probably the largest in any authority outside Greater London. The activities of the unit are available to officers and members of the county and the four district councils in the county. The unit's activities are contained within the following stated goals: to assist management to determine its policy and actions scientifically by providing an operational research service; to collect, maintain and distribute series of statistical information; to provide statistical analysis and forecasting services; to provide a social research service to keep the councils informed of the social conditions and opinions of their citizens; to provide advice and assist with the resolution of organizational and behavioural problems; to provide economic and general research services; to determine the research requirements of the five local authorities and co-ordinate the meeting of these needs.[12]

In the London Borough of Greenwich a Programme Planning Unit was set up in 1970 following the proposals of a study by management consultants the year before. Its purpose is to help elected members and officers in preparing a corporate or community approach. Specifically, the unit has been responsible for the following four main functions: the co-ordination, editing and production of much of the original material in the planning section of the community plan; research and analysis on behalf of committees and directorates; a central support and monitoring service through the presentation of regular network charts for a number of capital projects; the preparation and submission of periodic implementation reports to all service committees geared to the formal presentations on progress and results concerning most items in the community plan.[13]

In Wales, the Mid Glamorgan County Council established the Intelligence, Research and Development Unit in the Clerk and Chief Executive Department in 1974. The principal functions and objectives of the unit have been outlined by the County Clerk and Chief Executive as follows:

> The Unit has some purely Departmental functions, as well as functions relating to the corporate work of the Authority. Within the Department it helps by giving advice and interpretation on matters, generally technical, outside the normal scope of my Department, and also provides a library and intelligence service which is growing as the Unit's library and information collections develop. In the corporate sphere, the Unit has one broad objective, which is to seek to ensure that the best intelligence is available to policy makers at the right time. It seeks to achieve this objective

by ensuring that the Authority's own research and information facilities are appropriate to requirements and that it is kept fully informed of the results of research and development work carried out elsewhere.[14]

The metropolitan district council of Sunderland established a Programme Planning Unit in 1972, which later became a separate department. According to the Programme Planning Manager for Sunderland, the department has the following terms of reference. First, the design, implementation and development of the corporate planning system (known here as Achievement Planning); that is to say, the preparation of the annual budget which sets targets and priorities for all the Council's activities and relates them to the committees' stated objectives for three years, and quarterly reviews of achievement. Second, the development of community analysis/planning particularly in the inner urban areas of greatest need. Third, policy analysis of particular issues and policies for members, chief officers and committees, and providing advice for policy formulation and implementation. Fourth, general research and intelligence and support services especially for members either individually or in groups. And, technical support and servicing of the Management Review Sub-Committee.[15]

What are we to make of this maze of goals and objectives contained in the official statements and descriptions of planning units? A number of general observations and conclusions can be drawn.

In describing the arrangements of policy planning units in central government as they were in 1971, Geoffrey Fry concluded: 'the various government departments differ considerably in their approach to policy planning ... To some extent this diversity follows from the range and complexity of government activity'. Fry added that there was no clear pattern among the officially styled policy planning units. 'Perhaps, given the diversity of governmental activity and functions, the Fulton Committee discussed planning units with too great a degree of generality'.[16] However, to some extent there is a pattern in the official goals of policy units. In general, policy units do not carry any responsibility for the daily operations of existing policies and programmes. Their goals are designed to be separate from the administrative and executive tasks of departments and agencies. A number of the goals prescribed in administrative thinking are evident in the terms of reference of most policy units. At the same time, there are differences and variations in the range of unit goals, as well as other goals not envisaged by Fulton, Bains and other reports.

In connection with central government the official goals of policy units generally correspond with those recommended by the Fulton Committee. While none of the central government units contains all the Fulton goals in their mandate, the majority of policy planning units have, in one form or another, four of the Fulton goals. These are as follows: to identify and study future problems and needs; to be aware of and/or contribute to new thinking in the field; to see that daily decisions take account of future implications; to develop contacts with experts both inside and outside the Civil Service.

The relatively close correspondence between the Fulton goals and the official goals of policy units in the Civil Service is not surprising. The biggest growth in the number of central government policy units was during the five years following the publication of the Fulton Report in June 1968. To a large extent, the rapid growth of policy units in the Civil Service over the 1968 to 1972 period reflects both the impact of the Fulton Committee's recommendations and the Civil Service Department's active encouragement of such units.[17]

Two of the goals mentioned in the Fulton Report have not been widely incorporated into the mandates of policy units. The goal of using the relevant techniques of quantitative analysis is contained in the terms of reference of only a few units, such as the Systems Analysis Research Unit in the Department of the Environment and the Policy Analysis Division in the Treasury. However, it could be argued that this goal is implicitly contained in the mandate of other central government units like the CPRS in the Cabinet Office and the Research and Planning Division of the Department of Employment. Nonetheless, the role of statistical methods for planning and research was not usually reflected in the official goal statements of policy units. Furthermore, the goal that a unit provide an environment in which those who possess qualities of imagination and foresight can be identified and developed is not mentioned in the remit of any central government policy unit, although most units at both levels of government have embraced this as an actual goal in their internal organization.

A number of central government policy units have official goals not recommended in the Fulton Report. For example, the Central Policy Planning Unit (CPPU) in the Department of the Envrionment has the following two goals in its terms of reference: to co-ordinate the Department's contribution to the Programme Analysis and Review (PAR) Programme and to liaise with Central Policy Review Staff. The CPRS is another example of a unit having goals not proposed by the Fulton Committee. A key role of the CPRS is to play an important part in the extended public expenditure survey process.[18] The fact that the public expenditure survey is a pre-Fulton government process helps to demonstrate the particular and relatively narrow view that Fulton had of planning and policy planning units.

The Fulton Committee concentrated upon planning as long term policy formulation and review. Fulton saw policy units as concerned with the planning and research into future departmental problems and needs. This view of planning emphasizes the determination of long term policy aims, the assembly and analysis of information in order to develop alternative strategies for achieving the aims, and the monitoring and reviewing of current policies in relation to likely implications for the future. The Fulton concept of policy planning units emphasized what may be called a long term policy analysis view of planning, ignoring other Civil Service planning activities like resource allocation, economic analysis, administrative policies and management planning.[19]

There is some uncertainty over whether the main purpose of policy planning units in central government is to be centres of creative thought or to provide a bridge between the creative ideas of others and the executive activities of departments.[20] An examination of the official mandates of central government policy units provides no single answer. Some units such as the Home Office Research Unit and SARU in the Department of the Environment are intended mainly as research bodies to develop and analyse ideas and information. Other units like the CPPU in Environment are expected to provide co-ordination between organizations and between the ideas of others. Then again, such units as the CPRS, and the Research and Planning Division in Employment profess goals related to both innovation and co-ordination. This diversity reflects the complexity of government activity as well as differences among planning units themselves.

The official goals of local authority policy units generally correspond to those recommended by the Bains and the Society of County Clerks' Reports. Most local authority policy units have intelligence goals concerning common information and forecasting services, and research goals about consultancy services. A majority also have some form of goals with respect to corporate planning and/or corporate support services. While Bains suggested that detailed terms of reference would not be justified for corporate planning units in some district councils, the goals of the units in the five district authorities examined here were just as detailed as those for units in counties and London boroughs.

These reports had a significant impact on the development of corporate planning units and research and intelligence units. In large part, the close correspondence between the goals recommended by Bains and the Society of County Clerks on the one hand and the units' officials goals on the other, is resultant of the widespread establishment of policy units in local government over the 1973 to 1975 period. However, many of the corporate planning goals listed by Bains have not been widely adopted by local units. In general, these units have only a few of the goals related to corporate planning units as identified by the Bains Report. Probably the most common corporate planning goal is to assist departments or the authority in setting policy and programme objectives. Thus, there are some general patterns in the official goals of local government units. Intelligence and information services, research consultancy services and some corporate planning support services are evident in the terms of reference of most local units studied.

At the same time, considerable variations exist in the scope and mixture of local government unit goals, including goals not mentioned by the Bains Committee or the Society of County Clerks' Report. The R & I Unit of Cleveland, for example, has to provide advice and assist with the resolution of organizational and behavioural problems. The Cleveland unit is developing means of studying and improving interpersonal relationships within officer–member working parties and officer project teams.

Broad similarities appear between the official goals of central and local government policy units. The general purpose of policy units in British government is to improve the process and/or content of public policy and programmes. Units have staff oriented goals which are important for the policy process. Common goals of policy units at both levels of government relate to planning, usually of a long term nature, information collection, research or research advice, keeping abreast of new developments and liaison and co-ordination.

The most important difference between the official goals of central and local government policy units is in the area of corporate planning, that is, planning for a department or authority on an integrated basis. While a few units in central government have goals related to corporate planning like the CPRS and Corporate Planning Branch in Energy, local government units display a relatively greater concern and interest in corporate planning, objectives and priorities.

Official goals indicate administrative philosophy, early expectations and the general direction that policy units intend to move. They are less useful in describing what form policy planning and research processes do take, what information elected and appointed officials do require and receive, and how future problems are actually detected and related to daily decisions. Indeed, the organizational theorist Charles Perrow suggests, 'the type of goals most relevant to understanding organizational behaviour are not official goals, but those that are embedded in major operating policies and the daily decisions of the personnel',[21] namely, actual goals. The actual goals indicate what an organization is actually trying to do irrespective of what the official goals say. The idea of actual goals is an umbrella concept which includes a number of components. The components to be examined here are goal clarity, goal setting, organizational survival and the relationship between service goals and survival goals.

The goals of policy units in British government are distinguished more for their ambiguity than their clarity. Information related to unit goals has been incomplete or unavailable. There has been a general uncertainty both on the part of unit staff and on the part of others who interact with them about what the unit and its staff should be doing and how they should be doing it. A number of observers have noted the goal ambiguity of policy planning and research units.

In a study of planning units in central government departments, E.J. Razzell found, 'not a great deal of thought or research was put into their terms of reference'.[22] The Society of County Clerks have observed, 'Most research and intelligence units brought into existence in local government appear to have been created with no clear statement of their objectives'.[23] The society has noted that the realization of the need to rationalize information and policy planning systems in local government has not been accompanied by a clear understanding of what tasks should be assigned to a research and intelligence unit; where it should be located; how it should be staffed and the number of staff needed; and how its activities should be controlled. In a study of corporate planning units in the London boroughs, Mike Clegg found that in discussions with representatives from planning departments 'there appeared to be a good deal of ignorance about the work that the units were undertaking'.[24] Although most planning department officials were aware of the existence of a corporate planning unit within their authority they could not provide details about the unit. J. Skitt has also noted that a surprising number of senior officers know little about corporate planning and corporate planning units in their authorities.[25] Finally, on social services departments in local government, Andrew Leigh has concluded that the best ways of using the various skills of researchers have yet to be fully understood by policy makers.[26] Does role ambiguity matter? Is it not sometimes advantageous to have vague goals?

That the official goals of policy units have been stated in general and broad terms is understandable, since at the time most units were set up there did not exist a detailed set of ideas about how policy units should or could operate in specific organizational settings. In some cases policy units were established because they were 'modish'. As a consequence, officials usually had no clear idea of what a unit was intended to do. In some instances unit goals were deliberately ill-defined. This was done for a variety of reasons: so as not to constrain unduly the scope of activities which could be derived from the goals, to create and maintain a mystique around the role of the unit, and so as not to upset certain officials. The lack of information about policy units may also be a result of the belief held by some officials that units are not an important element in the operation of a department or a local authority.[27]

In both central and local government, the tendency has been to allow the officials charged with bringing policy units into being, normally the unit director, to indicate how the organizational goals will actually be pursued. Officials in many units stressed that their first job was to decide what, in fact, were the unit's responsibilities and how it should operate. The unit head in one local authority said: 'there was no blueprint when I arrived. I was given some general guidelines but the role of the unit was left to me to decide'. A former and original member of the CPRS said that on 1 February 1971, the first day of the CPRS, 'we sat around a table and Lord Rothschild asked: what are we going to do?'.

Policy units have not experienced total goal ambiguity. For example, the head of a unit in a county council recalled, 'when it was established, this unit was seen as a convenient source of statistics for the Clerk'. An official in a central government unit remarked that policy makers viewed that unit as a second source of advice on particular departmental issues and problems.

In general, planners and researchers believe other officers hold four expectations toward policy units. First, officials expect policy planners and researchers to be bright young people, offering more ideas than other officials, since they are free of operational duties and have the time to think. Second, unit personnel think other officials expect that some of their ideas will be wild and outrageous, again because unit staff are free from operational duties. Third, other officials expect these ideas will be subject to several drafts and redrafts and consultations. Fourth, many officials, at least initially, did not think policy units were necessary.

Goal setting as an interactive process

The setting and modification of unit goals can be understood as a process of interaction within a unit and between a unit and individuals and organizations in the unit's environment. In one central government department, the unit director said: 'our goals are the result of bargaining between advisers and administrators. The actual unit goals represent a negotiated settlement'. A local government policy planner stated, 'we got hints from the Bains Report and talked with senior officials and administrators in the department. The goals of this unit have changed as circumstances, key personnel and the range of policies open to the council have changed'. The planning unit in a major central government department engaged in what it called training seminars to help determine unit goals. The planning unit's staff had meetings with departmental officials from the various line divisions to discuss what the unit could do for them, what they would like to do for the divisions, on what topics and in what ways. Units at both levels use similar techniques of interaction and consultation. Such methods help units to define their role, promote themselves and generate some work for the unit. Consultation processes also help unit members get a better appreciation of their immediate organizational and task environment, as well as encourage participation in goal setting, build support for the unit and help avoid resistance to the goals themselves.[28]

To illustrate the interactive nature of goal setting, an illustrative case is given. The case shows how the organizational goals of a policy unit emerge and change over time in relation to factors in the unit's environment. The example considered here is the Central Intelligence and Monitoring Unit (CIMU) in the Greater London Borough of Lambeth. To understand the goals of the CIMU it is necessary to say something about the unit's establishment and the general context in which it is set.

The Conservative Party won the 1968 local government elections in Lambeth, gaining majority control on the council and ending thirty years of domination by the Labour Party. Upon taking control, the Conservative group retained a management consultant firm to study and advise on the management methods and structures. One result of this review was that the council replaced the existing post of town clerk with the new post of chief executive in mid-1970. The role of the chief executive, as set out in the terms of reference, stressed his co-ordination duties and indicated that he would be expected to bring forward proposals for financial and non-financial control systems as well as for the research and intelligence facilities required for his duties.

Initially, the chief executive established co-ordination procedures mainly through regular meetings with other principal and senior officers in the authority. After a few months the chief executive thought it necessary to consider how these procedures could be strengthened by control and monitoring systems and by research and intelligence facilities. Thus it was suggested by the chief executive and approved by policy committee that a corporate planning and programming officer be recruited and located in his office to develop these systems. Accordingly, Bill Kretchmer was appointed as corporate planning and programming officer in September 1970.

At about the same time, the council had accepted a proposal by the chief executive that an annual corporate plan (called the Community Plan) be prepared as a means regularly to review the council's objectives, activities and achievements. The goal of the corporate planning and programming officer was to assist in the preparation of the new community planning process. In particular, the officer would, in his own words, 'prompt and guide the work of seven interdepartmental working parties, set up to first prepare the new Community Plan and then to continue to update it and monitor progress'.[29] The first edition of the new Lambeth Community Plan appeared in March 1971.

Shortly after the first Community Plan was published, local government elections resulted in the Labour Party regaining control of the Council. But it was not the same Labour Party that had governed Lambeth in the past. As Cynthia Cockburn notes:

> The incoming Labour leader of 1971 was an economics teacher. Many of his colleagues, whose average age was undoubtedly the youngest ever known in this council, were not manual workers but professional and managerial people to whom the new ways came naturally. The Labour group took on and developed the management structure left by the Tories.[30]

Thus, when Labour returned to power in Lambeth in 1971 they accepted and used the planning process and documents that were in place. The new councillors, many of them also new to local government, found the seven volumes of the position statement a useful guide to the activities and duties of an inner London Borough. The head of the CIMU at the time has said he learned an important lesson: 'to serve in a central post guiding the decision making process of the Council, one is dependent on the political will of Councillors to support a corporate approach'.[31] The CIMU's role in prompting and guiding the community planning process continued. Although the seven inter-departmental working parties of senior officers were a key part of the corporate work on the Community Plan, the CIMU was still only a one person operation. It soon became evident, at least to Kretchmer himself, that the CIMU's role was beyond the capacity of one person.

To obtain more staff support for the CIMU, a report from the chief executive's office on Chief Executive's Control and Research Functions went to the policy committee in September 1971.[32] The report argued that the unit be built up to include six additional staff — four research officers, a senior assistant with editing and report writing skills, and an information and filing assistant. To support this request, the report proposed that the mandate of the CIMU be extended beyond prompting and guiding the Community Plan to include two further tasks in the corporate process: (i) to act as a co-ordinating focus for research, information and data, (ii) to be a co-ordinating focus for project monitoring and control systems. The reason why these new goals were proposed and subsequently accepted, lies in the officer management structure of Lambeth at the time.

Prior to the establishment of CIMU many departments (they are called directorates in Lambeth) were already collecting statistical data and carrying out studies. In addition, some departments such as development, social services, and housing and property services had units composed of staff specially devoted to research and intelligence activities. A similar situation existed in the area of monitoring. Much monitoring of achievements and progress in the council's activities was being done by individiual directorates which kept records and statistics, and reviewed the impact efficiency of the work of their staff. As regards the council's new building projects, the directorate of development had a project programming group which prepared regular reports on the progress of individual projects.

The prevailing belief in the authority's office structure, as manifested in committee documents, was that most research and intelligence activities and performance monitoring were best done in the individual directorates where the basic data are available and the activities under examination take place. However, some officers also argued there was a need for some form of central co-ordination. The case for central co-ordination was based on several grounds: to ensure that the information collected by the individual directorates could be presented to the chief executive for examination and action; to avoid duplication of effort either in research or monitoring; to ensure that each directorate knows what the others are doing; the many activities of different directorates impinge and react upon each other. It was therefore decided near the end of 1971, that the CIMU assume two new goals, becoming the co-ordinating focus for research as well as monitoring. With these new goals came new staff to assist Kretchmer. A corporate planner and two research officers arrived early in 1972 and two more joined later.

The goals of CIMU changed again towards the end of 1972 when the council added corporate project co-ordination to the role of the unit. Kretchmer explains the motivation behind this development: 'The Council had become concerned about delays in the housing programme and wanted more realistic forward projections, with detailed reports three times a year'.[33] During the early 1970s, as part of its housing programme, the Lambeth council were buying around 1,000 houses a year for eventual redevelopment. At the same time, however, the list of people waiting for a council flat was significantly growing; one in every four households in the borough lived in a shared dwelling; one in five of the borough's housing units had a life limited to fifteen years.[34] To deal with the delays in the housing programme a number of interdepartmental groups were set up to co-ordinate the implementation of all capital projects. For its new task of corporate project co-ordination, two further staff members were recruited to the CIMU.

The addition of this new goal significantly modified the role of CIMU, giving it a more interventionist dimension. As the head of the unit put it:

> Co-ordinating the corporate planning process was one thing, but monitoring the work of other people was a very different matter.

Outside the capital works programme, monitoring started mostly on the initiative of officers who were responsible for the activities they monitored, and it was done in their own departments. Indeed, this kind of monitoring has become more widespread over the year as a natural part of the Community Plan cycle; as the definition of targets improves, so does monitoring. The role of CIMU here remains prompting and guiding, and spreading the gospel.

In monitoring the capital programme its role is to ask questions, find out what is going right and what is going wrong, and making sure that the facts are reported to the Board of Directors and the Council's Committees. It means being a kind of watchdog over the building and other capital works programmes: barking and growling rather than prompting and guiding. Once corporate project co-ordination had been embraced, CIMU was cast in a dual role.[35]

In more recent years, other functions or goals have been added to the Chief Executive's Office which have affected the role of the CIMU. The new goals are associated with social, political and economic factors in the unit's environment.

In late 1977, an Inner City Unit was incorporated into the Chief Executive's Office. The Inner City Unit is composed of a leader paid by Lambeth and three secondees — one each from the Department of the Environment, the GLC and the Inner London Education Authority — who are paid by their own agencies. The origins of the Inner City Unit date back at least to 1972 when Lambeth was selected as one of three areas in Britain to be studied as part of DOE's Inner Area Studies. Briefly, the purpose of these studies was to determine the nature of multiple deprivation in inner city areas and to recommend a total approach or set of comprehensive policies to deal with inner area problems.[36] The studies were carried out by consultants appointed by the DOE. The CIMU assumed the role of acting as the link between the council and the consultants.

Following the Lambeth inner area studies, partnership arrangements are being established between the Lambeth council, the DOE and other public authorities. The CIMU's role in this policy area has been extended and formalized, resulting in greater differentiation within the CIMU itself. The Chief Executive's Office, of which CIMU is a part, expanded to encompass a new unit called the Inner City Unit. The aim of the Inner City Unit is to service the partnership. The duties of the new unit include assisting in the formulation, monitoring and updating of the programme to be established by the partnership, and providing administrative and research support to the partnership's officers steering group, which is chaired by the chief executive.

Another goal that has recently been added to the mandate of the Chief Executive Office concerns the promotion of employment in the area. In 1977, an employment promotion officer was appointed by the council and located within the chief executive's department. The role of this officer is to try to prevent businesses from leaving the borough, promote growth and employment and administer job creation schemes for the authority. In large part, the new goal and position were created because of the declining industrial base and high level of unemployment in the borough. These conditions in Lambeth are explained by a combination of market forces and central government planning: 'Lambeth is not a city but part of a city. Its economy is part of a metropolitan and national economy'.[37] Finally, a new post of co-ordinator of building programmes has been established in the Chief Executive's Office and will assume the same functions previously performed by the Project Programming Group. This development is the outcome of a report by a special review committee which the council established on taking office in May 1978.

This case study demonstrates that goal setting and modification is an interactive process. More specifically, the CIMU experience shows how the range and nature of goals are contingent upon a number of factors internal and external to the unit. Some of the main factors associated with goal setting and modification include the support for corporate planning and other rational methods by politicians, especially the ruling party and leader; the policy makers' interests in specific policy areas like housing redevelopment and employment promotion which, in turn, are conditioned by the state of the immediate and wider environment; the role of the chief executive officer and the management structure and style of the bureaucracy; and, the resources available to the unit, in particular human resources.

New goals can lead to changes in interorganizational relations between a unit and other officials. When the CIMU became responsible for monitoring capital programmes the unit became involved in barking and growling as well as prompting and guiding. On this dual role, Kretchmer has observed: 'it has not been particularly difficult to lead a slightly schizophrenic life (probably because our colleagues readily accepted it)'.[38] The last part of this statement deserves emphasis. A policy unit does not pursue goals by itself. Goal setting is essentially the relationship of a unit to its environment. A policy unit pursues goals in relation to other actors and organizations who can exercise influence on the unit through support, demands, opposition or indifference. To be effective, the goals of a unit must be related to and accepted by officials in the unit's environment. It is in the interaction between policy units and other organizational actors, that the actual goals of units are largely determined.

The role of the CIMU has gradually expanded over the 1970 to

1980 period with new goals being added to earlier ones, either formally or indirectly through a strengthening of Lambeth's administrative executive centre. Although the corporate project co-ordination staff were seen as part of CIMU after they were added in 1972–73, the inner city unit and employment promotion staff were at no stage considered to form any part of CIMU, although they report to the chief executive through the head of CIMU. The title Central Intelligence and Monitoring Unit is no longer used in Lambeth. This is mainly because the staff of two corporate planners and two research officers who make up the core of the unit now contribute substantially to the planning and administration of the inner area programme in addition to their original job of corporate planning and research co-ordination. Thus, the former CIMU, the inner city unit, the corporate project co-ordination and employment promotion staff and co-ordinator of building programmes all now operate under the general title of Chief Executive's Office.

While other policy units may undergo similar goal setting processes, the configuration of factors in any particular instance can lead to very different outcomes. Indeed, the experience of many policy units has been that after starting out with fairly ambitious goals, their roles have been reduced over time with certain goals being removed officially or simply withering away through organizational neglect.

Organizational survival as a goal

All organizations have two types of actual goals: to survive and to provide a service. Service goals refer to performance aims, achieving particular objectives, the delivery of a good or service, the production of an output. Service goals are usually contained in official statements and describe the reasons for establishing the organization. Survival goals deal with self maintenance, continuity, conservation, perhaps growth, prestige, internal integration and external acceptance and adaptation. The desire or the need to survive is rarely contained in the terms of reference of an organization but nonetheless it is a fundamental goal in reality.

Policy units in British government have emphasized both service and survival goals. In fact, units have frequently given priority to survival over service. The reasons are not hard to understand. The origins of policy units represent more an act of faith or a response to organizational fashion than a well considered step toward effecting and improving governmental activities. Policy units usually were given vague and general goals or were expected to suggest their own. Therefore they ran the risk of being unable to establish themselves within government and being abandoned as yet another reform which failed. Survival is important to nearly all organizations but is especially crucial to organizations like policy units that are relatively new, small in size, have fairly novel mandates, produce few tangible outputs and operate in a hostile or apathetic environment. As Anthony Downs points out, the survival of new organizations (he calls them bureaux) is often precarious. 'Their initial sources of support are usually weak, scattered and not accustomed to relations with the bureau. The latter must therefore rapidly organize so that its services become very valuable to the users. Only in this way can it motivate users to support it.' Hence, Downs suggests that 'officials in almost every new bureau place a high priority on creating conditions that will ensure the bureau's survival'.[39]

Officials in policy units have paid a great amount of attention to organizational survival. At times survival has been the overriding goal of policy units, and has been an ongoing concern for all units.

To survive, policy units use various strategies to build and maintain support as well as create a demand for their activities. One survival strategy commonly employed by units is to differentiate their activities from those performed by other officials and bodies. Many units have tried to develop a distinct area of competence. Another survival strategy is to establish a regular clientele and form routine working relationships with other officials. These considerations are nicely captured in the following comment by an assistant secretary who was in charge of the Crime Policy Planning Unit in the Home Office:

> If the planning unit is to succeed, it must be accepted by the Office as having a useful function and as doing something which either the rest of the Office cannot do or cannot do as well because it lacks the time or resources, but which it wants to have done. If it is not accepted by the organization which it is supposed to serve, there is a very real risk that it will be starved of the commodity upon which it chiefly depends, namely relevant information.[40]

The emphasis given to survival goals has had important ramifications for service goals such as policy advice and planning. A good deal of any policy unit's energies and resources are directed to self maintenance rather than directly to the pursuit of service aims. Secondly, questions of survival have conditioned and constrained policy units' service objectives. Consequently there is a gap between the official goals and the actual goals of most policy units. These new organizations are so dependent upon their environments for support that they have curtailed the pursuit of their professed goals so as to gain and retain support from a clientele. Policy units have in other words undertaken what I call *goal abridgement*. The abridgement of organizational goals is the process of curtailing or shortening the original mandate and selectively pursuing the intended objectives of the organization. This process is not a case of new more advanced goals succeeding old ones (goal succession), nor a case of original goals being displaced by unintended contrary ones (goal displacement). Instead, goal abridgement is an intentional reduction or abbreviation of original service goals aimed at gaining credibility and maintaining support. To go forward but not full steam ahead, to cut a long mandate short, this is goal abridgement. Some unit goals have fared better than others. As we shall see later in the book, policy units, through their actual operations and daily decisions, have emphasized research and intelligence and short term objectives at the expense of evaluation and planning, especially long term policy planning. Administrative politics, survival strategies and staffing practices have made for the incomplete realization of planning and research unit goals.

Notes

1. For example, see Richard H. Hall, *Organizations: Structure and Process*; Amitai Etzioni, *Modern Organizations*; Max D. Richards, *Organizational Goal Structures*; and Charles Perrow, 'The Analysis of Goals in Complex Organizations'.
2. *Report* of the Committee on the Civil Service, Cmnd. 3638, para.174.
3. Ibid., paras. 173 and 182.
4. *The New Local Authorities, management and structure*, p.79, para. 7.12.
5. Ibid., paras. 7.24, 7.25 and 7.31.
6. 'Research and Intelligence in the New County Councils', p.28, A Report to the Local Government Management Committee by A.J. Greenwell, W.U. Jackson and F.A. Stone. The report is reproduced in David L. Smith (ed.) *Research and Intelligence in the New Local Authorities,* pp.17—42. For other ideas on the possible goals of policy planning and research units in local government, see J.D. Stewart, *Management in Local Government: A Viewpoint*, especially pp.174—5; Bernard Benjamin, *Statistics and Research in Urban Administration and Development*, chapters 1 and 6; T. Eddison, *Local Government: Management and Corporate Planning*; and the Seebohm *Report* on Local Authority and Allied Personal Social Services, *chapter 15.*
7. *The Reorganisation of Central Government*, Cmnd. 4506, paras. 47—8.
8. *Programme of Research 1977—78*, Home Office Research Unit, p.iii.
9. Department of Employment and Manpower Services Commission, *Research 1976—77*, p.1 and p.8.
10. 'The Systems Analysis Research Unit', Department of the Environment, p.1.
11. Expenditure Committee (General Sub-Committee) Minutes of Evidence, Monday, 12 July 1976, Session 1975—76; 'Developments in the Civil Service Since the Fulton Report', Memorandum by the Department of the Environment, para.28.
12. Cleveland County, Research and Intelligence, *Annual Report 1976—77*, CR—157, June 1977, p.1.
13. Greenwich London Borough Officers' Management Committee, Appendix K, 'The Future of the Programme Planning Unit', p.1.
14. T.V. Walters, County Clerk and Chief Executive, Mid Glamorgan County Council, 'The Work of the Intelligence, Research and Development Unit', pp.1—2, paper presented to the Society

Based on information provided to the author by the Programme Planning Manager of Sunderland, August 1977.

16 Geoffrey K. Fry, 'Policy-Planning Units in British Central Government Departments', p.158 and pp.152–3. See also James Macdonald and G.K. Fry, 'Policy Planning Units — Ten Years On'.

17 See John Garrett, *The Management of Government*, chapter 2.

18 For a discussion of the PAR and PESC processes, see H. Heclo and A. Wildavsky, *The Private Government of Public Money*, chapter 5, and Sir Samuel Goldman, *Public Expenditure Management and Control*.

19 On different types of planning see S.D. Walker, 'Some Thoughts on Planning in the Civil Service'. John Garrett, *The Management of Government*, pp.113–15, compares the broad concept of planning units as envisaged by Fulton's Management Consultancy Group and the narrower concept held by the Fulton Committee.

20 R.G.S. Brown, *The Administrative Process in Britain*, p.248.

21 Charles Perrow, 'The Analysis of Goals in Complex Organizations', pp.854–6.

22 E.J. Razzell, 'Planning Units in Central Government', p.4.

23 A.J. Greenwell et al., 'Research and Intelligence in the New Local Authorities', p.19.

24 Mike Clegg, 'Corporate Planning, Corporate Planning Units and Planning Departments', p.60.

25 J. Skitt, *Practical Corporate Planning*, p.17.

26 Andrew Leigh, 'The work of social services researchers and its impact on social policy', p.109.

27 Interviews and Mike Clegg, 'Corporate Planning, Corporate Planning Units and Planning Departments'.

28 On the concepts of interaction and bargaining, see R.M. Cyert and J.G. March, *A Behavioural Theory of the Firm*; James D. Thompson and William J. McEwen, 'Organizational Goals and Environment: Goal-Setting as an Interaction Process'; Max D. Richards, *Organizational Goal Structure*, chapter 3; and Andrew M. Pettigrew, *The Politics of Organizational Decision Making*, Pettigrew shows how the task environment of specialist groups like policy units emerge over time through a process of negotiation.

29 Bill Kretchmer, 'The Central Unit in Lambeth', p.28.

30 Cynthia Cockburn, *The Local State*, p.6.

31 Bill Kretchmer, 'The Central Unit in Lambeth', p.29.

32 London Borough of Lambeth, Policy Committee, 15 September 1971, p.21/71–72, Agenda Para. 2c.

33 Bill Kretchmer, 'The Central Unit in Lambeth', p.30.
34 Cynthia Cockburn, *The Local State*, p.77 and pp.67–8.
35 Bill Kretchmer,'The Central Unit in Lambeth', p.30.
36 For an examination of recent neighbourhood policies in Britain, see Robin Hambleton, *Policy Planning and Local Government*, chapter 5.
37 Cynthia Cockburn, *The Local State*, p.68.
38 Bill Kretchmer, 'The Central Unit in Lambeth', pp.30–1.
39 Anthony Downs, *Inside Bureaucracy*, pp.7–8.
40 C.J. Train, 'The Development of Crime Policy Planning in the Home Office', p.377.

4 Policy and research personnel

If an applicant to this unit told me that he or she had majored in Agatha Christie, I'd say, Why not? Much of policy planning is detective work.

The Head of a Planning Unit

The proliferation of policy units throughout British government has resulted in a major growth in the number and status of policy planning and research personnel. Who are the people in these policy advisory roles? Are they political appointees or public servants? Insiders or outsiders? Generalists or specialists? Is there an élite corps of policy planners and researchers in the British public service?

In policy units there are two general types of members: (i) policy planners and researchers, and (ii) secretarial and clerical staff. While the importance of support staff should not be overlooked, this study focuses on the policy planners and researchers – the people who perform various policy oriented staff functions and are located within a policy unit. The label policy planners and researchers is a little misleading as only a few persons working in British government are officially designated as such, although many people in policy units actually use this label to describe themselves. They come from a considerable range of occupational categories and disciplines, principally statisticians, social science research officers, economists and the Administration Group of the Civil Service. The latter was created in 1971 from a merger of the administrative, clerical and executive classes.

The responsibilities of the senior staff in the Administration Group include advising and assisting ministers, the co-ordination and improvement of government machinery, and the control of departments of the public service. More specifically, their functions include: financial duties – forecasting expenditure, exercising financial and other control over the work of departments, reviewing the investment programmes of the nationalised industries; policy development – recommending, or advising on, new policies and policy options and writing the appropriate papers, and preparing legislation with members of the legal class; liaison – negotiating with local authorities, nationalized industries, private industry and members of the public on matters concerning the operation of existing government policies and regulations; executive support – preparing explanatory briefs on current policy, material for ministerial speeches and answers to parliamentary questions; administration–making decisions on individual casework arising from legislation; and acting as representative – on departmental and interdepartmental committees.[1] Middle and clerical officers perform a range of duties such as simple drafting and examining documents and submissions in relation to the conduct of departmental activities.

Economists are another major source of personnel for policy units at both levels of government in Britain. In central government, for instance, the Government Economic Service which was set up in 1965 now contains over 300 economists in addition to a large number of civil servants in other staff groups with degrees in economics.[2] The biggest employers of economists in the Civil Service are the Treasury, Department of the Environment, Department of Industry and Ministry of Overseas Development.

The work of economists in British government has been examined by a number of writers and can be summarized most conveniently in the words of Sir Alec Cairncross, the former head of the Government Economic Service.[3] Economic intelligence: 'This requires them to be experts on the available information of interest to their colleagues and to assess the current situation in light of the latest statistics as they come to hand'. Economic planning and forecasting: 'This is perhaps the most important operational role in which economists are used', and includes short term and longer term forecasting of a host of items. Economic co-ordination: this role requires the economist 'to see the way in which different elements in the economy interact and hence to form a judgement of the risks to which any programme is exposed and of the damage that its non-fulfilment might involve'. Economic research: 'Governments will always require the services of some economists to undertake research within Government or to follow, interpret and promote research work outside Government'. Policy advice: 'Advice on policy may be limited to a specific area (e.g. housing), or it may cover a wider field such as development assistance or investment policy, or it can be at the most general level of all and include advice on all the instruments of policy open to the Government'. Odd jobs: economists may also perform a range of odd jobs such as setting out replies to parliamentary questions, 'writing speeches, attending international conferences, coping with other economic advisers and trying to recruit more economic advisers'.

Statisticians abound in most central government departments and in many local authorities; there are currently about 400 staff in the Government Statistical Service. The objective of government statistical work has been officially described as 'to provide statistics to help in the formulation of policy, and statisticians are deeply involved in decisions about the kind of information which is needed, and are then responsible for the collection, analysis and interpretation of that information'.[4]

The research officer is another major occupational group represented in policy units. There are about 500 research officers working in various departments in central government, and over 1,000 corporate planning and research officers employed in local government services.[5] In central government there are two occupational groups for research officers: the Social Science Research Group and the Resource and Planning Research Group. In local government there is a wider variety of grades and titles for policy and research officers.

The work of researchers in British government can be described in general terms. The Social Science Research Group in the central government, 'is concerned with systematic approaches to discussion about patterns of behaviour among people in contemporary society, about the impact of government policies thereon, and about the implications for future policy'. The work of the Resource and Planning Research Group is similar, 'but concerned more directly with resource allocation, environment and infrastructure — physical or industrial, and local, regional, national or international'.[6]

Bernard Benjamin has identifed three main functions that may be performed by research workers in local authorities, especially within a central research and intelligence unit: first, a clearing house function which involves maintaining contacts with all research activity about any aspect of local government of interest to the authority; second, an advisory function of making advice on research available to departments which may need to conduct their own research; and, third, a research function of conducting individual research projects by themselves and assisting in the production of projects being carried out by fellow researchers.[7]

Two features can be noted about the relative importance of these occupations in policy units. In central government, a majority of unit personnel are from the Administration Group, that is, generalists. By contrast, most units in local authorities have relatively few general administrators. Rather they contain research officers, economists and information specialists. These differences and the reasons behind them are explored in the discussion of careers later in this chapter.

Though policy planners and researchers are drawn from several different disciplines and various occupational categories, they are nevertheless engaged in a similar range of activities. Their major intended activities include advising and recommending, forecasting and planning, liaison and co-ordination, research and intelligence. The work of unit personnel focuses mainly on the policy development and formulation process.

The direct participation of administrators in planning units is a significant development in the Civil Service. Until the late 1960s the research process within central government had largely been the preserve of the specialist classes.[8] With the formation of policy units, however, the research community has expanded to include both specialist and generalist occupational groups. Having career administrators as policy staff suggests units will not become too detached or isolated from the problems and feedback facing government departments in their day-to-day work. It promises that policy advice will be politically sensitive and have some immediate utility for operational needs, and that unit personnel will be better able to see how daily decisions can take account of long term applications. Moreover, it may mean that senior officials will become more aware of the contribution research and planning can make to policy development and general management. On the other hand, a reliance upon administrators to staff policy units raises several concerns. Can administrators be effective researchers and planners? Can they look far enough ahead to anticipate problems? Can they provide policy advice that is objective and independent, critical and evaluative? Other Civil Service occupational groups that include research staff are psychologists and scientific officers. Clearly, the role of various occupational groups in policy planning and research deserves much closer examination.

Everyday officials or whizz kids?

'Planning Units', the Fulton Report argued, 'should be staffed by comparatively young men and women. Thus some of the most able, vigorous and suitably qualified young civil servants will be able to have an early and direct impact on top policy-making'. Although Fulton did not define the term 'young civil servants', it appears they meant officials in their thirties and early forties.

A sample of unit personnel reveals that most planners and researchers are men, although women represent a sizeable proportion; they possess a high level of educational qualifications and are comparatively young.

The majority of planners and researchers surveyed were male (71.9 per cent, or 105 of 146). Considerable variations exist between policy units in terms of the sex of personnel. A number of units contain no women as policy planners and researchers while in other units women are widely employed and in a few units predominate. If temporary and part time staff are included, the proportion of women employed in policy units probably increases by a marginal amount. Data on the employment of women in the Civil Service as of 1971 show that the proportion of women in the policy units studied (28.1 per cent) is significantly higher than women as a percentage of those in the middle and upper grades of the Administration Group (14.5 per cent at the higher executive office grade, and dropping steadily to 3.0 per cent at under secretary and above). Moreover, the proportion of women in policy units is somewhat closer to, but still higher than the percentage of women in the specialist classes like statisticians (20 per cent) and economists (13.5 per cent).[9] Relatively speaking, policy units are important employers of women in the public service.

Precise figures were obtained about the age of fifty-two unit staff. As of 1980 about half of the staff were in their thirties (53.9 per cent) and an overwhelming majority under forty (86.6 per cent). In comparison, officials in the administrative and executive classes tend to be older. A survey done for the Fulton Committee found that only about one-third of those in the administrative and executive classes were under forty.[10] These figures are in accord with the Fulton Report's suggestion and are partially confirmed by other studies.[11] A recent examination by Razzell of the age of staff in central government departmental planning units found that with the exception of planning unit heads, the staff appear to be on the young side. Sir Alec Cairncross, writing in 1968, said of the age of government economists: 'The majority are young economists, still in their twenties or early thirties'. Given the turnover of economists in central government, there is no reason to suppose the situation is very different now.

Not only are policy planners and researchers often 'kids', they also have 'whizz'. A distinguishing characteristic of unit staff is their high level of educational attainment. Virtually all have a bachelor's degree and many have graduate degrees in various disciplines. Similar characteristics are exhibited by other policy personnel in British government, as well as by equivalent personnel in the administrative systems of other countries such as Canada and the United States. For example, of the twenty-eight political or special policy advisers serving British cabinet ministers in 1976 the majority were male (85 per cent), comparatively young (67.9 per cent under forty) and had a high level of educational attainment (including at least three doctors and two professors). A recent study of policy advisory groups in the Canadian federal public service found that policy planners tend to be young (median age 30–34 years), male (82 per cent), and with a high level of formal education (92 per cent with a bachelor's degree, over half had graduate degrees).[1][2]

Thus policy planners and researchers exhibit the characteristics of youth and expertise, in short, they are whizz kids rather than everyday bureaucrats. As bright young persons within government bureaucracies they are expected to be conversant with the latest analytical techniques and ideas, and display some initiative in policy development. However, as Macdonald and Fry recently have noted, ' "Youth" may well be a quality of the directors and staff of these units, but in this framework, while the practice of public administration is learned but not yet taught, youth is no unmixed blessing'.[13] That the attributes of policy planners and researchers can have both positive and negative consequences for units will be evident from an examination of their interorganizational relations and their personnel management processes.

Recruitment, training and career prospects

Most of the policy units in central government are composed wholly or largely of civil servants, even though the Fulton Report proposed that planning units should also employ people from outside government on temporary secondments to the Civil Service. This is because of the norms of secrecy within government and the political neutrality of public servants, mixed with tactical considerations of recruiting staff likely to gain acceptance by administrators and able to work with civil servants.

In a study of the Department of Education and Science, the House of Commons Expenditure Committee commented on the absence of outsiders in that department's planning organization. The committee suggested that this approach 'has the advantage for the DES that discussion within the planning group can be unconstrained by tactical considerations about relationships with and between various outside groups'. Yet, on the other hand, the lack of outsiders has 'the disadvantage that local authorities, teachers' organisations and others having a legitimate interest in the development of educational plans are not associated at first hand with "the actual planning process" '.[14]

Acceptability to the larger bureaucracy is another important consideration in the recruitment of unit staff. An assistant secretary formerly in charge of the Crime Policy Planning Unit in the Home Office has given the following reasons why the Office has relied on recruiting from the ranks of the Civil Service instead of using outsiders: 'We have gone for the use of insiders on the grounds that acceptance by the Office and an ability to understand the work with it are of paramount importance'.[15]

There are a few notable exceptions to this general approach in central government, one of which is the CPRS in the Cabinet Office. The CPRS has adopted a staffing policy of recruiting half its staff from within the ranks of the Civil Service and half from outside. Recruiting outsiders is intended to help the CPRS keep in touch, more readily than central government departments, with a wide range of opinion and contacts outside Whitehall. This approach adds some flexibility to recruitment allowing the CPRS to be less dependent upon departments for staff, and to blend outside perspective with inside experience. The method of recruitment for those positions to be filled by insiders differs from those to be filled by outsiders. For outside recruits on a short term secondment to the CPRS, the Civil Service Commission is not involved.[16] If, however, an outside recruit wanted to stay on in the Civil Service, which has happened in a few cases, then the Commission and the regular appointment procedures are involved.

Compared to central government experience, most policy units in local authorities are composed of people both from within and outside the local authority service. The actual mix of insiders and outsiders can vary between units and local authorities. In cases like Tyne and Wear or Avon, which were completely new authorities in 1974, outside recruits comprised the entire policy units' staff. In other authorities like Cheshire, the origins of the central R & I unit staff, at least initially, were from other departments within the authority. Most local authority policy units are somewhere between these two positions, but typically have a greater proportion of outsiders than central government units. The main reason for this has to do with the different emphasis given to the career argument for policy units at the two levels of government.

A career structure for policy units' personnel such as economists and statisticians, as existed in central government, was absent in local government. Local authorities have traditionally encountered real difficulties in attracting and holding information specialists. Thus an important argument for policy units in local government was that they would aid in the recruitment and retention of information and research specialists. Outsiders were therefore recruited because the desired skills were not available in the authority and/or were outside the normal local government professions.[17] Generally, outsiders were from other local authorities, not infrequently originating from another unit, and from universities and polytechnics, where they were teaching or had recently graduated. Occasionally, outside staff to local authority units come from central government or the private sector.

In planning units in central government departments the general attitude of departments seems to be that ability is the main condition of appointment. In local government units, researchers themselves have said that the technical abilities required for information collection and analysis include such skills as computing, forecasting, statistics and survey methodologies.[18] While ability is undoubtedly a major consideration in the appointment of staff, such broad statements do not provide much understanding of the recruitment process.

Policy units in British government employ a wide array of criteria in the recruitment of their personnel. Some common considerations, however, can be noted. Academic qualifications, normally at degree level, professional or technical qualifications if appropriate, work experience and knowledge of the substantive area(s) with which the unit is concerned, are emphasized in varying degrees in the recruitment of policy unit personnel. Furthermore, many officials stress the importance of personal traits and skills. For instance, Lord Rothschild has described the persona of the planner in terms of certain gifts of mind and of character; planners must be intellectually and morally honest, philosophical, patient, brave, tenacious and capable of very hard work.[19] Yet, there is a danger in setting forth the ideal personal traits and skills of policy planners and researchers which are mentioned in interviews and which also appear in job advertisements — statements such as, must be a divergent and quick thinker, and should be self starters. 'It is very easy to move from broad statements of this nature', says corporate planner D.E. Hussey, 'to long lists of disciplines and personal traits which should characterise the good corporate planner'. The outcome of such an approach is 'the impression of a saint-like creature, barely human, the identification of whom would defy the efforts of the most skilled and efficient of management headhunters'.[20]

A better understanding of the recruitment process of policy units is gained by taking into account the factors which can affect the criteria for recruiting unit personnel. In respect to any policy unit, there is a range of factors which may influence recruitment. These factors include the overall number of unit staff, the number and types of specialist skills, the staff grades, the organizational goals of the unit, the organizational location of the unit and whether other such units exist in the department or authority.

Organizational location and tradition can affect the type or types of people recruited to a unit. For example, in some central government departments, such as Environment and Transport, statisticians and economists work together in mixed divisions. In other departments like Health and Social Security, these specialists operate separately. Similarly, in staffing research and intelligence units in local authorities, 'in a Treasurer's department, the basic skills are more likely to be those of economist and accountant; in a Planning department, the geographer and land use planner'.[21] In short, a unit located in a professional or service department will tend to recruit specialists oriented to the functions of that department.

The larger organizational context of which a unit is a part may also condition the recruitment criteria. The Central Research and Evaluation Unit in Avon is intended to serve the whole authority. There are, however, a number of other units located within various departments of the authority. As a consequence, rather than maintain a multidisciplinary unit which would overlap and possibly conflict with specialists in other departments, the central unit has deliberately recruited only specialists in numerate disciplines. Thus, the composition of the three person unit changed from its original composition of one statistician, one historian and one geographer to two statisticians and one mathematician. The recruitment approach adopted by the Avon unit demonstrates that recruitment may be affected by other factors. For instance, the role skills and conception of the unit head were important. With his own experience and background in statistics, the unit head was inclined to look toward recruiting other personnel from the statistical field. Another influence is the concern for organizational survival and the idea that nothing succeeds like success. Since the inception of the Avon central unit, its statistical role has been accepted and recognized as worthwhile by other departments and has developed into the main function of the unit. Finally, the small size of the unit was an influencing factor. The unit head believed that with only three members it would be very hard to be multidisciplinary and have an effective role in the authority.

In contrast to the Avon approach of specialization, many units do try to achieve a representation of professional, organizational or even geographical expertise within their ranks. The CPRS, with regard to the half of its staff that comes from inside the Civil Service, tries to recruit one person from each major department who has done a range of jobs in the department and is familiar with the work of the department. With regard to staff from outside the Civil Service, the CPRS tries to get a balance of skills and experience and normally has representatives from the oil companies, merchant banking, industry and universities. When the Economic Planning Staff of the Ministry of Overseas Development was founded, some economists were recruited for their special knowledge and experience of particular geographical areas in the world. 'In fact', as some members of the staff have recorded, 'a point was made of requiring geographical economists to have some previous experience of actual service in the areas in which they were to be assigned'.[22] In sum, policy units in the British public service have been staffed by insiders and some outside specialists. The politicization of policy units, staffing units with personal supporters of a government or minister or by the temporary appointment of outside party policy experts, has not happened. If any, there are only a small number of political appointees in policy units.

In the Civil Service and local government service, public servants undergo various forms of induction training, management and development, and vocational training programmes. These types of training are well established and quite extensive. In comparison, the training people receive *as members of a policy unit*, is characterized by a reliance on informal, although often deliberate, methods which occur on an ongoing basis. Policy unit heads recognize that staff training is important to unit effectiveness, and attempt to train and develop their personnel through a variety of means. Bernard Benjamin, a former director of the GLC's research and intelligence unit, emphasizes the importance of indoctrinating unit staff. 'There are a number of matters concerning professional behaviour on which staff need to be carefully indoctrinated and it would be useful for the Director to take an immediate opportunity to talk to the newly recruited staff about his policy on these matters.' In addition, the Director should speak to the staff collectively. 'This will give him the opportunity to begin to cultivate the team spirit within the Unit on which success depends'.[23] Benjamin suggests that the best way a unit head can indoctrinate new members is by talking with them and explaining what has worked in the past. He believes, as do many other unit heads, that it is very difficult, however, to instill professional behaviour into staff through training programmes.

George Shagory has commented that 'on-the-job training is by far the most important and lasting that a planning staff member receives. As in other fields of endeavour, there is no substitute which compares with actually doing the work'.[24] The importance of on-the-job training is due to the small size of policy units and the type of people recruited. Robert Pinkham, of the Programme Planning Unit in Greenwich, has pointed out that social science researchers in government 'will seldom be experts in their fields of study. Only the largest local authorities can afford the luxury of employing all the relevant expertise which any given study seems to require'.[25] In addition, as Andrew Leigh notes in a discussion of social service departments, 'the decision by departments to hire people with research skills who can then learn about social work, rather than taking specialists in social work and turning them into researchers has meant that there is inevitably quite a lengthy period before even the most skilled researcher can get to grips with what the agency does, how it tries to do it and above all the relevant questions to begin asking'.[26]

Little attention is paid to induction training of unit personnel because of the prevalent belief in British administrative culture that learning and training are best realized by doing. The small size of policy units is also a key consideration. The recruitment process of units is generally incremental in that only one or two people are recruited at a time. Given this situation, some unit heads argue it is not cost effective to set up an induction course.

Moreover, the lack of induction training is linked to the relative novelty of policy planning and policy units as explicit processes and structures in British government. A number of unit heads have said they are not sure what an induction training programme for policy personnel would contain and how it could be taught without becoming abstract and terribly dry. Peter Kershaw, the Programme Planning Manager in Sunderland has underlined this uncertainty: 'In Sunderland we are working in a developing situation. Nothing is final. Nothing is fixed. New systems, new data, new ideas can and will be used'. Kershaw emphasizes that a high degree of flexibility is needed by planners and other officials to enable quick adaption to changing circumstances. Sunderland's basic approach to corporate planning and management is one of open experimentation since little is known about corporate management/planning in practical terms. 'It is axiomatic to this form of approach that there should be a readiness to admit mistakes, change course and, if need be, start afresh building on past experience'.[27]

The induction training that does occur in policy units usually involves new recruits talking with the person that they are taking over from, talking with other unit personnel and reading over past and current work of the unit.

In a real sense, policy unit personnel are in a continuing training and learning process. Training is done through attaching new and junior staff to more experienced and senior policy planners and researchers. 'The new staff member not only performs his own work but seeks to learn all he can under the wings, so to speak, of the experienced staff'. Another training method utilized is job rotation. Unit staff are divided into work groups, and are rotated from one group to another after each project or a fixed period of time. From this method, unit personnel 'can gain diversified experience in a relatively limited area instead of attempting to learn all that is required at once'.[28]

Thinking the unthinkable is a common technique used in units. This involves thinking about activities and options that are clearly beyond the bounds of current government or council policy. Unit staff suggest that this technique helps to inform their thinking as policy advisers by stretching their views as to what is possible and by highlighting the interrelation of various factors in a policy area. Unconventional thinking may also serve to protect policy units from pressures of conformity in their organizational environment.

Other training and staff development methods include informal group discussions, meetings during which all unit members can exchange views, report on their work and help plan future work projects, role playing exercises and weekend retreats.

The large majority of personnel in units are full time and hold established or permanent positions. Many units at both levels of government also use part time and temporary or fixed period appointees, such as other officials within the department or authority. These part time members are co-opted to a unit usually because they have some expertise on a subject and/or are a representative of a particular organization. In addition, a few units, in local government, recruit staff from the general public on a temporary basis. The Cleveland R & I Unit and the Central Research and Intelligence Unit in Tyne and Wear, for instance, have trained field forces of interviewers for surveys as required.

For some people in central government and for relatively more in local authorities, working in a policy unit offers career opportunities – a means of making a living and pursuing a course of personal advancement. This difference in career structures reflects the greater emphasis given the career argument in local government.

Although the Fulton Report suggested that planning units could provide better career opportunities for research officers, it did not place much emphasis on the career argument as a justification for the units. Except for the head of the unit, Fulton said people should not normally remain in these units beyond their mid-forties. Instead, after a period of service in a unit, people should return to the operating sections of their departments or, if they are outsiders, return to work outside government. The career patterns of unit personnel in central government are in accordance with the Fulton Report. The personnel are mostly civil servants from the Administration Group, each of whom does a one to three year stint in the unit as part of their general work within the department. These units are not a career for people but typically operate on a system of short term secondments. The policy units in central government that do provide career opportunities are usually staffed by specialists like statisticians and research officers. Thus, units like the Social Research Branch in the Department of Social Security, the Research and Planning Division in the Department of Employment and the Home Office Research Unit have provided career opportunities for research officers in the Civil Service.

In local government, policy units have created career opportunities for a significant number of research and specialist personnel. The career structure and prospects that exist are more in the form of horizontal job change than upward hierarchical mobility. Career prospects for policy planners and researchers within a particular unit or authority, that is to say, vertical job mobility, are generally limited. Most units are not big enough in terms of the number of positions and grades to permit the creation of a long career ladder. The most common size of the units sampled is between one and five people. Moreover, as one senior staff officer has suggested, many researchers

80

have a 'preference for investing their energies in intellectually stimulating enquiries rather than clawing their way into administrative oblivion'.[29] Thus the career pattern of policy unit personnel in local government frequently takes the form of horizontal mobility, with staff moving from a unit in one local authority to a unit situated in another authority. Although individually most policy units are too small to provide a career structure for their staff, as a group there are sufficient units to provide a career network.

The establishment of policy units has therefore improved the ability of individual local authorities to attract research specialists, although, having attracted them, the small size of units limits the ability of authorities to hold them. The horizontal mobility of unit personnel means that on the one hand authorities lose experienced staff knowledgeable of the council's activities, but on the other hand gain new blood with experience and ideas from other authorities and organizations.

The rate of turnover in many local authority units has slowed in recent years because of a general tightening in the job market, and resource constraints in most authorities. The present relative lack of job mobility in and between units possibly 'tends to deemphasize new ideas and stress continuity'.[30] This situation has both benefits and costs. One unit head remarked in an interview that because his staff had remained unchanged for two years some of them were growing stale. Policy planners may develop vested interests and deliberately offer advice that confirms previous work done by themselves. However, low turnover at this stage of unit development probably allows them to consolidate and gain some stability.

A new profession?

The people in a policy unit normally share a certain *esprit de corps*. This is in large part due to the relative novelty of their organizational role, the small size of these units and the obvious dangers in the environment. Most see themselves as different in some ways from other officials in government. In many cases people in policy units have more training and skills in the use of quantitative techniques than other officials. As a type of official most could be classified as advocates. In addition, policy unit personnel perform a similar range of staff functions and probably tend to have 'more confidence than politicians and other staff in the value of policy research'.[31] All of these factors contribute to an ethos among policy and research personnel. However, a sense of unity among officials in different organizations does not constitute a profession. 'To be a profession it is not sufficient merely to believe it oneself; it is necessary to secure wider social recognition of the claim.'[3][2]

Policy planners and researchers exhibit only a few of the attributes of a profession and lack most of the other attributes. Working in a policy unit has the professional features of being a full time, non-manual occupation with a financial compensation for providing a service to someone else. Furthermore, policy unit roles involve relationships with clients based on confidentiality and trust. However, the official who wants policy advice is often free to choose from a number of people and organizations both inside and outside government. Policy planners and researchers do not have a monopoly over their skills. Moreover, there is no national association of policy unit personnel with a community sanctioned monopoly over recruitment, training and certification of members. There is no formal code of ethics or standards of work performance. There are also no degree granting schools or institutes of policy planning and research in Britain and no unified professional structure.

Writing in 1972, a special adviser in the Treasury observed: 'It will be particularly interesting to see whether the Civil Service will encourage any marked specialization in strategic planning as a field of management'.[3][3] In part, the Civil Service Department has encouraged such specialization through its active support of establishing departmental and interdepartmental arrangements for planning and research. Indeed, a number of steps have been taken toward occupational specialization in policy planning both in central and local government.

Several central government organizations, including the Bank of England, Civil Service Department and the Departments of Energy, the Environment, and Industry are corporate members of the Society for Long Range Planning. The Society was founded in 1967 with the following objectives: to awaken the need for, and understanding of long range planning in both the private and public sectors of the economy. To enhance the skills of long range planners. To exchange and extend the information available to long range planners. To bridge the gap between long range planners in industry, government and the academic world. The Society publishes a bi-monthly journal, *Long Range Planning*, and holds conferences, seminars and study groups, which are organized on a subject and regional basis.

The Civil Service College offers courses in analytic and decision making techniques and has sponsored seminars on policy planning units. For instance, a seminar was held in 1977 on 'How Departments Are Developing Planning Units'. About ten central government departments participated and a number of officials gave presentations on their departmental planning arrangements and experience. There is a realization among people in policy units in the central government that many of the problems and issues facing them are similar, although communications between these units is an intermittent process. Apart from the odd telephone conversation very few officials in the different departmental units have contact with each other. Officials acknowledge that Civil Service College seminars are useful, but some officials believe there is a need for a more regular planning network between departments to provide a means for keeping in touch with one another.

With the creation of the CPRS in the Cabinet Office, some commentators suggested there might follow more uniformity between departmental planning units.[34] This has not happened. It has not been the responsibility of the CPRS to co-ordinate or act as the link between all the various units in the departmental arena. Departments have continued to staff their policy units and use them largely according to particular departmental needs and within existing staffing arrangements. It is very unlikely that the people working policy units in the Civil Service will be organized and recognized as a separate service to become, say, HM Government Policy Planning and Research Service.

In local government, there have been relatively greater efforts made toward professionalism. The fact that nearly all local authority departments are professional organizations has probably encouraged policy unit personnel to move towards professionalism. As Stanyer points out: 'In the local government context it is highly advantageous to be able to "prove" that one's occupation is a true profession because this is the way to higher salary, higher status and greater working autonomy within the local political system'.[35] Moves for the recognition of policy planning and research as a profession in its own right have occurred at the local level along a number of distinct fronts, with the possibility that there may eventually be two, three or more professions of policy unit personnel. A number of associations and organizations have been established in recent years which have contributed to the emerging professionalism of unit personnel in local government. The Institute of Local Government Studies (INLOGOV) in the University of Birmingham has served an important catalytic role in most of these developments.

The British Urban and Regional Information Systems Association (BURISA) was set up in 1972 as a self-supporting independent association of people whose common interest is the research, development and management of information systems. BURISA aims 'to be an organization working for that "invisible college of experts" whose job it is to develop information systems'.[36] Since 1972, BURISA has published a bi-monthly newsletter which reports activity about information systems and major trends of thought in urban and regional research. Since 1974, BURISA has held annual conferences to provide a more immediate face-to-face opportunity for members to exchange views and ideas.

The Social Services Research Group (SSRG) was launched in 1972 as a result of a conference held at INLOGOV. The general purpose of SSRG is to provide an association for research staff in social services departments. The aims of the SSRG cited in its constitution are as follows: (a) to provide a forum for the exchange of ideas on research into the social services; (b) to promote high standards of social services research; (c) to encourage collaboration in social service research activities; (d) to develop an informed body of opinion on social service research.[37] The SSRG operates through a national committee as well as regional groups throughout England, Scotland and Wales and several special interest working parties. It periodically publishes a newsletter and encourages members from researchers in universities and institutes and social workers.

Also set up in 1972 was the Corporate Planning Steering Group composed of officers from various local authorities concerned with corporate planning and management. Since that year there have been annual corporate planning workshops in which officers from many authorities participate in a two-day conference. Papers on various aspects of corporate planning are presented and discussed. Since 1974, a journal, *Corporate Planning*, has been published three times a year by INLOGOV. The journal is intended to provide a medium of communication between people developing corporate planning in local government. It contains short articles by practitioners on selected themes and contains information on problems and innovations in the field.

The Research and Intelligence Group was set up in 1974 after a seminar had been held at INLOGOV on Research and Intelligence in 1973. The purpose of the Group is to enable officers in R & I units to inform each other of their activities and to discuss a number of issues of common interest, such as staffing, functions and the organizational location and relations of units. Annual seminars have been held for heads of R & I units as well as annual conferences for research officers since 1974. INLOGOV periodically publishes a Register of Research Projects in Research & Intelligence Units. The Register provides in one document summaries of the projects being undertaken by R & I units in local authorities, and allows a contact for those wishing to follow up this work.[38]

Another organization in local government related to the emerging professionalism of policy planners and researchers is the Programme Management Group (PMG), set up in 1974, to seek development and improvement in local authority management processes. The PMG invites membership from all those associated with forward planning/corporate management regardless of disciplines, specialization, qualification or viewpoint. The PMG promotes a range of activities including a newsletter, local area groups, special study groups and annual seminars. In conjunction with INLOGOV, the group published in 1978 a *Corporate Planning Yearbook* which provides a survey of developments in corporate planning in local government throughout England, Scotland and Wales, and a *Corporate Planning Handbook* in 1979.

Many policy planners and researchers are actively contributing to the development of working in a policy unit as a profession. Officials have given talks and published papers describing their role and the problems they face. Communications among policy units in local government have become regular due to the various organizations set up and the role of INLOGOV as a forum for many of these developments. The creation of journals and research registers demonstrates efforts to develop a common body of knowledge.

The arguments for and against the professionalization of policy planners and researchers can be illustrated by examining an attempt by the R & I Steering Group in 1976 to gain recognition as a professional association. This brief case study indicates a number of the issues that unit personnel are likely to face as they pursue professionalism.

Associated with the Research and Intelligence Group set up in 1974, is the R & I Steering Group. This Steering Group is an informal and self-created body comprised of about eight to ten heads of policy units in various local authorities. In 1976 the Steering Group decided to apply for formal recognition from the Society of Local Authority Chief Executives (SOLACE) as the professional association of officers in charge of research and corporate planning in English and Welsh local government. The Steering Group acknowledged that there were variations in the roles, responsibilities and professional qualifications of unit heads. However, the group contended that these variations, rather than being arguments against the formation of an association, made it all the more probable that by exchanging views and information on research and corporate planning, local authorities could benefit from each other's experience. The Steering Group argued that a forum representing research and intelligence, and policy and corporate planning activities was justified since all of these activities are fairly well established in many local authorities, and because several facets of their functions have not yet been comprehensively examined. Furthermore, the group argued that existing forums play specific, often topic oriented roles, which do not embrace the several professional, technical and administrative aspects to the conduct of these functions. These aspects relate to standards of research, professional etiquette, analytical practices, validation of research and methodological issues, training of staff, career structures and prospects. Therefore, the Steering Group suggested an additional forum might play an embracing part in representing the interests of research, intelligence and corporate planning in local authorities on all issues, as well as serve as backup support to the local authority side in all matters where research was relevant to negotiations with central government.

To date, SOLACE has not given formal recognition to the Steering Group and it seems unlikely recognition will be given in the foreseeable future. Two reasons may be suggested why SOLACE has not recognized the Steering Group as the professional association for researchers and corporate planners in local government. A great many of these units are located within chief executive's departments and chief executives and *their* professional association may be reluctant to lose control over these staff. Many chief executives view policy units as an essential component for supporting their leadership and co-ordinative roles in a local authority.[39] Secondly, not all researchers and corporate planners believe it is important or desirable to seek recognition as a profession. Indeed, there is considerable debate over whether policy unit staff should become a profession. Some policy personnel are very strongly opposed to the professionalization of their role. They believe their positions were originally established in local government because of the narrow specialism and professionalism of other occupations which tended to encourage departmentalism. Greater professionalization could restrict their creative and innovative capabilities and broad outlook on issues. Some officials suggest that a danger of professionalism is insularity: it will lead to researchers and policy planners talking only to other researchers and policy planners about research and policy planning. A number of officials point out that unit personnel come from a variety of backgrounds and should continue to do so, implying that professionalism would restrict the range of skills recruited.

Nonetheless, working in a policy unit has taken the first few steps along the professionalism path. A number of groups and associations are in place for unit personnel. On what further steps, if any, are likely in coming years, it is worth quoting what the chairman of the Social Services Research Group believes that association cannot aspire to:

> Firstly, it cannot become a trade union, not least because such matters as would be dealt with are already the province of large and powerful bodies like NALGO [National Association of Local Government Officers]. SSRG is also too small and there would be no agreement among the memberships that this should be how SSRG should develop. Secondly, it cannot become a super professional body, a watchdog on standards and ethics because of the variety of practice, the pragmatism built into social services research, and a lack of consensus about what is good practice. Thirdly, it cannot become a pressure group or campaigning organization for substantive social change because it is too small and

other bodies are already in existence for this purpose.[40]

If we take the Social Services Research Group as an example, then, the personnel management process for policy units will not easily become professionalized. Policy planners and researchers come from a variety of occupations, the most common are researchers associated with various social science disciplines, statisticians, economists and administrators. While individually unit personnel may belong to a particular profession, collectively people working in policy units do not represent a new profession in British government. As a group, the practitioners of policy planning and research are in the embryonic stages of professionalism, and a number of initiatives, especially at the local level, have been taken to organize better the unit personnel. However, the success of policy planning and research is not realized merely by the introduction of personnel into new positions: a critical factor is to provide supportive organizational arrangements in which the personnel can work.

Notes

1 *The British Civil Service*, Central Office of Information, Reference Pamphlet 122.

2 *Economists, Posts in Government Service*, Civil Service Commission, p.3.

3 The list and quotations are taken from Sir Alec Cairncross, 'The Work of an Economic Adviser', pp.5–7. See also Peter Self, *Administrative Theories and Politics*, pp.211–15, and Sir Alec Cairncross, 'Economists in Government'.

4 *Statisticians, Posts in Government Service*, Civil Service Commission, p.3. See also Dr B. Benjamin, 'The Statistician and the Manager', and The Right Hon. Harold Wilson, 'Statistics and Decision-making in Government – Bradshaw Revisited'. The figure of 500 statisticians is from *The Times*, 31 May 1977.

5 See E.M. Davies, *The Central Research Function in Local Government*, and Andrew Leigh, 'Researchers in the Social Services'.

6 Civil Service Department, 'The Response to the Fulton Report – Part 3', an abridged version of a memorandum submitted by the CSD to a Sub-Committee of the House of Commons Expenditure Committee, printed in *Management Services in Government*, vol. 32, no. 1, (February 1977), p.47.

7 See Bernard Benjamin, *Statistics and Research in Urban Administration and Development*, pp.38–9.

8 John Garrett, *The Management of Government*, pp.108–9. See also David Judge, 'Specialists and Generalists in Britsh Central Government: A Political Debate'.

9 CSD Management Studies 3, *The Employment of Women in the Civil Service*, pp.44–5.

10 This sample is much smaller than that on sex since it was more difficult to obtain precise figures on age of personnel. *Report* of the Committee on the Civil Service, vol. 3(1), p.16.

11 E.J. Razzell, 'Planning Units in Central Government', p.5. See also, 'Improving Policy Analysis – The D.H.S.S. Approach', p.13, and Sir Alec Cairncross, 'The Work of an Economic Adviser', p.7.

12 See *HC Debates*, vol. 908, c.28 and vol. 872, c.151–3, and Michael J. Prince, 'Policy Advisory Groups in Government Departments', p.289.

13 James Macdonald and G.K. Fry, 'Policy Planning Units – Ten Years On', p.432.

14 Tenth Report from the Expenditure Committee, 1975–76 Session, p.xvii.

15 C.J. Train, 'The Development of Crime Policy Planning in the

Home Office', p.384.

16 See the evidence from Sir Kenneth Berrill, Head of the CPRS, and others, before the Expenditure Committee (General Sub-Committee), 6 December 1976.

17 Cynthia Cockburn, *The Local State*, p.22.

18 Geoffrey K. Fry, 'Policy-Planning Units in British Central Government Departments', p.149; E.J. Razzell, 'Planning Units in Central Government', p.5; and E.M. Davies, *The Central Research Function in Local Government*.

19 Lord Rothschild, *Meditations of a Broomstick*, pp.166–7.

20 D.E. Hussey (ed.), *The Corporate Planner's Yearbook, 1974–75*, p.85.

21 A.J. Greenwell et al., 'Research and Intelligence in the New County Councils', p.37.

22 *Report* of the Committee on the Civil Service, vol. 5, no. 2, Memorandum No. 124 submitted by 'A Group of Members of the Economic Planning Staff of the Ministry of Overseas Development', p.558.

23 Bernard Benjamin, *Statistics and Research in Urban Administration and Development*, p.103.

24 George E. Shagory, 'Development of Corporate Planning Staff', p.72.

25 Robert Pinkham, 'Effective Social Research for Local Government', p.24.

26 Andrew Leigh, 'Researchers in the Social Services', p.55.

27 Peter Kershaw, 'Management Information', p.18.

28 George E. Shagory, 'Development of Corporate Planning Staff', p.73.

29 Andrew Leigh, 'Researchers in the Social Services', p.54.

30 Anthony Downs, *Inside Bureaucracy*, p.230.

31 Arnold J. Meltsner, *Policy Analysts in the Bureaucracy*, p.53. See also Anthony Downs, *Inside Bureaucracy* on the concept of advocate.

32 Brian Smith and Jeffrey Stanyer, *Administering Britain*, p.194. The literature on professions is legion. For a general introduction, see D.J. Hickson and M.W. Thomas, 'Professionalization in Britain: A Preliminary Measurement'; H. Wilensky, 'The Professionalization of Everyone?'; and R.H. Hall, 'Professionalization and Bureaucratization'. On the professionalism of policy advisers see H. Laswell *A Pre-View of Policy Sciences*, chapters 7 and 8; and Arnold J. Meltsner, *Policy Analysts in the Bureaucracy*, Introduction.

33 R.J. East, 'Comparison of Strategic Planning in Large Corporations and Government', p.7.

34 Geoffrey K. Fry, 'Policy-Planning Units in British Central

Government Departments', p.150.

35 Jeffrey Stanyer, *Understanding Local Government*, p.158.
36 *BURISA*, no. 1, October 1972, p.1.
37 *BURISA*, no. 3, February 1973, p.11.
38 See A.G. Bovaird (ed.), *Register of Research Projects in Research and Intelligence Units*; E.M. Davies (ed.), *Research and Intelligence: Papers delivered at the annual conference 1979*; and *INLOGOV Register of Research Project — 1979 Update*.
39 On the role and views of chief executive officers in local government, see Margaret Lomer, 'The Chief Executive in Local Government 1974—76'; Stewart Ranson, 'Notes on a Conference — Education and Corporate Management'; and R. Greenwood et al., *In Pursuit of Corporate Rationality*.
40 Linda Challis, 'The Role and Development of the Social Services Research Group', pp.2—3.

5 Internal organization

... one of the fundamental things about a civil service job is that it has no particular significance in itself, but it gets its significance from its place in an organization.

Sir William Armstrong

The head of a policy unit is the crucial link between the planning and research personnel and the larger administrative and political systems. The Fulton Report and Society of County Clerks' Report both prescribed a model for the unit head. How do they compare to actual practice in British government? Recent administrative thinking also recognizes the importance of policy units as formal organizations. Indeed, how unit heads perform is influenced not only by their own role conceptions, but also by the size, structure and working climate of their policy units.

The policy unit head

The Fulton Committee, upon proposing that each major central government department create a planning unit or units, recommended that a senior policy adviser be head of the unit. The committee made a number of suggestions both with regard to the official role of unit heads and of the particular individual that should occupy this role.

Concerning the official role, the committee said that the prime job of a senior policy adviser would be to look to, and prepare for, the future and to ensure that day-to-day policy decisions are taken with as full a recognition as possible of likely future developments. It would also be the duty of the senior policy adviser to know the other experts in the field, both inside and outside the service, at home and abroad, and be aware of all the relevant important trends in new thinking and practice.[1]

As head of the unit staff, the policy adviser should have the chief responsibility for the forward planning of departmental policy, and be the minister's main adviser on long term policy questions and on their implications for the day-to-day policy decisions. The adviser should be the official chiefly responsible for a department's major policy planning and research, with the permanent secretary keeping responsibility for the daily operations and affairs of the department.

The Fulton Committee considered that properly to discharge their duties, senior policy advisers must have direct and unrestricted access to their minister, both personally and in writing. In addition, they should be free to determine, after consultation with the permanent secretary but subject only to the approval of the minister, what problems their planning unit should tackle.

Given the varying needs of different departments and wishes of ministers, Fulton did not wish to make specific recommendations about the senior policy adviser's rank. They foresaw a top post and high status for the adviser commensurate with being the minister's main adviser on long term policy questions. In the end, Fulton did in fact recommend that the rank of senior policy adviser should not normally be below that of deputy secretary.

Besides these official attributes, the Fulton Committee made three suggestions concerning the characteristics of the individual who should occupy the role of unit head. In terms of skills, the senior policy adviser 'should be an authority in the department's field of activity. Where a department's responsibilities are so varied that no single adviser can be an authority on all of them, he would be a specialist in a major part of the department's work'. The committee suggested that in departments with wide fields of activity it might be necessary to have more than one senior policy adviser to ensure that various departmental specialisms are included in the unit.

In terms of age, Fulton said the adviser would often be relatively young, probably in his or her mid-forties. The committee thought 'considerable advantages are gained in France and Sweden from the system by which the average age of the French directeurs du cabinet is 46 and of Swedish under-secretaries 45. The average age of Permanent Secretaries in Britain is 56'. As a member of the committee explained later, 'the argument was that the Senior Policy Adviser should normally be a relatively young man so that we could have people in the British civil service who carried the same kind of responsibilities for forward thinking at a relatively early age as do the Directeurs and the Under Secretaries in the French and Swedish civil services'.[2]

In terms of origins, Fulton said senior policy advisers should normally be career civil servants with long experience in and expert knowledge of, the field covered by the department, and that it would be advantageous if advisers also had some experience outside the Civil Service. Occasionally, senior policy advisers might be appointed by a minister from outside the service to give new impetus to its forward thinking.

On the recruitment and possible replacement of the senior policy adviser, Fulton hoped that whether career civil servants or outsiders, senior policy advisers would be selected on the basis of technical competence and vitality, and ministers would therefore not normally wish to replace them. However, since the role was partly intended to increase the control of ministers over the formulation of policy in their department, Fulton recognized that in some cases the minister may wish to change the individual in the role. Thus, Fulton suggested that a minister should be free to replace a senior policy adviser 'when a new Minister finds the current holder of this office too closely identified with, or wedded to, policies that he wishes to change; or when an adviser's capacity for producing and making use of new ideas declines'. This proposal allows for government sympathizers and politically committed experts to be appointed as senior policy advisers in some departments, with the possibility that the units would become politicized.

The Fulton Committee's recommendations on the senior policy adviser provoked much interest and debate in Parliament and the civil service world. In November 1968, during the House of Commons debate about the Fulton Report, Sir Edward (now Lord) Boyle, who had been a member of the Fulton Committee, singled out the senior policy adviser suggestion as one of the recommendations which had most widely attracted criticism. Indeed, other MPs in their speeches on Fulton discussed the policy adviser concept, including the then Paymaster-General, Mrs Judith Hart, and the Leader of the Opposition, Mr Edward Heath.[3] At about the same time, Sir James Dunnett, then Permanent Under Secretary in the Ministry of Defence, who had also been a member of the Fulton Committee, observed: 'It is the recommendation in favour of having Senior Policy Advisers which has perhaps created the most excitement among retired Permanent Secretaries who have spoken to me'.[4] Undoubtedly, the recommendation also excited existing permanent secretaries, and created much discussion and different views within Whitehall.

Much of the discussion centred on the proposal that the adviser should have direct and unrestricted access to the minister. Edward Heath supported the recommendations for planning units and policy advisers. However, Mr Heath argued that they should operate and report through the permanent secretary and not directly to a minister, to ensure the units do not become detached from policy formation and those who are handling the day-to-day issues. Other MPs suggested that direct access of policy advisers to the minister may raise problems of ministerial favourites, or difficulties within the department. Sir Edward Boyle admitted during the parliamentary debate on Fulton that he had doubts as to whether the senior policy adviser should have an independent line to the minister, bypassing the permanent secretary.

Speaking on behalf of the Government, Mrs Hart argued against 'those rigidities which in any way circumscribe the particular contributions that can be made, either by policy advisers or the Permanent Secretary and the senior officials'. She said that advice to ministers had traditionally been given 'not only by the Permanent Secretary, but by all the senior officials; by the deputy secretaries and under secretaries, according to the particular area of importance, and the subject which was of concern to them'. However, she admitted that officials and advisers normally put forward their views of policy through the permanent secretary and only on the odd occasion direct to the minister.

In his 1971 study of policy planning units in central government departments, Geoffrey Fry concluded, 'no posts of Senior Policy Adviser of the type envisaged by the Fulton Committee have been created'. Fry made the following observation: 'The heads of the various planning units, even when of Deputy Secretary status, as in the Ministry of Defence's arrangements, do not enjoy the privileged access to the Minister that the Fulton Committee proposed'.[5] Fry found that their relationship with the minister is much the same as other senior administrators, with no sign of permanent secretaries being bypassed in the manner that Fulton described. This conclusion, however, is based only on two aspects of the senior policy adviser role as described by Fulton; that is, rank and access to the minister. The extent to which unit heads correspond to the role suggested by Fulton can only be fully understood if one takes into account all the suggested organizational and personal attributes, and compares them with actual practice.

With respect to organizational role, most unit head posts do not exhibit the Fulton features. The label senior policy adviser is rarely used as the official title of unit head posts in the Civil Service. The posts are normally described by rank, such as under secretary, assistant secretary or senior economic adviser. More important, the post of unit head has not been recognized nor designed as the main adviser to ministers on long term policy questions in departments. The general opinion in the Civil Service on this is perhaps best captured in a Civil Service Department paper written by S.D. Walker in 1974.[6] Walker says post-Fulton developments in the organization of departmental policy planning and analytic activities indicate that the task of co-ordinating this work 'is one for top management and not for a "planing unit" '. Policy units in central government departments are seen as providing various forms of support to the permanent secretary and senior officials. 'But', Walker adds, 'the ultimate responsibility for co-ordinating policies, for allocating resources and for deciding the priorities between competing policies cannot be allocated to a "planning unit" '.

Most unit heads do not hold the rank of deputy secretary that Fulton thought would be the status senior policy advisers should normally have. One notable exception is the CPRS, in which the post of unit head is at the rank of permanent secretary and the assistant head is at the deputy secretary level. Usually, though, unit heads are at the under secretary or assistant secretary level.

In general, the relationship of unit heads to ministers is similar to that of other senior officials, operating through permanent secretaries and senior policy and management committees. Unit heads do not have direct and unrestricted access to a minister on a regular or institutionalized basis, although in some cases a unit head may directly brief a minister. Indeed, most unit heads have only limited access to their permanent secretary. Finally, unit heads are not free to determine what problems the unit should tackle subject only to the approval of the minister, although a good deal of the work that units do and the problems they tackle are suggested by the unit themselves. Nearly all units are active in generating some of their own work after consultation with senior officials and administrators.

Thus, the heads of policy planning units in the civil service are on tap but not on top. They do not enjoy free access to ministers nor do they manage departmental planning systems. A number of obstacles facing the senior policy adviser concept can be noted which suggest why this Fulton proposal was not implemented. As proposed by Fulton, the senior policy adviser role breaches the principle of unity of command whereby all departmental officials report to ministers through the administrative head, the permanent secretary. The role also challenges the principles of the neutrality and anonymity of civil servants and the confidentiality of their advice to ministers. The appointment of outside party sympathizers to senior level advisory roles would politicize the central bureaucracy. Moreover, for some officials, the Fulton concept was based on a false dichotomy between the planning and administration functions. In the words of Sir Richard Clarke, 'There is perhaps a false antithesis between "management" and "policy", for it is assuredly the Permanent Secretary's responsibility both to advise the Minister on policy and strategy of the department, and to create the instrument by which the Minister carries this out'.[7] In short, the senior policy adviser concept was contrary to the deep tradition in the public administrative culture in Britain 'of the regular civil service as ministerial advisers, of the view of ministers as temporary heads of permanent organisations, and of the distrust of political forms of staff assistance'.[8]

The individuals that occupy unit head positions in the civil service are in closer accord with the criteria the Fulton Committee proposed. Virtually all unit heads are career civil servants. They are selected on the basis of competence and their experience in at least one major part of the department's responsibilities. Furthermore, the age of the unit head is generally in line with the Fulton proposal that the heads be relatively young; unit heads are often in their mid-forties or younger. However, this is because the actual rank of most unit heads is lower than that proposed by the Fulton Committee.

Overall, policy unit heads in the civil service do not correspond to the organizational features of the post as described by Fulton. One important qualification is that much of the work done by units is self initiated. With respect to the personal features of the post holder, unit heads do generally correspond to the age, origins and skills criteria that the Fulton Committee recommended. Hence it would be incorrect to say that senior policy advisers à la Fulton have not taken root in the Civil Service. To be sure, the position has not come to fruition but the actual people in the role of unit head do reflect the Fulton philosophy.

The importance of the director of research and planning units was also clearly emphasized in local government administrative philosophy. For example, the Society of County Clerks' Report, in recommending the creation of a research and intelligence unit in the new county councils, said: 'the success or failure of a central unit will largely depend upon the standing and personal qualities of the Director of the unit'.[9]

In regard to the organizational role, the Clerks' Report suggested a comparatively senior rank for unit heads. On the basis of information obtained on experience in Cheshire, Kent and Greater London, and an examination of statisticians' salaries in the Civil Service, they suggested, the director of a central unit will need to be graded as equivalent to third tier posts in departments. Regardless of the organizational location of the unit in the authority, the head of the unit should be accountable directly to the chief executive and the management team, and the unit's work programme be controlled and ultimately approved by the chief officers' management team.

On the type of person who should occupy this post, the Clerks' Report recommended the unit head should be an experienced statistician or economist who is knowledgeable about local government, which meant being conversant with inter-departmental relationships, methods of working and the priorities of the local authority. Unlike Fulton, the Society of County Clerks' Report did not consider the age of unit heads.

Policy unit heads in local government do reflect the attributes proposed by the Society's Report. The majority of unit heads are at fairly senior grades, normally at the principal officer rank, and in a few cases at the assistant chief officer or chief officer level. A survey of central research units in local government conducted in 1978 found that in the response group of seventy-three unit heads, about half were third tier officers while nearly a third were chief or deputy chief officer rank.[10] Senior ranking unit posts are found in nearly all types of departments, and unit heads in counties tend to be in higher grade positions than those in other types of local authorities. Policy unit heads with a chief officer rank, such as in Bolton, Cleveland and Rugby, are in charge of independent units with a departmental status.

In local authorities, unit heads frequently report to the chief executive officer (or assistant) and/or the chief officers' management team. Indeed, most *central* research units in local government are directly responsible to the chief executive officer. In some authorities unit heads are responsible to a departmental chief officer or deputy chief officer. In only a relatively few cases does the head of a unit report to a third tier officer.

Generally, the arrangements for setting the work programme include some form of approval by a chief officer or group of senior officers. In a few cases, such as the Programme Planning Unit in Sunderland, unit heads are independent chief officers not subject to control by the chief officer's management team but with a loyalty to the leader of the council and the chief executive. Such an overt allegiance to the governing political party is not widespread among unit heads in local government. In Sunderland the central unit's primary responsibility is to ensure that the elected representatives are adequately informed. This requires the unit to be pragmatic, politically aware and close to everyday pressures.

Operating within such an environment clearly has a bearing on the unit's work programme and on the type of person best suited to be a unit head. Like their central government counterparts, local authority units exercise some discretion and self initiative in generating their work programme. In terms of personal attributes, most unit heads studied have a background in a numerate discipline such as economics, statistics, operational research or accounting, and nearly all are knowledgeable about local government in terms of personal work experience.

A fuller picture of the policy unit head in British government can be obtained by examining the roles or patterns of behaviour and activities associated with this position. The behaviour of unit heads can be grouped into six basic roles: personnel manager, policy planner, research manager, representative, promoter and protector. While not all unit heads necessarily perform all these roles, they generally depict the functions that unit heads should and do perform. These roles are not performed exclusively by unit heads; some duties may be delegated and/or performed by other unit personnel.

One group of activities that policy unit heads deal with are personnel management roles. Unit heads are concerned with the recruitment, training, staff development, morale and motivation of unit members. This may involve discussing career prospects with members, finding the right staff and trying to keep the good staff. It also involves building morale by telling staff they are making contributions to policy, asking their opinions on issues and assigning them pieces of major work. If the unit is multidisciplinary in composition the unit head will have to ensure there is genuine respect and interaction between the various disciplines and some balance in the use of the unit's various skills in specific projects.

Secondly, the unit head is a policy planner. This function deals with being the planner of policy for the unit and may include developing procedures on the confidentiality of advice or the advocacy and selling tactics to be used by the staff. In part, then, the policy planner role is concerned with the internal working processes of units. In addition, this role can also mean that the unit head is a policy planner specialist who performs analytical and planning activities similar to other unit personnel. Thus, unit heads often carry out operational functions along with their managerial tasks. A proper balance between these sets of activities is crucial to the survival and effectiveness of policy units in government.

A third group of responsibilities constitute the research manager role. Some of the main activities related to research management include defining and interpreting the unit's goals, managing the overall development of the work programme, deciding upon the division of labour and resources within the unit, and monitoring the progress of projects being undertaken by the unit members. The role also involves ensuring the work is actually done and in accordance with some standards, such as meeting client needs and avoiding undue bias, and resolving any conflict that might arise between unit members doing a study. The head of the unit is ultimately responsible for the work of his or her members, and many heads see part of their role as overseeing the quality of work, refining and amending it when necessary and trying to make it as high a quality as possible.

Unit heads engage in a fourth range of activities that deal with representative roles. These roles involve the unit head linking or relating the unit to its external environment. One unit head summed it up with the remark, 'I'm the formal link between the unit and the rest of the world'. The head of a policy unit may represent the unit formally and informally at council, council committees, departmental or interdepartmental official committees, working parties, meetings with politicians and senior officials, other local authorities, and a host of public and private organizations. The unit head may be showing the flag, giving advice, communicating the unit's views, presenting and interpreting reports, or representing the department or authority on aspects of policy planning and research. There is nothing simple about showing the flag. It requires constant alertness and awareness, coupled with the ability to manipulate or exploit each situation as it arises.

In this representative role the unit head acts as a bridge and often as an interpreter between unit staff and administrators and politicians. The linking role can help unit staff appreciate the needs and priorities of policy makers and help make policy makers aware of the best ways of using the unit's skills and resources. As the director of research in a social services department has expressed it: 'In playing this role the research manager is essentially bringing together the differing realities and values of policy makers and their researchers'.[11] In which case, the ability to communicate with and gain the confidence of the layman is of major significance to the unit director.

A fifth group of activities consists of promotional roles. Most unit heads partly see themselves as salespersons or promoters, trying to sell other officials on the importance of policy planning and research, the unit's role and the competence of its staff. Activities of the unit head as promoter include the following: anticipating, cultivating and suggesting possible work topics; fostering the use of the unit by departments; developing, building and maintaining relationships of trust with officials; promoting the operation of related corporate management and policy planning procedures and information systems; and, selling the unit's completed work in such a way as to maximize its acceptance. These activities are all related to the goal of organizational survival. Policy units have placed a high prority on creating conditions that will ensure their survival and the role of the unit head reflects this concern. In essence, the role of promoter includes ensuring that the voice of the unit is heard and that the unit is involved in the policy and management processes of British government.

There is a sixth group of activities that may be called protection roles. Whereas the role of promoter can be viewed as the active, positive side of the survival coin, the role of protector is the negative, reactive side. This role can involve protecting members from all the bureaucratic paper work, and discouraging inappropriate or impossible demands being placed upon the unit, such as rapid results on complex problems. Another aspect of this role consists of the unit head fighting for the unit in getting a fair share of available resources. Finally, the unit head may frequently fight on behalf of the research team at top management level to justify and explain why the researchers want to extend a project or expand the original research problem or to explain why the researchers have turned against the conventional wisdom of the client.[12]

The roles of personnel manager, policy planner, research manager, representative, promoter and protector are carried out by unit heads in varying styles and methods. To some extent, the manner in which a unit head performs these roles is dependent upon the size and internal patterns of structure of the policy unit.

Small is beautiful: the size of policy units

A number of official inquiries and academic studies in British public administrative thought has considered the question of the size of policy units. A common theme running through much of this literature is that, in terms of the number of personnel, policy units should be small organizations.

The Fulton Committee thought that policy planning units in central government departments should be relatively small, although no precise figure was given. The units were to be small since they would not be responsible for any of the day-to-day operations of departments. Fulton also implied that a small unit would provide an environment in which qualities of imagination and foresight seen as essential for long term planning could be encouraged. Even in large departments with a diverse range of activities, Fulton suggested that instead of one big unit spanning the various policy fields it may well be that more than one planning unit should be set up.

The 1970 White Paper on *The Reorganisation of Central Government* announced the establishment of the CPRS in the Cabinet Office. The CPRS was described as a small multidisciplinary staff. A major objective of the CPRS was to produce a strategic definition of the priority to be given the government's policies and programmes. The White Paper described this task as a new and formidable one which can only be approached gradually. The small CPRS was therefore seen as a beginning, the first step toward producing a comprehensive definition of government strategy. Moreover, the number of staff in the CPRS was to be small since the unit was not to duplicate or replace the analytical work done by departments in their own areas of responsibility.

Administrative thinking in local government has also emphasized a small size for policy units. The Bains Report, for example, spoke of a small research and intelligence unit located in a county clerk's department, possibly meaning four or five people including support staff.[13] Bains also preferred very small corporate planning units in local authorities, perhaps only one or two staff members, operating through officers from other departments of the authority. The small size of policy units was defended on two grounds.

First, small size meant the corporate planning unit would be kept in close touch with the reality of what was actually happening on the ground. Professor J.D. Stewart made a similar point around the same time: 'Such a unit should not be built up to a point where it removes so much of the work of local authority policy planning from the departments that they lose all sense of involvement with it'.[14] Second, with a small permanent staff in a central policy unit, Bains suggested 'those officers within departments who serve within the unit will be given valuable experience in the broad management problems of the authority as a whole'.

On the staffing of central research and intelligence units in local government, the Society of County Clerks' Report stated, 'even the largest of the new Counties ... will not need, for the foreseeable future, a unit having more than 12 professional and clerical staff' to undertake information, research consultancy and corporate planning support devices. The Society's Report proposed a larger sized policy unit than Bains because they emphasized the career potential of units. They believed that a central unit with twelve staff would be large enough in most counties to offer an attractive career structure to qualified staff who would otherwise have only very limited outlets in the field of local government. Moreover, a central unit with several staff would be better able to attract and retain the skills needed for corporate management and research, than to have such staff dispersed throughout departments. Similar arguments were made in the early 1970s by a number of students of British local government that a unit of about six to ten full time members would 'be able to work more quickly and enable an across the board approach to be pursued'.[15]

Policy planning and research units in British government are *small* organizations. Most have twenty or fewer full time planners and researchers. Small policy units are common at both levels of government, although units in central government tend to be relatively larger in size. Central government policy units also appear to have a comparatively bigger supportive component. The average size of central government units sampled was twelve persons whereas in local government it was eight. When support staff are included, the average unit size in central government rises to fourteen and in local government to nine people. It is very difficult to measure the number of part time staff that units employ since the number of temporary staff is often flexible, expanding and contracting as work demands change. It can be mentioned, however, that a few units, particularly in county councils, employ comparatively large numbers of part time staff to conduct household surveys.

This finding that policy units in British government are small organizations is in line with the results of other recent surveys done in the United Kingdom on the number of personnel in various research and planning organizations in government and business.[16]

The view that all organizations have inherent tendencies to grow in size has wide acceptance. As one organization theorist, Richard Hall, puts it: 'Even in a no-growth economy, public and private organizations try to grow at one another's expense'.[17] Hall claims that all organizations have an orientation toward growth and a momentum toward greater organizational size. If this is true, it should be expected that unit members would exhibit strong growth oriented attitudes. And since most policy units are small in numbers, it might be assumed that this type of organization would, through time, display actual growth or at least attempts at greater organizational size.

Yet, most policy units are small and, more interestingly, they have *remained small*. It is also interesting that many unit members do not express growth oriented attitudes. To be sure, some units have grown, and some officials do express interest in larger policy units. Nevertheless, the proposition that all organizations inherently tend toward growth can be overemphasized. In particular, such a proposition does not accurately portray the motivations of many policy advisers nor the experiences of most policy units.

Environmental conditions have tended to promote the small size of units and inhibit their organizational growth. One of these environmental conditions has been recent public administrative thought in Britain. The prevailing belief about the organizational size of policy units is that units should be of a small size. Another external condition has been the shortage of qualified and experienced research and statistical specialists. This has meant that many local authorities, at least during the early and mid-1970s, were unable to establish fully staffed units. The situation in recent years of no real growth and, in some cases, resource reductions in government, has also tended to inhibit the growth of units. Indeed, many units have experienced a decline in size. For example, the Home Office Research Unit has decreased from over sixty to about fifty professional staff over the past several years. The Central Research Unit at Mid Glamorgan has declined from sixteen to eleven staff in less than five years. Other units of even smaller size at both levels of government have experienced a contraction by vacant posts not being filled.

Key actors in the immediate organizational environment of policy units have tended to prefer that units remain small in size. Even senior officials who could be regarded as natural allies of units, such as chief executive officers in local authorities, generally believe units are required but should be small in size.[18] As one corporate planner in a district council explained, 'we have the research staff but now we need the chief officers who will support and use that staff'. Officials

102

at both levels suggest that if planning or corporate management firmly take hold in government then perhaps policy units should expand in size but that at present there is not sufficient support nor demand to justify such expansion.

A second reason for the lack of growth in policy units is that many unit heads have not pursued or advocated organizational expansion. This situation is intriguing as it seems to conflict with the conventional view of the relation between organizational members and organizational growth. This view is demonstrated by Hall when he states, 'growth is a major way in which organizational decision makers or elites demonstrate their contributions to the organization'.[19] Likewise, Downs has argued: 'The expansion of any organization normally provides its leaders with increased power, income and prestige; hence they encourage its growth'.[20] However, many policy planners and researchers do not regard organizational growth as organizational success, nor as the best way to demonstrate their contributions. Here, for example, is the view of a former leader of the CPRS, Sir Kenneth Berrill, on the desirable size of that unit: 'I do not think that is ever a part of our job to try to create the expertise in all the possible lines of government. If we tried to do that, even a little bit, a unit of under 20 would by definition expand quite a lot'.[21]

Both Sir Kenneth and Lord Rothschild, the first head of the CPRS, felt strongly that a bigger unit would be a different one and not so successful. A corporate planner in a local authority conveys a similar view: 'Nor am I convinced of the legitimacy of big units (say 10+ staff) with large work programmes, don't they exist to bludgeon departmental colleagues into submission?'[22]

Unit heads and members *are* interested in gaining more status for themselves and their organization. The promotional and protective roles of unit staff are obviously linked with maintaining and developing organizational and occupational status. However, organizational growth is not always a means by which increased status can be realized. In fact, given the environmental conditions in which policy units operate, attempts at organizational growth could conceivably lead to a decline in unit status. To some extent this preference for small units may indicate a rationalization by unit members of their existing situation and environmental conditions.

Policy advisers offer the following reasons why units should remain small in size: to avoid spending a lot of time on such administrative matters as holidays, replacements and co-ordination; in a large unit there is little incentive to keep reports short and crisp; it may be difficult to find enough work for a large unit; and, to avoid a bureaucratic organization which prevents a group discussion and close working relationships. Indeed, these views are partly supported by research on the relation between organizational size and the relative size of the administrative component. The percentage of an organization devoted to administrative and supportive tasks such as supervision and control, increases disproportionately in size as the organization expands at the initial stages of growth. The proportion of the administration component then decreases with further growth.[23] These findings are of particular importance to policy units. Being at the low end of the size scale, any additional growth, although probably small in absolute numbers, would likely mean a significant increase in the administrative task.

Changes in the size of an organization have more significance for behaviour at certain points along a scale of size than at other points. A unit much bigger than twenty members would be a very different one. Indeed, one organization theorist has argued: 'If a work crew with fifteen members is doubled in size, its structure and its activities are quite certain to change, because the pattern of close interaction possible among fifteen persons is improbable among thirty'. Yet, in contrast, 'a work group of two hundred members might be doubled in size without any striking changes in its structure'.[24]

An important goal of all policy units is organizational survival. It has frequently been suggested in administrative theory that an organization's chances of survival increase with expansion and growth. However, contrary to this view, policy planners and researchers contend that by remaining relatively small in size, units have a better chance of survival than if they attempt to develop into large organizations.

Guy Benveniste has pointed out in his analysis of planning and advisory teams: 'The team should remain small, by bureaucratic standards, because a large staff is too visible and therefore too vulnerable to attack on other than professional grounds. Any large, expensive staff of experts is easily accused of wasting resources and can be eliminated before it has a chance to defend itself'.[25] By remaining small, the unit avoids creating the appearance of Big Brother or empire building which can often aggravate interorganizational relations. A small sized unit permits flexibility in that the unit can expand as the planning process develops, being augmented with personnel from other organizations which allows potentially friendly groups inside or outside the bureaucracy to be involved, making it more likely that a unit's work will be accepted. Thus, the common belief that all organizations have an inherent orientation toward growth must be investigated and should not be taken as a universal tendency. For policy unit personnel, at least, small is beautiful; survival is a more categorical imperative than growth.

Informal bureaucracy: structure and climate

Policy units are informal bureaucracies; their official hierarchy of roles are joined with a pattern of informal and adaptive working relations. The internal structure of policy units can be fruitfully examined in relation to the following dimensions: the number of major subdivisions (horizontal differentiation); the criteria used in allocating work among unit staff (the allocation of functions); the number of hierarchical levels (vertical differentiation); the degree to which staff and physical facilities are spatially dispersed (spatial differentiation); and, the extent to which the various members and subdivisions in a unit interact and are brought together (integration). Besides these structural dimensions, the concept of organizational climate permits some observations on internal working relationships.

With regard to horizontal differentiation, policy units generally are not very complex organizations. Most units have only one major subdivision. As might be expected, those units with several subdivisions are the comparatively larger units.

Policy units employ a variety of principles in grouping the work among their staff. Units may be subdivided on the basis of occupational categories. The Housing Analysis and Monitoring Unit (HAMU) in the Department of the Environment is subdivided along generalist—specialist lines. Like the Departmental Planning Unit in HM Customs and Excise, and the Corporate Planning Unit in the Department of Energy, HAMU has an administrator and a specialist as joint heads. The dual heads of HAMU are an assistant secretary Administration Group, and a senior economic adviser, assistant secretary equivalent in the Government Economic Service. Under these heads are parallel hierarchies of generalists and specialists.

Some units are subdivided according to policy area. An example is the Social Research Branch in the Department of Health and Social Security which consists of two sections, one related to health and the other to social security. Several units are organized on the principle of function. The Central Research and Intelligence Unit at Tyne and Wear, for instance, is comprised of three sections — policy analysis, intelligence services and information services. A fourth criterion according to which units may be internally differentiated is time. The Corporate Planning Division in the Department of Energy at one time included three sections, one charged with long term planning and a second charged with the medium term. The third section was based upon the principle of type of advice; that is, planning techniques and methodology, which may transcend a policy area or time period.

Units can also be subdivided on the basis of clients served. The Corporate Planning Unit in Plymouth allocates the work among its three members by assigning to each member responsibility for two of the council's committees. Geographical area is still another principle on which units may be subdivided. The Foreign and Commonwealth Office Planning Staff, whose individual members deal with European problems, Africa and so on, is an example. Finally, units are organized on a task force or team basis. Probably the dominant principles upon which policy units are internally organized are team basis and function.

In regard to the number of levels between the unit head and the junior position in a unit, most policy units have multilevel hierarchies, while some units have just one or two levels. Many have between three to six levels, the most common number probably being five levels. Overall, full time staff in central research units in local government, for example, span about nine grades of authority from clerk to principal officer and higher.[26] In this sense, policy units do display a formal or mechanistic structure with a hierarchy of offices. In virtually all units the personnel are concentrated in one location. In other terms, units have a low degree of spatial differentiation. Many units also operate within an open concept physical setting which means staff are in close physical and visual proximity to one another.

The co-ordination and integration of unit work is achieved through discussions and meetings, job rotation, flexible working roles between subdivisions and an emphasis on team work. The changing environment in which policy units operate, facing fresh problems and unforeseen tasks, means that their work cannot always be broken down or distributed to certain roles. Units have established integrative methods to adapt to their environments, particularly the team approach to internal organization.

When the Programme Planning Unit in Greenwich was set up there was a clear division of functions between the staff engaged in research and analysis under the senior research officer and those who were employed in programme planning in relation to the community plan. Figure 5.1 shows the structure of the unit as it was originally conceived. This structure was found to be unworkable in practice. The workload of the unit, particularly on the planning side, varied considerably throughout the year, and during the first few annual reviews of the community plan, the research staff worked on planning. To the staff there appeared little point in attempting to create an artificial distinction between planning and research when the dividing line was so blurred. This distinction has almost wholly disappeared. The unit now operates in a fairly flexible manner and Figure 5.2 shows how the unit generally functions in practice. Apart from the work of the three project co-ordinators, the remainder of the staff are given both a research and planning role.

The Greenwich experience illustrates a planning organization which started along mechanistic lines with the duties of each position clearly set out in an organization chart and with a hierarchical system of

FIGURE 5-1

INTENDED STRUCTURE OF GREENWICH PROGRAMME PLANNING UNIT, 1970

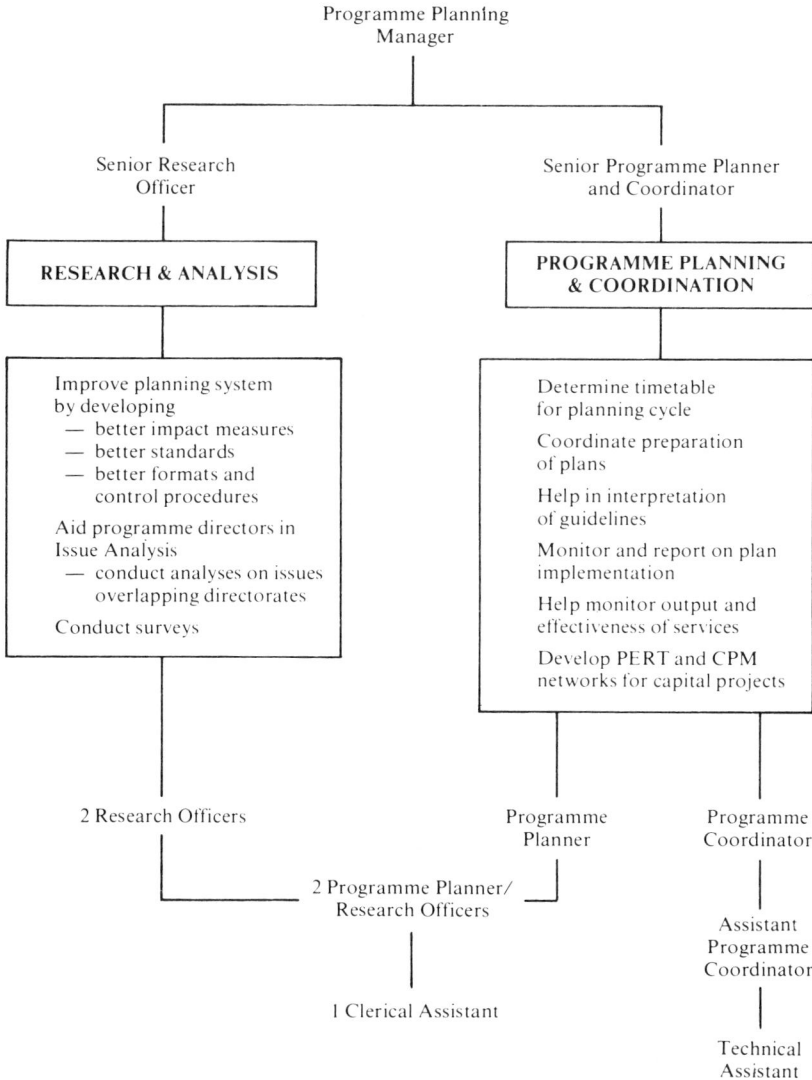

Programme Planning
Manager

Senior Research
Officer

Senior Programme Planner
and Coordinator

RESEARCH & ANALYSIS

**PROGRAMME PLANNING
& COORDINATION**

Improve planning system
by developing
— better impact measures
— better standards
— better formats and
  control procedures

Aid programme directors in
Issue Analysis
— conduct analyses on issues
  overlapping directorates

Conduct surveys

Determine timetable
for planning cycle

Coordinate preparation
of plans

Help in interpretation
of guidelines

Monitor and report on plan
implementation

Help monitor output and
effectiveness of services

Develop PERT and CPM
networks for capital projects

2 Research Officers

Programme
Planner

Programme
Coordinator

2 Programme Planner/
Research Officers

Assistant
Programme
Coordinator

1 Clerical Assistant

Technical
Assistant

FIGURE 5-2

THE GREENWICH PROGRAMME PLANNING UNIT IN PRACTICE

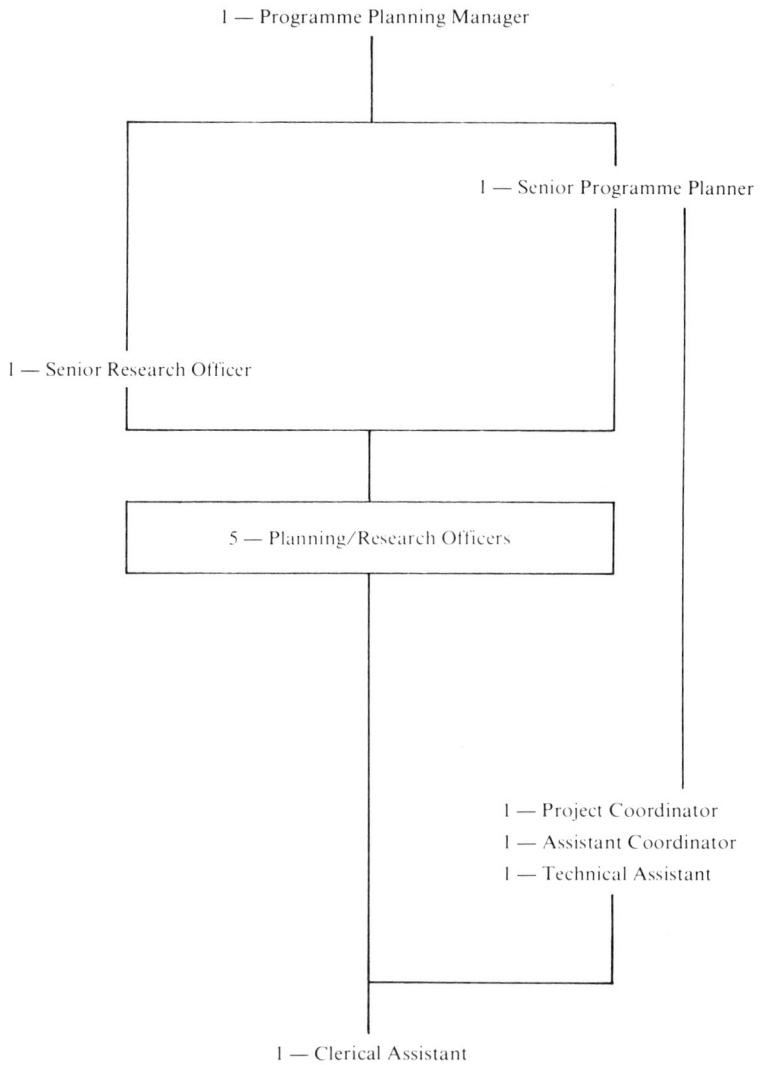

1 — Programme Planning Manager

1 — Senior Programme Planner

1 — Senior Research Officer

5 — Planning/Research Officers

1 — Project Coordinator
1 — Assistant Coordinator
1 — Technical Assistant

1 — Clerical Assistant

responsibility. Yet as the unit staff learned about their environment and the dynamic nature of their responsibilities they found they could not effectively and quickly respond to changing demands. The Greenwich unit therefore adopted a relatively different organization structure more along organic lines with a fluid and collegiate pattern of work duties. Some elements of bureaucracy still remain however.

The integration and internal co-ordination of policy units is facilitated by the widespread use of teams as a working method. This type of work method as used in the Central Policy Review Staff has been described as follows: 'Members of CPRS usually work in small teams, consisting of between two and five people. Most people will be members of, say, three teams. Wherever possible, the teams are made up of people from different backgrounds, so that different kinds of expertise can be brought to bear on particular problems'.[27] The result is that unit members are likely to find themselves dividing their time between a major piece of work and smaller jobs — some longer term, some shorter term.

Most units, it seems, prefer to operate on a team basis. This may then mean that all members of a unit are engaged on any one project throughout its life. More frequently it may involve the consideration of a problem and its likely solution by the entire staff followed by the delegation of the project to a team consisting of some of the unit's members. Another variation to the team approach is that responsibility for a project is given to one unit member and throughout the life of that project the member may draw on other unit members when their particular skills are required. The team approach has several potential benefits. In terms of work load, neither the unit as a whole nor any individual within it will become over-burdened. Operating on a flexible team basis enables a unit better to respond to the changing work load it may face. Some policy unit staff believe the team approach results in improved consideration being given to precise problem formulation and a broader consideration to an appropriate research method and possible recommendations. Finally, each member is encouraged to take a view beyond their own sphere of specialization and to integrate various forms of advice. Thus, the team approach to internal organization serves as a useful method for training and job development.

The organizational climate or work atmosphere of policy planning and research units has been prescribed by a number of writers. The Fulton Committee, for example, believed policy units could help generate the thrust and drive needed for long term planning and also provide an environment in which those who possess qualities of imagination and foresight could be developed. Similarly, Yehezkel Dror has urged, 'The organizational climate and work patterns of policy research organizations must encourage frank mutual criticism, uninhibited creativity, breakdown of disciplinary boundaries, continuous learning by staff and constant freshness of approach'.[28]

What is it like to work in a policy unit in British government? What is the organizational climate of policy units? Do planners and researchers more or less share a distinctive set of perceptions and methods of work? Indicators of organization climate to be considered here include perceptions of the degree of structure, the character of internal unit relations, and the leadership style of unit heads.[29]

Policy planning units are officially structured organizations according to a formal hierarchy of authority. This is not only an inevitable result of being within government, but it allows one recognizable opinion to emerge from the unit and therefore assist the unit head in his or her relations with other officials. While policy planners and researchers see their units as being officially structured, in actual practice they see them as unstructured and non-bureaucratic. Typical comments are: this unit is not hierarchical; we are non-bureaucratic and non-routine — we are stepping out into all directions; we work in a very organic or unstructured way; and, we use very few standardized rules and procedures. Officials suggest that units have fluid internal structures because the advisory nature of their work means operating in a dynamic environment. The small size of units also allows informal and unstructured patterns of work.

In terms of working relations within units, officials frequently say they operate in an easy going atmosphere, and that relations between unit members are personal and very relaxed. Unit members believe they have some freedom in choosing and handling projects. The assignment of tasks within units tends to develop around the type of people rather than the other way. Policy units have attempted to provide a working climate or environment in which imagination and foresight can be developed. Their operational norms emphasize flexibility in roles and a team approach to problem solving.

Unit heads generally exhibit a participatory leadership style. In this type of leadership process the unit head has high influence, subordinates enjoy some influence and freedom, and there is frequent contact between them.[30] Unit heads enjoy high influence in that their position is at the apex of the authority structure of policy units. Unit heads normally approve all work proposals and final studies, and try to resolve conflicts that might arise between unit members. Another indication of the high influence of some unit heads is that all external letters and written communications must be signed or at least seen by the unit head. This enables the head to remain aware of all unit activities. Additionally, unit heads encourage staff to keep aware of developments in their field, to develop contacts with clients, other officials and groups both inside and outside government, and to pursue educational and professional affiliations. Unit members

110

are often given considerable scope and flexibility in their work.

Putting planning and research functions into separate organizations has led to unit heads performing the roles of personnel manager, planner, and research manager, representative, promoter and protector. It has also meant that unit personnel have some discretion in generating policy advice. The small size of units can be seen to encourage a pattern of close working relationships among planners and researchers and, hence, to contribute to their professional development. The organizational climate of policy units includes a low degree of structured behaviour, easy going work relationships and a participatory leadership style by unit heads. Small size can also impose restrictions on a unit's ability to offer policy advice, which may induce greater doubts about their efficacy.

The analysis in this chapter partly challenges and subsequently refines the conventional view of the structure of policy planning and research units. To describe units as organic structures, as 'teams organised in flexible, collegiate rather than hierarchical structures' is the truth but not the whole truth.[31] Policy units contain both organic and mechanistic elements of organization design.

Alongside the fluid and collegial relationships among policy personnel, some degree of official structure, hierarchy and management control are found. This suggests that two apparently contradictory principles of structure exist in policy units. As the Greenwich unit experience illustrates the two principles must be kept in some balance. Moreover, both principles can contribute to the effective performance of policy units. Formal integrative measures assist the co-ordination of unit staff and policy ideas, and a management hierarchy facilitates the communication of advice from a unit and helps a unit relate to its interorganizational context. A low degree of formal differentiation enables policy units to remain flexible and responsive to their environment. A team approach permits a reliance on informal rules and provides a blending of disciplines.

This portrait of planning and research units is more complex than the one usually provided in the organizational theory literature. We may be moving toward a new way of thinking about management and organization patterns. Rather than treating organic and mechanistic elements as contradictory principles along a single dimension of more or less formality, they may in reality be two separate dimensions. Perhaps organic and mechanistic traits are not the obverse of each other but instead are distinct dimensions of organizational behaviour.

Of course, planners and researchers not only operate within a policy unit but carry on relationships with other organizations in British government. It is therefore appropriate to turn to an examination of the location and relationship of policy units within the larger political and administrative system.

Notes

1 *Report* of the Committee on the Civil Service, vol. 1, para. 182. The following remarks draw from paras. 182–4.
2 Sir James Dunnett, 'The Fulton Report – Equipping the Civil Service for its Tasks', p.25.
3 *HC Debates*, (1968–69), vol. 773, c. 1665–6, 1572–3, 1628 and 1680.
4 Sir James Dunnett, 'The Fulton Report', p.24.
5 Geoffrey K. Fry, 'Policy-Planning Units in British Central Government Departments', pp.149–50.
6 S.D. Walker, 'Some Thoughts on Planning in the Civil Service', p.8.
7 Sir Richard Clarke, *New Trends in Government*, p.114.
8 Peter Self, *Administrative Theories and Politics*, p.132. See also, John Garrett and Robert Sheldon, *Administrative Reform: The Next Step*, pp.3–4; and James Macdonald and G.K. Fry, 'Policy Planning Units – Ten Years On', pp.430–1.
9 A.J. Greenwell et al., 'Research and Intelligence in the New County Councils', p.37. See also Bernard Benjamin, *Statistics and Research in Urban Administration and Development.*
10 E.M. Davies, *The Central Research Function in Local Government.*
11 Andrew Leigh, 'The Work of Social Services Researchers and Its Impact on Social Policy', p.109.
12 Andrew Leigh, 'Researchers in the Social Services', pp.60–1.
13 *The New Local Authorities, Management and Structure*, paras. 7.26–7.28. The figure of four or five is suggested since the report was probably referring to the unit in Bain's own authority, Kent County Council.
14 J.D. Stewart, *Management in Local Government: A Viewpoint*, p.174.
15 J. Skitt, *Practical Corporate Planning*, p.159; and Michael Greenwood, 'Corporate Planning Units', p.500.
16 See Elisabeth Cherns and Norman Perry (eds), *Demand for Social Knowledge: The Role of Research Organizations*; Anne Wedgewood-Oppenheim, 'A Look at Research Staff in Local Authority Social Service Departments'; Mike Clegg, 'Corporate Planning, Corporate Planning Units and Planning Departments'; David L. Smith (ed.), *Research and Intelligence in the New Local Authorities*; Geoffrey K. Fry, 'Policy-Planning Units in British Central Government Departments'; E.J. Razzell, 'Planning Units in Central Government'; S.J.M. Al-Bazzaz, 'Contextual Variables and Corporate Planning in 48 U.K. Companies'; and E.M. Davies, *The Central Research Function in*

Local Government.

17 Richard H. Hall, *Organizations: Structure and Process*, second edition, p.7.

18 A.J. Greenwell et al., 'Research and Intelligence in the New County Councils', p.37; and Stuart Ranson, 'Notes on a Conference – Education and Corporate Management', p.78.

19 Richard H. Hall, *Organizations*, p.7.

20 Anthony Downs, *Inside Bureaucracy*, p.17.

21 Sir Kenneth Berrill, evidence to the Expenditure Committee (General Sub-Committee), 6 December 1976.

22 R. Allen, 'Current Practice Review', p.49. At the time Allen was a corporate planner at Swindon, Thamesdown.

23 See F.C. Terrien and D.C. Mills, 'The Effect of Changing Size Upon the Internal Structure of an Organization'; and Richard H. Hall et al., 'Organizational Size, Complexity and Formalization'.

24 Theodore Caplow, 'Organizational Size', p.484.

25 Guy Benveniste, *The Politics of Expertise*, p.154. See also Michael Greenwood, 'Corporate Planning Units', p.500; and Robin Hambleton, *Policy Planning and Local Government*, p.63.

26 E.M. Davies, *The Central Research Function in Local Government*.

27 Sir Kenneth Berrill, 'The Role of The Central Policy Review Staff in Whitehall', p.125.

28 Yehezkel Dror, *Design for Policy Sciences*, p.94.

29 For a detailed discussion of the possible characteristics and the problems of measuring organizational climate see Donald Hellriegel and John W. Slocum Jr., 'Organizational Climate: Measures, Research and Contingencies'.

30 Howard Baumgartel, 'Leadership Style as a Variable in Research Administration'.

31 Brian Smith, *Policy Making in British Government*, p.164. See also R.G.S. Brown, *The Administrative Process in Britain*, and Robert J. Haynes, *Organization Theory and Local Government*.

6 Organizational relations

There is nothing more difficult to take in hand, more perilous to conduct or more uncertain in its success than the introduction of a new order of things, because the innovator has for enemies all those who have done well under the old conditions and lukewarm defenders in those who may do well under the new.

Machiavelli

To survive and succeed policy advisers must grapple with a jungle of organizations; some are friends, others are foes. Relationships with other organizations have important implications for the status and independence of units and the nature of their policy advice. This chapter analyses some structural and behavioural features of the location of policy units and their relations with other organizations, officials and politicians.

Organizational locations

Most policy units in central government are at the upper levels of departmental hierarchies. In general, units are found at the assistant secretary or equivalent level and occasionally at the under secretary level. Figure 6.1 illustrates the location of a policy planning unit within one central government department, the Department of Education and Science. This figure shows many of the organizational features that central government departments have in common. Departments are headed on the political side by ministers and on the official side by a permanent secretary. Most departments are structured into divisions, co-ordinated by deputy secretaries, which in turn are divided into branches headed by under secretaries or the equivalent specialist grades.[1]

Policy planning units in central government departments are often

FIGURE 6-1

DEPARTMENT OF EDUCATION AND SCIENCE

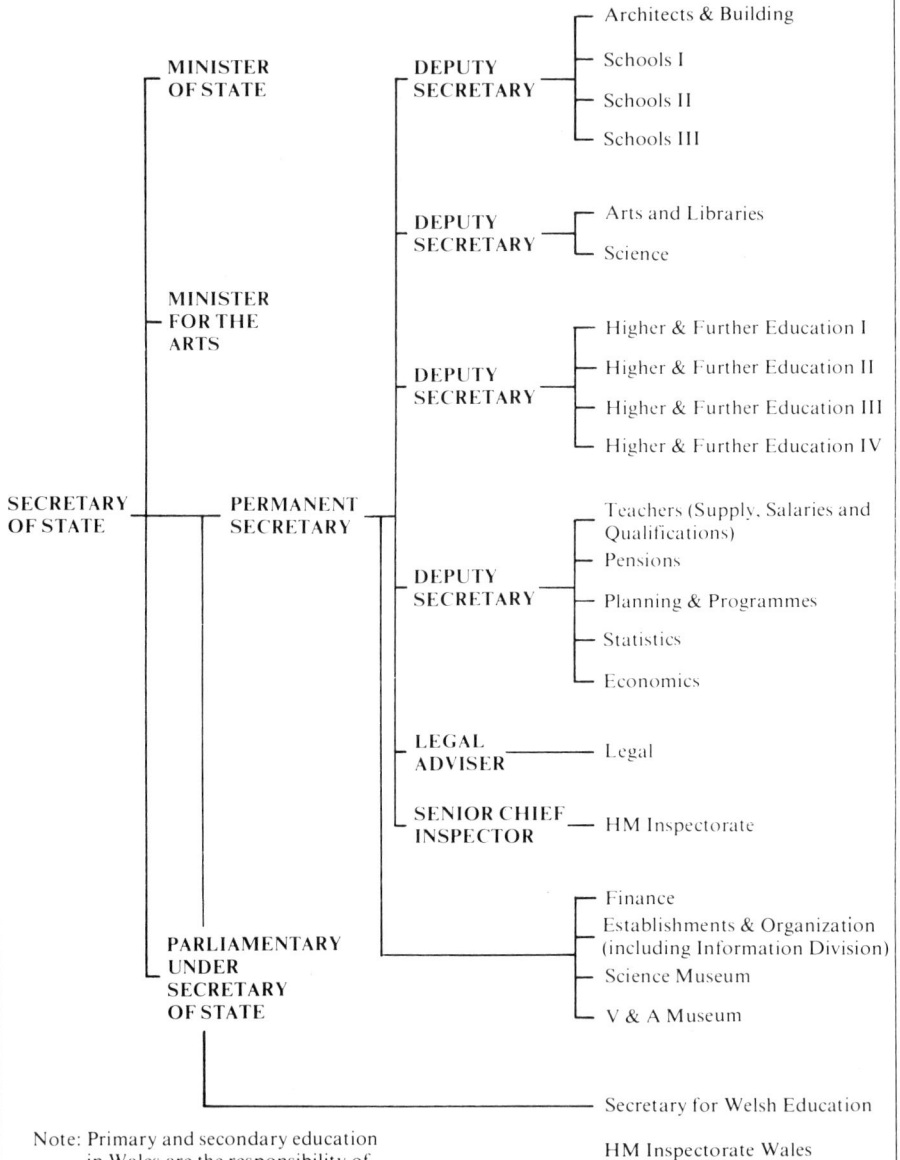

SECRETARY OF STATE

- MINISTER OF STATE
  - DEPUTY SECRETARY
    - Architects & Building
    - Schools I
    - Schools II
    - Schools III

- MINISTER FOR THE ARTS
  - DEPUTY SECRETARY
    - Arts and Libraries
    - Science

- PERMANENT SECRETARY
  - DEPUTY SECRETARY
    - Higher & Further Education I
    - Higher & Further Education II
    - Higher & Further Education III
    - Higher & Further Education IV
  - DEPUTY SECRETARY
    - Teachers (Supply, Salaries and Qualifications)
    - Pensions
    - Planning & Programmes
    - Statistics
    - Economics
  - LEGAL ADVISER
    - Legal
  - SENIOR CHIEF INSPECTOR
    - HM Inspectorate

- PARLIAMENTARY UNDER SECRETARY OF STATE
  - Finance
  - Establishments & Organization (including Information Division)
  - Science Museum
  - V & A Museum
  - Secretary for Welsh Education
  - HM Inspectorate Wales

Note: Primary and secondary education in Wales are the responsibility of the Secretary of State for Wales.

source: *How the DES is Organised*, pp. 6-7. The chart depicts the organization as of January 1977.

116

located within a specialist division. Specialist divisions or branches are a major unit of organization comprised of members from specialist categories such as statisticians, research officers and scientists, and headed by a professional or scientific civil servant at the under secretary level. Examples include the Central Policy Planning Unit of the Department of the Environment's Economic and Statistics Division, the Unit for Manpower Studies in the Research and Planning Division of the Department of Employment, and the Social Research Branch in DHSS situated within a Statistics and Research Division. Some units are located in combined administrative/specialist branches and a few units are in policy divisions. In a sense, the CPRS with its own permanent secretary, is a mini-department. Although physically and constitutionally in the Cabinet Office, the CPRS operates as a distinct unit rather than as a regular part of the Cabinet Office.

These organizational locations have important effects on the authority and role of policy units. Operating within regular governmental hierarchies means units have had to adjust to the administrative culture of public organizations with its concern for risk avoidance, the short term and the practical. This context delimits the planning and research functions making them specific to a particular set of legislative and administrative concerns. It also means that units in the Civil Service do not enjoy free access to ministers but rather report to senior officials.

Central government policy units normally report to an under secretary or deputy secretary who is also responsible for about three other branches. Thus, the immediate superior of a unit has a relatively narrow span of control. It is also frequently the case that units report to one or more committees including a steering group of senior officials within the department chaired by the permanent secretary and composed of deputy secretaries and, in some departments, professional equivalents, as well as other planning committees at the under secretary and assistant secretary level.

While individual policy units are in the business of giving advice they are often part of a planning industry in their departments and a planning economy within the governmental system as a whole. In several departments there is above the policy planning unit a policy planning organization made up of a series of official committees that co-ordinate, approve and discuss the unit's work. Departmental planning systems have been established in Education and Science, Environment, Employment, Health and Social Security and Transport among others. In some cases the head of the unit may sit on such committees. Being part of a larger planning process has resulted in some units playing more the roles of co-ordinator and secretariat than of long term planner and analyst.

A few units, such as the Unit for Manpower Studies and the Systems Analysis Research Unit (SARU) also report to interdepartmental committees. This is because their areas of study go well beyond the direct responsibilities of the department in which they are located. SARU reports to both the director general of research in the Department of the Environment and an interdepartmental committee of officials at the deputy and under secretary level from the Department of Energy, Ministry of Agriculture, Fisheries and Food, Overseas Development Ministry, Department of Industry and the Department of Health and Social Security. The Unit for Manpower Studies, though formally part of the Department of Employment, reports to an interdepartmental committee which meets twice a year to assign and approve the unit's work. The committee is chaired by a senior official from the Department of Employment and has representatives from the Departments of Education and Science, Industry, Health and Social Security, and Environment, as well as the Treasury, Central Statistical Office and the CPRS.

Local authority policy units are situated at the upper hierarchical levels of departments, usually at the third tier officer level.[2] In some authorities, for instance Sunderland, Lambeth, Cleveland and Tyne and Wear, the unit head is of chief officer status. In all these cases the units are *central* policy units in that they officially have a mandate with regard to one or more functions for the whole of the authority, just as the CPRS does for the central government. While having central functions is perhaps a necessary condition for a unit to be located at the very senior level of a department or authority, it is not, by itself, a sufficient condition; most central unit heads are not at the chief officer level but at the second or third tier level.

Three basic organizational locations for policy units are evident in local government. A policy unit may be situated within the chief executive officer's department, within a service department, or stand as a separate department. In a survey of 293 authorities in England and Wales over the 1973–75 period, Greenwood and his associates found that the most likely organizational location for corporate planning and research and intelligence functions was the chief executive's department and the least likely location for both functions was separate departmental status.[3] Figure 6.2 shows the location of the corporate planning unit in the chief executive and town clerk's department of Plymouth City Council. This chief executive, as his full title indicates, has retained some of the traditional functions of committee administration and legal services. In many authorities the chief executive's office contains both corporate planning and research functions and more traditional town clerk functions, although a number of chief executive officers in local government do not have a large department.

When units are located in departments other than the chief executive's they frequently are in central services or horizontal depart-

118

FIGURE 6-2

DEPARTMENT OF CHIEF EXECUTIVE AND TOWN CLERK: PLYMOUTH CITY COUNCIL

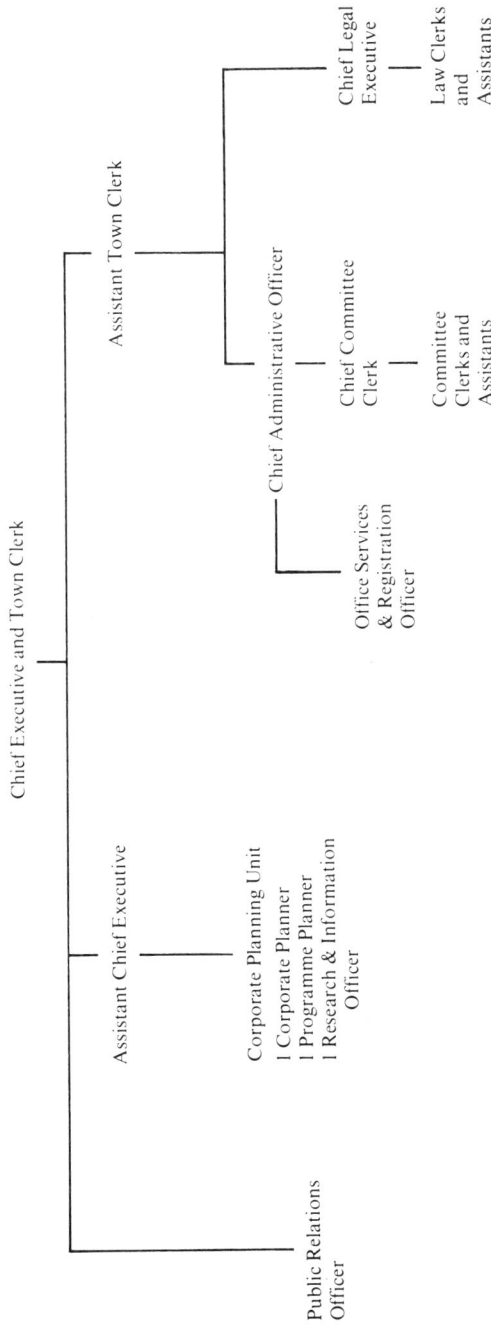

source: Based on official organization chart as of September 1977, and adapted by the author. Administrative and clerical posts have been eliminated.

ments such as management services and planning.[4] These departments are horizontal in that their activities cut across most other structures in the policy making process of the authority. Policy units with separate departmental status are non-existent in central government and quite uncommon in local government. The Tyne and Wear Central Research and Intelligence Unit, the Cleveland R & I Unit, and Sunderland's Programme Planning Unit are examples of units as independent organizational entities.

On the officer side, most local authority policy units report to an assistant chief executive officer and/or to the chief executive. Policy units with departmental status have a formal or informal link to the chief executive officer besides reporting to a chief officers' management team. One unique case is the corporate planner in Exeter District Council. Here the post of chief executive officer was abolished in 1977 and the corporate planner now reports to a committee of three senior chief officers.

On the member side, there is considerable variation among local authority policy units as to their reporting arrangements. Probably the most common format is where units report to a policy and resources committee or one of its sub-committees. Units may also deal with other council committees depending upon the client and the content of their work. An example of the relationships of a corporate planning unit with officers and members in a local authority is given in Figure 6.3. The figure demonstrates some typical elements of local authority management structures. There is a series of departments or directorates each based on a professional service headed by a chief officer, the director. There is also a chief executive officer. In Lambeth the chief executive has no department other than his corporate planning unit. The chief executive chairs the chief officers' management group, in Lambeth called the Director's Board, and plays some role in encouraging a corporate approach. On the members side there is a series of committees, each of which supervises the work of one or more departments. In Lambeth there is one committee for each directorate.[5]

Being located at the upper hierarchical level of the administrative system in both central and local government, policy units often engage in providing advice that is value oriented and closely linked to political decisions. Policy and research personnel can relate to both the political and managerial tasks of government. However, even at the upper echelon of the administrative system, the perception of policy questions and nature of policy advice probably varies to some extent between grades.

The fact that central government units are normally at the assistant secretary level means they are less likely to have a broad overview of the work of departmental divisions than if they were located at the

FIGURE 6-3

LAMBETH BOROUGH COUNCIL CORPORATE STRUCTURE

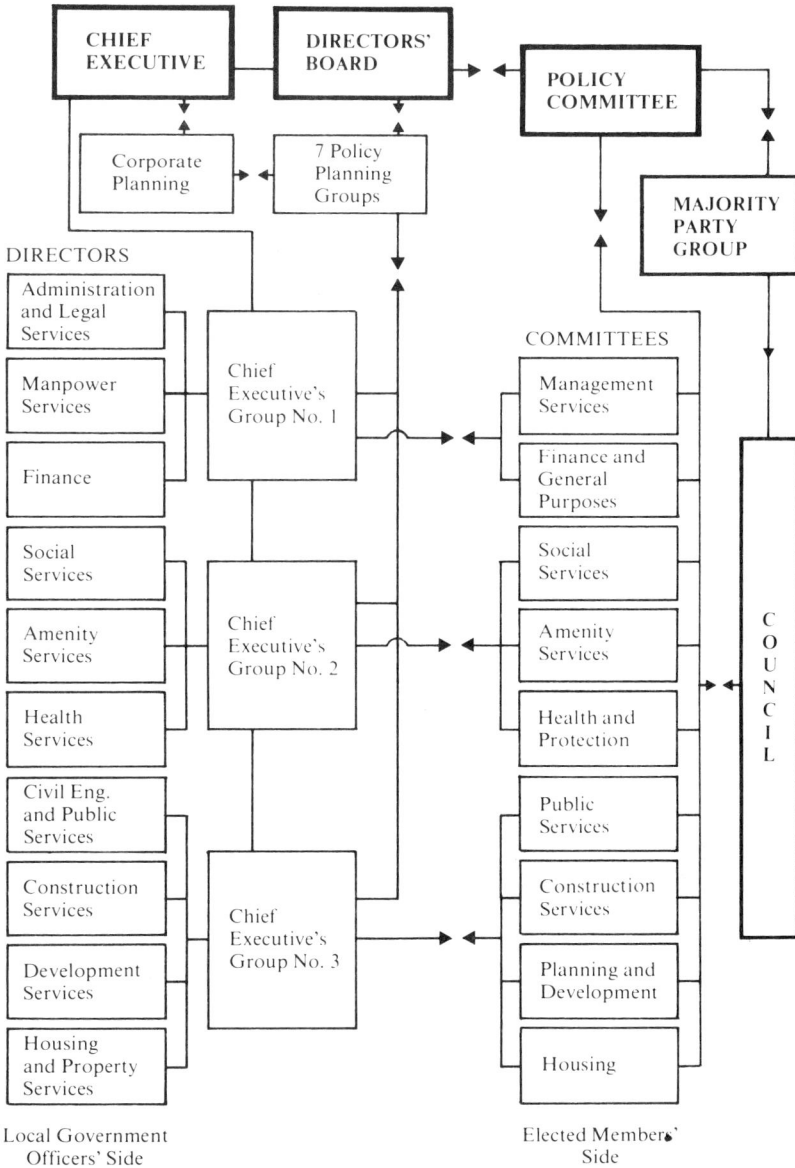

source: C. Cockburn, *The Local State*, p. 27. This chart shows the structure as it was in 1974.

deputy secretary level as Fulton proposed. If unit heads were deputy secretaries they would enjoy the formal authority accorded these positions to co-ordinate and direct the work of divisions and therefore possess a greater number of opportunities to become involved in the broad policy issues and work areas of a department.[6] And since most unit heads are at the third and fourth levels of the administrative hierarchy, they are not normally members of the senior policy and management committees in central government departments, nor of the chief officer management teams in local authorities.

Most units have been organized in specialist structures, such as research planning divisions or branches in central government and research sections in local authority departments. Such an arrangement means that policy units are somewhat organizationally separate and distinct from the structures responsible for line management and the administration of current policies and programmes. While this arrangement minimizes the danger of policy units becoming bogged down in day-to-day operations, it does little 'in resolving the very difficult problems of co-ordination and choice between different policies and of allocation of available resources in accordance with policy objectives' between administrators and policy units.[7] Moreover, the separation of policy units from daily operations can create resentment among administrators toward these units.

Keeping policy units organizationally distinct from administrators can result in isolation and a short life for some units. For example, Grey and Simon argue that the Home Office Research Unit has been like an academic institution, concentrating almost exclusively on models and information, with little effect on the Office's policy making divisions. In order to have a greater impact on policy making the Research Unit has made a concentrated effort in recent years to develop closer links with administrators. Grey and Simon also argue that the failure of the Department of Economic Affairs, created in 1964 and abolished in 1969 by the Labour Government, resulted in part because the economic planning division separated specialists from administrators.[8]

In British local government circles, two contending schools of thought have developed in recent years over the preferred organizational location of the corporate planning and research and intelligence functions. If a corporate planning or research unit is to be introduced in a local authority, where in the structure should it be located? Should policy planners and researchers be housed in a central department and promote corporate management or work in a service department and promote professional management? This debate is worth exploring as it deals with differing ideas on the extent of integration and the extent of concentration in policy analysis needed in a local authority.

The centralist perspective, as represented by the Seebohm Report, the Society of County Clerks' Report and the Paterson Report on Management in Scottish local authorities, holds that a policy unit should be centrally located and probably part of a central department such as the chief executive, county secretary or director of administration.[9] This school of thought argues that a central unit is more objective because it avoids the problems of loyalty to the head of a service department and a particular departmental viewpoint which could inhibit the unit's work. There is a tendency for departmental research staff, especially in larger departments, to be saddled with one aspect of the service, whereas central researchers should be able to foster management relationships at a higher level with the backing of a central department. A central unit ensures consistent forecasts, common statistical bases for survey work and a better awareness of the range of information about the local authority as a whole. A centrally located unit may also prevent or reduce the duplication of research throughout the authority, and is not restricted in the recruitment of specialist staff needed. It will not be seen to be aligned with the professional disciplines of any particular professional department and will offer an opportunity for specialist staff, such as statisticians and economists.

If there is to be a genuine move towards corporate management in an authority, the centralist view argues that the key research and information services required to support forward planning throughout the authority should be part of the framework for corporate planning. To aid corporate management, units should be centrally located in order to have access to central management processes and officials. Moreover, in the larger authorities the chief executive office should have a policy planning director and unit to provide formal support to the chief executive's co-ordinative role in policy planning and to ensure that the chief executive does not become isolated from the administrative process.

A corporate planner in the central unit at Thamesdown argues that their experience indicates the benefit of the unit reporting directly to the chief executive:

> Corporate planning is a central function, with the Chief Executive as 'Chief Corporate Planner'. Hence the benefits of the unit *being seen* to be in a central position. Some planners report to the Secretary, Directors of Administration (ugh), of Management Services, to Chief Planning Officers/Treasurers etc. — they must run the risk of many departmental research functions in taking a 'branch' rather than corporate view. Effective planners must be able to influence (hopefully for the good) key decisions of the authority rather than sub-decisions.[10]

In summary, the corporate perspective contends that centralized units have the following benefits: a greater degree of objectivity and comprehensiveness in work, economies of scale and support for corporate management and the chief executive.

The second school of thought advances a departmental or decentralist view that there are good reasons why policy units should be located in service departments. Andrew Leigh contends that the centralist arguments are not entirely convincing. 'Researchers in central units have had no more or less freedom to choose research subjects, or present facts. Economies from holding researchers centrally are mainly illusory, and few councils are big enough to create one research team sufficiently large to generate savings solely due to size'.[11] There is 'no convincing evidence ... that the overall results of centralized research is noticeably better or more effective at bringing about better information or change than research based within individual departments'.[12] A unit located within a service department may be more conversant with departmental operations, better able to advise on where and when research is needed, and have a better chance of establishing relations with officers within the department and other service departments. The Bains Report advocated a departmental or decentralized format for corporate planning specialists on the grounds that it would be workable and more acceptable to officers and members.

Central units could be located in a service department, although relatively few units are actually in that category. In this location the central unit could in theory fall back on the department's work if the corporate work dries up, though the departmental location may cause suspicion and prevent corporate work forthcoming. Finally, a central unit can create tensions by highlighting the conflicts between policy alternatives and solutions between departments and between officers and members.

How have local authorities themselves responded to these competing ideas in terms of the organizational position of policy units? In many authorities, 'a typical British compromise has been adopted' with policy units located both in service departments and in a central department, usually the chief executive department. As Leigh notes, 'This decision probably owes as much to the determination of directors to keep control of their own research effort as any careful appraisal of the ultimate effects that this would have on prospective research work'. It is interesting to note that most of the writings on where a unit should be located in a local authority do not discuss the organizational form where the unit is of separate departmental status and the unit head is a chief officer. For instance, both the Bains Report and the Society of County Clerks' Report appear to assume that corporate planning and research and intelligence are specialist services

124

which do not justify separate departmental status but should be located within a department.

Policy planning units in British government are examples of what Michael Watson calls piecemeal pragmatism, 'change has not involved a major reshaping of the administrative structure; planning bodies have simply been added alongside existing structures, and not substituted for them'.[13] Similarly, Macdonald and Fry assert that, 'the attention which has been paid to planning since 1968 has in fact extended and consolidated the regularities of British administrative procedure'.[14] Policy planning units in the civil service do not break with structural and procedural traditions in departments and are not new, independent sources of advice.

It is true that most policy units are grafted on to existing administrative structures, but units have had some effects on the organizational form and processes of administrative systems in Britain. Policy units have contributed to departmental organizations becoming more differentiated and institutionalized. The creation of a unit introduces another organizational structure into the administrative system, and the institutionalization of previously implicit or diverse functions. Furthermore, the creation of units has led to the diffusion and differentiation of policy advisory roles and structures within government, introducing in some instances persons embued with bureaucratic ideologies that support policy planning and research.[15] Policy units have diversified advice perhaps not in the sense of providing independent and direct sources of ideas to ministers but as new and additional forums for advice.

While having increased the division of labour in administrative organizations, the establishment of many units can be seen as a device for achieving greater integration of activities. Units may co-ordinate activities such as research and corporate planning carried on within a department, among departments or between a department and outside bodies, such as nationalized industries, royal commissions or regional authorities. Units can also serve as a forum for interorganizational relations and the development of co-operation between various organizational units in a central government department or local authority. For example, the Research and Planning Division in the Department of Employment held a seminar in 1974 on 'The Transition from School to Work'. The seminar was attended by professional and administrative civil servants as well as academics. Its purpose, as described by a member of the Research and Planning Division, was 'to enable the Department to learn about recent academic thinking and research in this area and to create a forum within which a fruitful. interchange between academics and civil servants could take place'.[16]

Policy planning units contribute to integration by highlighting the relationship of different programmes to overall policy objectives and by assisting senior officials in playing a greater role in programme design and implementation. In some cases the formation of units has led to the establishment of other integrative structures such as planning steering committees and research liaison groups within and between departments.

A few units in central government departments are structural innovations in that they are not based on the traditional separation of generalists and specialists but rather are integrated or joint hierarchies. Administrative, executive and specialist grades are merged together in some branches and divisions jointly headed by a specialist and administrator. Examples of this organizational form are the Housing Analysis Monitoring Unit in the Department of the Environment, Departmental Planning Unit in Customs and Excise and the Corporate Planning Unit in the Department of Energy.

Conflict and co-operation

Two types of interorganizational relations are particularly important for an understanding of policy units in British government. The first is conflict and the second is co-operation between policy units and other organizations and persons in the bureaucratic and political arenas.

Many policy unit staff perceive or feel some form of resistance and negative expectations from other officials and politicians. Many also believe that officials and organizations were hostile, defensive or apprehensive about the introduction of policy units. As the head of a central unit in a local authority put it, 'reaction ranged from suspicion — what are they doing? do we really need them? — to open hostility'. An assistant secretary in charge of a unit in a central government department recalled that his under secretary and deputy secretary knew this job would have more than the usual frustration attached to it. Commenting on reactions to the introduction of his policy unit to a district council, a corporate planner remarked, 'It's lucky that murder is a capital offence!'. The director of a research and intelligence unit admitted that if you are not prepared for punishment and fighting, don't become the head of a research unit.

Why have policy units encountered conflict in their interorganizational relations? The head of the Programme Planning Department at Sunderland has explained, 'Experimentalists are rarely greeted with enthusiasm, particularly in local government, because their activities disturb the even flow of routine'.[17] Large bureaucracies tend to be conservative and organizational innovations are likely to appear to be threatening and therefore are resisted. Besides this tendency to fear and resist change, the fact that policy units are novel organizational forms means new and additional uncertainties and ways of working are introduced. This novelty was accentuated in local authorities because the formal departmental structures established at the time of local government reorganization in 1974 were largely those of the pre-reorganization period.

The introduction of policy units implies a criticism of past planning and research activities in government, and may suggest to some administrators and politicians that they lack the ability to perform these functions. As one policy adviser put it, 'this feeling that if we suggest something new it means that they aren't doing it right now makes it very difficult to make constructive criticisms without leading to cynicism by officers'.

Civil servants, it is said, generally follow the wishes of their political masters in executive office.[18] However, there is evidence of resistance by civil servants to implementing ministerial intentions concerning planning structures and processes. Barbara Castle has reported her difficulties with civil service obstruction at the Ministry of Transport in gaining acceptance for the concept of integrated transport planning.[19] Richard Crossman has recorded in his diaries as Minister of Housing that 'as long as the Dame [Dame Evelyn Sharp, Permanent Secretary from 1955–66] was there I had tremendous difficulties even in building up an economic intelligence inside the Department'. When Crossman tried to establish a central appraisal unit in the department and recruit more statisticians and economists he met 'nothing but resistance'.[20]

When Anthony Crosland as Secretary of State for Education and Science, wanted to create a planning branch in DES, it was one of only a few rare instances where he faced opposition from officials in the Department. Crosland later said that the opposition 'was based partly on general conservatism and partly on administrative argument. The administrative argument was that a Department like Education didn't need a central planning division because the planning function was already being carried out in the separate operating branches — teacher supply, school building, further education and so on'.

Crosland did not agree and he made clear his decision to set up the planning branch by sending a minute to Herbert Andrew, the Permanent Under-Secretary of State for Education and Science, saying ' "I would be grateful for your final advice on this matter as I propose to make a public announcement in a fortnight's time." ... An experienced civil servant can always tell when the argument is over and he's lost the battle'.[21] Though the battle had been lost the war was not yet over. Crosland was not at DES long enough to guarantee the branch adequate status in relation to other branches of the department. In 1971, after a departmental reorganization, the planning branch was replaced by a smaller planning unit and a flexible network of committees of officials drawn from the operating branches.

A common reason for conflict in the interorganizational relations of policy units is that officials are not familiar with or have a clear understanding of the actual roles of units. Administrators are often unfamiliar with the methods, techniques and language used by policy staff. This uncertainty can also arise because the role of policy units has not always been fully or properly explained and, more importantly, because most policy units do not have a clearly defined occupational identity.[22]

Policy unit personnel are not identified with a single defined field but with many fields, bodies of knowledge and methods. With regards to the value system that justifies the occupation, the underlying ideas are multiple and of varying applicability to central government and local authorities. There is no clearly articulated and widely accepted view of the mission that the field serves nor of the activities that are proper to the field. As part of a new type of government organization, the relationship between policy planners and researchers themselves, and between them and other officials has often been characterized by ambiguity. The absence of a structured role and clear division of labour between advisers and other officials can be a source of inter-organizational conflict. As J.A. Stockfisch has noted of the initiation of systems analysis within government bureaucracy:

> The lack of clarity regarding functions creates tensions, the tensions generate suspicion, and the suspicion promotes struggle. Struggle, in the form of competition, is not bad per se. It is essential, however, that competition take place within some coherent set of ground rules. Without ground rules, the struggle becomes one in which power can become an end for its own sake. Individual behaviour in such a context is governed by a form of jungle ethics.[23]

Many of the sources of staff—line conflict that might be expected between unit personnel and administrators are very evident throughout British public administration. Policy units are sometimes seen as a control organization checking up on administrators and possibly gathering data of a damaging nature. Units are viewed as encroaching on the influence and power of professional competence in local authorities and the administrator's role in central government departments. Furthermore, there is not a complete congruence between the values and interests of policy advisers and administrators; policy advisers are perhaps more versed in new techniques, inclined to collect information, more concerned with finding a logical answer than one that is suitable, and, more inclined toward change and a longer time orientation than administrators. Indeed, many policy advisers believe it is part of their job to be different.

The individual characteristics of policy unit personnel have exacerbated staff—line tensions. The young age of staff is one irritant. Older officials do not like to admit that younger officials can tell them something they did not already know about their own work. The presence of policy unit 'whizz kids' at senior officer grades has also caused some resentment. In addition, some local authority units were staffed mainly with people from outside the authority and, in a few cases, with little, if any, local government experience. Where suspicions and defensive feelings toward a unit already existed, the outsider aspect of unit staff was another potential source of conflict.

The conflict relationships that policy units have are clearly related to the larger organizational situation in government, that is, the extent to which units impinge on the resources, interests and power bases of other agencies. Moreover, policy units have had to deal with various organizational value systems within British government. Government organizations with relatively large power bases and a culture of autonomy are more apt to be hostile toward policy units than are organizations with less power.

In local government, the departments that seem to be the most hostile to central policy units are education, planning and the treasurer's, while engineering and surveying departments tend to be defensive. These departments are repeatedly identified by policy advisers as the organizations most likely to view policy units as threats to their relative influence, status and share of resources.

Education departments with their relatively large budgets are frequently hostile to central units and corporate planning and management because they have the most to lose in the reallocation of existing resources and the allocation of new resources. Chief education officers, especially those who entered local government in the 1940s, often see their role exclusively in terms of developing and expanding the local education service. Education officers are often reluctant to support corporate planning and management because of their traditional autonomy and centrality within local government.[24]

Policy units have had difficult relations with planning departments because, historically, planners have usually done whatever research, statistical and intelligence functions many units are now doing.[25] Also, the development of corporate and community plans co-ordinated by central units, has replaced the structure plans formulated by planning departments as a council's overall framework. Some treasurer's departments think they should have the statistical capacity rather than a central policy unit, say, in the chief executive's department, and because an authority's corporate plan is related to the budgetary process, policy unit staff are sometimes seen as stepping on the treasurer's toes. Of course, a policy unit with a limited mandate located within a service department probably would not face this kind of resistance.

In some authorities a centre—periphery split has occurred, aggravating the organizational relations of policy units and other corporate management structures. Much of corporate planning activity has been concentrated in the centre of local authorities. The centre of a local authority includes the policy and resources committee, the chief officer's management team, parts of the chief executive's, finance and administration departments, as well as those members and officers who are 'abreast of the subtleties of the developing ideas and scheme of things'. The establishment of planning units in the centre of some authorities has highlighted the traditional centre—periphery split. As Robin Hambleton states, 'members and officers at the "centre" are likely to approve of the changes taking place but what about the others — the back bench members and the great majority of officers? Those on the "periphery" may not be hostile but there is every chance that they will be unenthusiastic and lack commitment to the new ideas'.[26] Thus while the ideas of a policy unit may be quite feasible they may provoke apathy or hostility simply because the advice is seen as coming from the centre.

The world of the policy unit is not all darkness and conflict. Policy units encounter co-operative interorganizational relations when they join together with one or more other organizations for the production, provision or allocation of resources or activities; when they exchange resources with other organizations bearing some relevance to their organizational goals such as departmental information for unit advice; and when unit staff have memberships formally linking the unit with other organizations.[27]

As members of staff organizations with little or no administrative responsibilities, unit personnel are in the position of giving advice and information to other officials and organizations. This raises several fundamental questions for policy advisers. Who are their allies? Who are their clients? What does a client expect from the policy unit?

Unit personnel identify individuals and groups in their immediate organizational setting as allies and clients. In most cases the official goals of policy units identify clients the unit may serve. The CPRS serves ministers collectively, while the Research and Planning Division in the Department of Employment advises policy divisions. The terms of reference of the Central Policy Planning Unit in the Department of the Environment mentions as clients the policy and management group, various functional directorates and internal departmental task forces and working parties. The mandate of the Research and Intelligence Unit in Cleveland identifies the county council and the four district councils as possible clients.

A policy unit can have a wide range of clients in its organizational setting. Unit members in local authorities may have any combination of the following as clients: the council, its committees, individual or groups of councillors, the chief executive officer, the chief officers' group, individual chief officers and departments, interdepartmental working parties, other local authorities and public authorities, individual citizens and local voluntary and business agencies. In central government, the clients of units may include the cabinet and its committees, individual ministers, the permanent secretary and other senior officials, administrative divisions and inter and intra departmental working groups. Thus, unit personnel see themselves as policy advisers and co-ordinators to people above them, below them, and — if they are in a corporate or central unit — people across the organizational hierarchy, and, perhaps, to people and groups in the community.

In British government there are processes and structures such as PESC, PAR and policy and corporate planning steering committees that provide some regular, institutionalized support for units. As well, some units are comprised of administrators who have links with policy line divisions. Some officials mention a deputy secretary, permanent secretary or, occasionally, a minister who is an ally and supporter of a unit.

Apart from personalities, a key factor in determining co-operative relationships is the size and type of organizations. In local government small departments look upon policy units as allies in the budgetary process, giving them a better chance against larger departments in resource allocations. In some authorities, the corporate approach, of which policy units are a part, is seen as a 'leveller', reducing the dominance of big departments. Departments frequently cited as co-operative and supportive toward units are social services, housing and recreation/leisure. While many social service departments have a research capacity they may also use central policy units to provide statistical skills and advice. Many housing and recreation departments do not have a research and analysis capacity because of their relatively low professional status in local government. Therefore, when policy units were set up, housing and recreation services were sympathetic toward the corporate planning and research and consultancy services provided by the units. Chief executive officers are also potential allies but their degree of support depends upon their own role conception, skills and behaviour. A number of unit officials describe their chief executive as more consensus oriented than a corporate leader which, they argue, limits their planning role.

E.S. Quade has raised the interesting question of who is the *real* client or sponsor of an adviser who works in government, and whether or not the adviser should be fully the client's agent. 'When the sponsor is a public official or agency, the analyst may sometime feel he should consider himself more than the agent of that particular official or agency alone. In other words, he may consider himself an agent of a wider society, of his country perhaps, or even of the world'.[28]

Policy advisers see themselves generally as agents or aides to particular appointed and elected officials within government agencies. Such a perspective is understandable given that policy units are not administrative organizations; they normally do not provide goods and services directly to the public nor do they regulate public activities. However, some unit members do take a wider view of who is their client. For example, some advisers believe their work is for the community as much as for the county council; reports are generally available in the members' library and the public libraries in the county. Other planners and researchers claim they work for anybody who wants their service — from the CEO and department heads, through committees, to community groups and associations.

Most policy planners and researchers that consider they have clients beyond their immediate organizational context work in local authorities. To a large extent, this broader view of client probably stems from the special nature of local government. What local authorities usually do has immediate and obvious implications for people. 'Central government is insulated from the citizen by layers of organization and deals with the general rather than the particular, whilst individuals and individual organizations have a continuous effect on local authority operations through feedback arising from daily operations.'[29] Furthermore, the relatively greater emphasis on a corporate or community outlook in local government undoubtedly encourages local policy planners to take a broad view of who is their client.

Client expectations and relations

Clients have mixed feelings about policy advisers. As a social services researcher has observed: 'There is a temptation to treat researchers as either high powered consultants who can solve any problem, or as magicians who by mouthing mysterious mumbo jumbo like "regression analysis", "probability", or "confidence limits", dematerialize the problem'.[30] To these views one can add that clients might expect researchers to justify a decision or position that has already been taken, give only an appearance of action or concern, or make the client appear progressive by using a fashionable administrative technique.

The following remarks illustrate the range of client expectations of policy unit work from the policy planner's point of view: clients

132

expect a fair range of information they would not normally receive; our client wants a broad view on issues; they expect research that is relevant to policy formation or evaluation; he wants us to do critiques of other departments' work and activities; and, they expect planning that is politically and financially realistic. Clients expect policy advice to allow decisions to be more readily defended in public, to improve the quality of decisions in the short run, to get better control of achieving goals and policies, to inform thinking about the next few years, and to ask questions and provide answers to questions such as, are we getting value for money from this programme?

In terms of scope, policy advisers expect clients want a relatively broad or comprehensive perspective on issues and problems. In terms of content, they believe clients want and need advice that is both critical and practical. These expectations of policy advisers appear to correspond with client requirements in practice. For example, most cabinet ministers wish to make a significant contribution to policy and therefore require from their Civil Service advisers loyal implementation of ministerial or party objectives and programmes; advice on a range of alternative objectives, priorities and programmes; expert advice, that is, advice based on timely specialist knowledge on the likely consequences of implementing alternative policy options.[31]

A number of policy planning units in central government have endeavoured to respond to these requirements and expectations of cabinet ministers by developing statements of alternative objectives and programmes and by considering ministerial interests in analytical work. In other words, the policy planning unit is helping to meet the minister's need for policy advice. Only a very few units are providing ministers with secretarial support for such political work as general cabinet duties, dealing with parliamentary questions and drafting speeches. None of the Fulton styled units are acting as a political brains trust to their minister. This is because units are staffed by civil servants rather than political appointees. In a few cases, such as in the Home Office, a minister's special adviser has sat in on departmental planning steering committees, but they have not been members of planning units.

Most policy planners and researchers realize and accept that their work methods and advice must relate to the client's needs and their organizational and political context. Consider the premises of the policy planning organization in the Department of Education and Science. Planning must directly involve those who have to administer the policies that have been planned. Second, educational planning cannot get far without specialist skills and these must be built-in in such a way as to ensure that they can make a creative contribution to policy formation. Third, the planning machinery must keep close to ministers exploring, among others, options that reflect their known views, and seeking ministerial guidance and endorsement from time to time. Fourth, the planning must be consistent with current government thinking about resource prospects. Furthermore, the planning organization must take account of the ideas of enthusiastic reformers and pressure groups.[32]

A view held by most policy advisers is that clients often do not know what their problems are or what kind of help advisers can give them. As one local government researcher says, 'The policy maker may be unwilling or merely unable to explain the nature of the problem'.[33] Policy advisers believe their clients, politician clients especially, need to be helped in identifying their information needs and diagnosing how to meet these needs. This results in a process of interaction between advisers and their clients in setting the work programmes of policy units.

Relations between policy units and politicians are generally indirect. In many cases, particularly in central government, policy planners and researchers advise politicians through other senior officials and the top administrative structures. Most MPs and councillors probably have little awareness, interest and understanding of policy units. Since its establishment in 1957 the Home Office Research Unit has been scrutinized periodically by parliamentary committees. Martin Davies has described politicians' attitudes towards the Research Unit as follows: MPs are critical about the Unit, unclear about the role of research specialists, generally expect research to lead directly to action, and are suspicious that researchers may be trying to pull the wool over their eyes.[34]

Shortly after the Fulton Report was published in 1968, R.G.S. Brown wrote: 'there is a risk that planning units will become particularly vulnerable to inquisition by specialist parliamentary committees. The possibility of such probing may prejudice their ability to range freely over policy options, popular and unpopular alike'.[35] However, the risk of parliamentary criticism concentrated on planning units has not developed. Indeed, since the publication of the Fulton Report there have been very few parliamentary questions about central government departmental policy planning units. By contrast, the Central Policy Review Staff or Think Tank has received greater attention both in parliament and the media, undoubtedly because of its close proximity to the cabinet and prime minister, and the flamboyance of its first director, Lord Rothschild. A number of CPRS reports have been published and have attracted parliamentary and public attention. CPRS members have appeared before the Science Sub-Committee of the Select Committee on Science and Technology, and the General Sub-Committee of the Expenditure Committee, providing evidence and information about their work and activities.

A few departmental planning units as in Education and Science,

Environment and the Home Office have come under scrutiny by parliamentary committees, and while there have been some criticisms, such inquiries have not restricted the role of planning units. When the planning organization in the Department of Education and Science came under heavy fire it was because the planning system had not considered a wide enough range of policy issues and problems. In effect the critics were calling for a more comprehensive planning activity.[36] The few parliamentary inquiries that have dealt with policy units have actually provided an opportunity for planners and researchers to explain and promote their activities. It is possible that such probings have provided some greater legitimacy and external support for the planning and analysis functions.

Since its announced creation in November 1970, the CPRS has been the subject of a large number of parliamentary questions. While some of these questions relate to the work programme of the CPRS many more questions concern the composition of the CPRS. MPs have asked the prime minister if various specialists or specific people would ·be appointed to the Think Tank. Periodically an MP will ask if the prime minister will abolish the CPRS. In short, MPs have used parliamentary questions about the CPRS as a device to make a partisan point or to raise a particular problem in the House of Commons and ask the Government if they are going to do something about the issue. As John Mackintosh has remarked, 'MPs are political animals and far more interested in scoring political points than in understanding the administrative processes'.[37]

What has been the CPRS's relation with prime ministers and cabinet ministers? The CPRS has survived several changes in government and appears to have enjoyed the support of all four prime ministers it has worked under. On the other hand, relations with other ministers are a mixed record. For example, when the CPRS was first formed some Conservative ministers were suspicious of the CPRS, thinking it was designed to strengthen the role of the prime minister at the expense of the cabinet. Moreover, during the 1970–74 Heath government, a number of Conservative ministers apparently were not impressed by the CPRS strategy meetings held about every six months. These meetings were discontinued by the Wilson government in 1974.

In discussing the relationship between policy units and politicians in local government, a distinction can be made between executive councillors in the centre of the authority (party leaders, policy and resource committee chairpersons and members) and other backbench councillors on the periphery. Awareness, contact and detailed knowledge of a policy unit is frequently confined to executive councillors. Backbench councillors usually have only a vague idea of what a policy unit does, aware perhaps only that the unit is in some way connected with the annual corporate plan which many members may regard as a useful reference.[38]

The lack of awareness by councillors about policy units is due in part to councillors' tendency to emphasize representative roles over policy making roles. George Jones has divided British councillors into three role categories: (i) representative of a geographical area, a broad section of the population, particular organized groups, another local authority, and individual citizens; (ii) specialized policy makers concerned with one or two services or functions; and (iii) broad policy makers concerned with the overall policy and the setting of priorities of the local authority's activities. Jones estimates that about 75 per cent of councillors are primarily representatives, about 20 per cent are specialized policy makers and only about 5 per cent are broad policy makers.[39] Furthermore, many policy unit staff believe it is unwise for a unit to become close to councillors or to be seen to be close to them. While in the short run it may be necessary for a unit to rely on councillors for support and work, if units are closely identified with councillors in the long run, a change in the majority party could cause the decline and possible abolition of a unit.

Besides having limited knowledge of policy units, councillors may be suspicious of units and view a unit's identification and measurement of public needs as supplanting their representative role. Members do not like the idea of highly paid people sitting around and thinking all day, telling politicians that they are not meeting public needs, especially during conditions of resource constraints. Some members see the measurement of client needs and programme impacts as restricting their political manoeuverability; they do not want to know the precise impact of policies but are more concerned to be seen to be doing the right thing.[40]

In some instances policy units have developed close working relationships with politicians, be it a cabinet committee, minister, councillor, or group of councillors. Direct and regular contact between unit personnel and politicians is more common in local government than in central government. Local government central research units have a fairly high degree of formal contact with members being directly represented at committee meetings and members' working parties. In most cases, the head and/or other unit personnel may attend such meetings. Elected members as a client group are served by a large majority of central units in local authorities. While much of the contact with members is to do with corporate planning, units also provide direct support for member committees, answer inquiries from members, and offer press cutting, library and other information services for elected officials.[41]

This finding is consistent with differences in the constitutional position between the Civil Service and the local government service in the area of elected member–official relations. In local government, administrative responsibilities are delegated by the council to committees rather than to individuals. Thus, there is no concept of ministerial responsibility. The heads of the local authority departments service those committees and they are in more frequent contact with elected representatives than are civil servants.[42]

What are the consequences of these organizational relations and reactions toward policy units? How do officials and organizations translate their attitudes towards a policy unit into actual behaviour?

Information is the life blood of policy units. Hence a fundamental question is whether units are obtaining the information they need and want to perform their tasks. Officials suggest the problem is not so much that other organizations refuse to give information, but that the information made available is not recorded in a form useful for the unit's work. Other difficulties concerning information for government research have been described by the Seebohm Report:

> A great deal of information is currently assembled by local authorities and central departments as a by-product of their other functions or because as a matter of standing practice, specific pieces of information have always been collected in a particular form. The difficulty is that some of this material is not the most useful, and is not always collected and published in a comprehensible, comparable or standardized way.[43]

Ambushes — organizations giving false information and/or withholding vital information until after a unit presents a report — appear to be rare. With respect to negative behaviour toward units, policy planners and researchers more frequently experience not receiving any work from a department, or being asked to do inappropriate and trivial tasks, such as a statistical oriented unit being asked to compile an inventory of all the periodicals the authority receives.

In general, organizations play fair, though they can drag their feet by providing information when it's too late or by saying they lack resources to provide the requested information at the moment. Units get around this problem in some instances by going to client groups as well as outside experts and organizations for information and ideas, and in other instances by creating their own estimates and then confronting an organization with them. Sometimes a unit may say in a report that the information was not as good as it could have been. This tactic can lead to elected members giving a unit support to get more and better information.

The ultimate form of hostility toward a policy unit is organizational murder. The Social Research Branch in DHSS and the Programme Planning Unit in Greenwich have faced threats of abolition. Some units such as those in the Department of Education and Science and Ministry of Agriculture, Fisheries and Food have been reorganized and reduced in status and function. Indeed, the unit in MAFF was disbanded during the 1975–77 period. The Programme Evaluation Group in the Ministry of Defence was destroyed by the Chiefs of Staff in the mid-1960s, and the Central Intelligence Unit at Birmingham City was abolished in 1976.[44]

Due to environmental apathy and hostility, policy staff have paid considerable attention to organizational survival and promoting and protecting their units in the organizational jungle. A significant degree of resources can be devoted to these activities over a long period of time. The planning unit in DES, which has been in existence for over a decade, is still having to promote itself to the operational and policy branches in headquarters through meetings with branch officials. The Central Planning Division in the health side of DHSS has held seminars with officials from various line divisions to help generate work. Similar promotional activities have been done by local policy units. A member of the Central Research and Intelligence Unit at Tyne and Wear, for example, has given a series of lectures on statistics to people in other departments. The R & I Unit in Cleveland publishes an annual report which describes the unit's work and indicates by example ways in which the unit has and can assist county departments and district councils.

The organizational context of policy units described here supports the conception of central government and any given local authority as a series of coalitions of values and interests, each coalition potentially including one or more groups of officials, and one or more groups of politicians attempting to benefit at the expense of other groups.[45] Having encountered both negative and positive relationships has meant that policy planning units have investigated certain topics and not studied others. It has also meant that units must devote considerable time and energy to gaining acceptance and overcoming resistance, resources which might otherwise have been spent on planning and research activities. How this organizational context influences the work programme of policy units is considered next.

Notes

1 For a discussion on the internal structure of central government departments see John Garrett, *The Management of Government*, pp.70–81; Brian Smith and Jeffrey Stanyer, *Administering Britain*, pp.144–50; and D.C. Pitt and B.C. Smith, *Government Departments: An Organizational Perspective*.

2 On the structure of local authorities and local authority departments, see Jeffrey Stanyer, *Understanding Local Government*, pp.156–62; Ralph Rowbottom et al., *Social Services Departments*, chapter 4; and Royson Greenwood et al., *In Pursuit of Corporate Rationality*.

3 R. Greenwood et al., *The Organisation of Local Authorities in England and Wales*, tables 16–19, pp.57–60.

4 On the concept of common service or horizontal departments and spending or vertical departments, see J.M. Lee et al., *The Scope of Local Initiative*, pp.10, 132–4 and 153–7; and T.E. Headrick, *The Town Clerk in English Local Government*, pp.169–83.

5 For a more detailed although dated discussion of the internal organization of Lambeth, see Cynthia Cockburn, *The Local State*, chapter 1. For a broader picture of the internal structure of local authorities, see Jeffrey Stanyer, *Understanding Local Government*, chapters 7 and 8.

6 On the relation between types of advice and levels in the administrative system, see Peter Self, *Administrative Theories and Politics*, pp.209–15. See also Arnold J. Meltsner, *Policy Analysts in the Bureaucracy*, pp.288–9. On the role differences between the permanent and deputy secretaries and under secretaries and assistant secretaries, see John Garrett, *The Management of Government*, pp.70–2.

7 S.D. Walker, 'Planning in the Civil Service', p.7. See also Michael J. Prince and John A. Chenier, 'The rise and fall of policy planning and research units: an organizational perspective'.

8 Alexander Grey and Andrew Simon, 'People, Structure and Civil Service Reform', pp.301–2. On the DEA, see George Brown, *In My Way*, chapters 5 and 6.

9 For the centralist perspective, see A.J. Greenwell et al., 'Research and Intelligence in the New County Councils', contained in R. Greenwood et al., *In Pursuit of Corporate Rationality*, pp.148–52; Paul A. Taylor, 'The Role of Research and Intelligence Units in English Local Authorities', pp.15–17; Desmond Keeling, *Management in Government*, pp.192–3;

Seebohm *Report on Personal and Allied Social Services*, pp. 144–5; and the Paterson Report, *The New Scottish Local Authorities, Organisation and Management Structures.*

10 R. Allen, 'Current Practice Review', p.49. Emphasis in original.
11 Andrew Leigh, 'Researchers in the Social Services', pp.53–4. See also David Cranston, 'The Case for Decentralization'; Paul A. Taylor, 'The Role of Research and Intelligence Units in English Local Authorities', pp.15–17; and J. Skitt, *Practical Corporate Planning.*
12 Andrew Leigh, 'Researchers in the Social Services', p.53.
13 Michael Watson, 'A Comparative Evaluation of Planning Practice in the Liberal Democratic State', p.462.
14 James Macdonald and G.K. Fry, 'Policy Planning Units – Ten Years On', p.437.
15 On the concept of bureaucratic ideology, see Anthony Downs, *Inside Bureaucracy*, chapter 19. See also Fred A. Kramer, 'Policy Analysis as Ideology'.
16 P. Brannen (ed.), *Entering the World of Work*, p.2.
17 Peter Kershaw, 'Community Dialogue', p.507.
18 Bruce Headey, *British Cabinet Ministers: The Roles of Politicians in Executive Office.*
19 Barbara Castle, 'Mandarin Power'.
20 Richard Crossman, *The Diaries of a Cabinet Minister*, vol. 1, pp.614 and 31.
21 E. Boyle, A. Crosland and M. Kegan, *The Politics of Education*, pp.177 and 183.
22 On the concept of occupational identity, see Andrew M. Pettigrew, *The Politics of Organizational Decision-Making*, p.100.
23 J.A. Stockfisch, 'The Genesis of Systems Analysis Within the Bureaucracy', pp.10–11.
24 See Brian Neve, 'Bureaucracy and Politics in Local Government: The Role of Local Authority Education Officers'; Stewart Ranson, 'Notes on a Conference – Education and Corporate Management'; Ernest Butcher and Jasmine Sawkins, 'The Corporate Approach in Local Government – An Education Viewpoint'; and Royston Greenwood et al., *Patterns of Management in Local Government*, p.56.
25 See Brian McLoughlin and David L. Smith, 'R and I and Development Plans', p.61; and Cynthia Cockburn, *The Local State*, p.30.
26 Robin Hambleton, *Policy Planning and Local Government*, p.62.
27 I. Adefolu Akinbode and Robert C. Clark, 'A Framework for Analyzing Interorganizational Relationships', p.162.
28 E.S. Quade, *Analysis for Public Decisions*, p.273. See also

K.A. Archibald, 'Three Views of the Expert's Role in Policy-making'.

29 Jeffrey Stanyer, *Understanding Local Government*, p.84.

30 Andrew Leigh, 'The work of social services researchers and its impact on social policy', p.109.

31 Bruce Headey, 'Cabinet Ministers and Senior Civil Servants: Mutual Requirements and Expectations'. See also L.J. Sharpe, 'Governments as Clients for Social Science Research'.

32 Tenth Report from the Expenditure Committee, 1975—76 Session, p.8.

33 Andrew Leigh, 'The work of social services researchers and its impact on social policy', p.109.

34 Martin Davies, 'Government and Research Policy', pp.54—5.

35 R.G.S. Brown, *The Administrative Process in Britain*, pp. 253—4.

36 Organization for Economic Cooperation and Development, *Educational Development Strategy in England and Wales.*

37 J.P. Mackintosh, MP, *Specialist Committees in the House of Commons*, quoted in S.A. Walkland, 'The Committee Structure of the House of Commons and the Relevance of Small Group Theory', p.6.

38 See Cynthia Cockburn, *The Local State*; Mike Clegg, 'Corporate Planning, Corporate Planning Units and Planning Departments'; W.J. Taylor, 'The member and corporate management'; the journal *Corporate Planning*, vol. 4, no.1, devoted to the theme political parties' views of corporate planning; John Cartwright, MP, 'Corporate Planning in Local Government — Implications for the Elected Member'; and Kim Quaile Hill and James C. Coomer, 'Local Politicians and Their Attitudes to Planning'.

39 G.W. Jones, 'Problems of City Government', p.226.

40 See Andrew Leigh, 'The work of social services researchers and its impact on social policy', pp.109—10; Mike Clegg, 'Corporate Planning, Corporate Planning Units and Planning Departments'; Michael Greenwood, 'Corporate Planning Units', p.498; Paul A. Taylor, 'The Role of Research and Intelligence Units in English Local Authorities', pp.18—19; and C.A. Collins, 'Councillors' Attitudes: Some Research Findings'.

41 E.M. Davies, *The Central Research Function in Local Government.*

42 Brian Smith and Jeffrey Stanyer, *Administering Britain*, p.187. See also Jon G. Davies, *The Evangelistic Bureaucrats*; R. Batley et al., *Going Comprehensive: Educational Policy-Making in Two County Boroughs.*

43 *Report on Personal and Allied Social Services*, p.143.

44 See Hugh Hanning, 'Our first defence need is better machinery

for taking the big decisions'; John Earwicker, 'The Birmingham Saga'; and R.J. Haynes, 'The Rejection of Corporate Management in Birmingham in Theoretical Perspective'.

45 See Royston Greenwood and C.R. Hinings, 'The Study of Local Government: Towards an Organizational Analysis'; Robert Pinkham, 'Effective social research for local government'; Hugh Heclo and Aaron Wildavsky, *The Private Government of Public Money*; A.J. Pettigrew, *The Politics of Organizational Decision Making*; and Richard Cyert and James March, *Behavioural Theory of the Firm.*

7 The market for policy advice

Research is no more than the art of discerning the possible.

John Croft, Head of
the Home Office Research Unit

Policy units in British government operate in a market where they obtain work or permission to conduct work from other officials and attempt to sell their products of advice and research. The market for policy planning and research is the link between policy advisers and clients, policy units and the administrative and political systems. Who determines the work programme of a unit? To what extent are projects and tasks undertaken in response to assignments and to what degree are they initiated by a unit? Do planning and research organizations only respond to client initiatives or do they have some capacity for detached work? What criteria are used in the identification and selection of work topics? Are certain kinds of topics improper or too difficult for a unit to do? Who defines the problems and issues that a unit works on? A case study will be presented to illustrate the different types of projects, different project stages and the language used by policy planners and researchers. Furthermore, this chapter will explore how units try to gain acceptance of their work. How do units market their advice to other officials? What strategies and skills are employed to market the work of policy units? A discussion of these issues should contribute to a better understanding of the interaction between policy advisers and other officials, and the general work processes of units.

Work programmes

In speaking of a programme of work for policy units it should be emphasized that not all units have a coherent and explicit programme, 'with all parts of the research integrated nicely within a common framework'. It is often more accurate to speak of a research 'menu' — 'a varied collection of items reflecting the ideas and tastes of many cooks'.[1] Work programmes are likely to be of varying degrees of complexity and ambitiousness. 'The extent to which a programme is formalized, written down, and made widely available depends on whether this is seen to be a worthwhile activity since it may involve the production of a complicated document showing all the various stages through which the research projects on hand are expected to pass.'[2] Yet every policy unit can be said to have a work programme or set of matters to which attention is being given, whatever the degree of formality of the programme.

Although the work of a policy unit can originate from a number of different sources, the following general features can be noted about the work programme of most units: a limited role by elected representatives; a significant but variable role of departments and divisions; a self-initiated role by units; and, an interactive process between the units and their clients.

Elected representatives at both levels of government generally play a limited direct role in the determination and selection of work for policy units. In central government, ministers may periodically suggest a particular research or planning topic or comment on the relative priorities of the current programme. For example, the Policy Analysis Division in the Treasury and the Departmental Planning Unit in Customs and Excise may be asked to do some work for the chancellor, especially around budget time. The Central Policy Planning Unit in the Department of the Environment directly briefs the secretary of state on matters of industrial democracy but does not try to brief the minister on policy matters within the Department so as not to make enemies. The CPRS is an exception in that its major pieces of work are usually triggered by a cabinet committee, occasionally by the prime minister or a single minister and only seldom by two ministers.[3]

The typical role that a minister plays in setting and supervising the work programme of a departmental policy unit is probably similar to the arrangements at the Department of Education and Science. In 1976, Sir William Pile, then permanent secretary of DES, said that occasionally ministers suggest projects but that 'the initiative does tend to rest with officials, knowing what Minister's policies are, to support a relevant programme of research'. Sir William added that:

Every now and then a Minister may say 'What is happening on research' so we parade ... a list of the current programme, and he or she may say, 'There is too much of this or not enough of that. Is there not a gap here?', and we have a discussion. If it is clear that something ought to be done, then we can act accordingly.[4]

The extent to which ministers are interested and involved in the planning and research programme depends on the personal manner and thinking of each particular occupant of a ministerial role. Sometimes it is difficult to get ministerial guidance and therefore the setting of a unit work programme involves interpretation and guidance on ministerial wishes from the permanent secretary. It seems that ministers only occasionally play a direct, active part in the policy planning and research organizations in departments. For example, they do not normally preside over the steering groups which supervise and approve the research and planning projects of a department. Other demands and burdens on ministers limit them to playing an active role in only a few key issues at any given time.

Ministers are, of course, kept informed of what goes on in departmental planning organizations. The Secretary of State for Education and Science, for instance, 'receives regular reports as to the work in progress and is consulted about future work to be commissioned, so he has full information about what is going on and is in a position to change the course of the planning effort if he does not like it'.[5]

In local government as well, elected members play a limited role in directly setting the work programme of policy units. Councillors who request work are usually those in the centre of the authority, that is, council leaders, policy committee members and perhaps service committee chairmen. A few units, such as the Corporate Planning Unit in Harringay and the Central Research Unit in West Glamorgan, have attempted, through meetings and questionnaires, to solicit ideas and suggestions from members on what they wanted examined. However, they found a lack of interest from some members and topics suggested were pet projects and not necessarily issues of priority and real importance.

Members can often have an impact on the work programme of units through the chief officers and their management team. For example, a senior researcher in a central research and intelligence unit produced some figures on unemployment in the authority and region for a council committee report concerned with development and employment. The researcher wanted to do some further work on female unemployment in the area as the preliminary figures produced showed a surprisingly very high rate. The unit head approached his superiors, the assistant town clerk and the chief executive, who said that the topic was not on at this time. Shortly afterwards, however, a councillor who read the committee report picked up the figure regarding female unemployment and wanted to know whether any attention was being paid to this problem. Because of the councillor's comments in committee, the unit researcher was asked to do further work on the question of female unemployment in the authority.

Although this example shows that a clear distinction cannot always be made between political and administrative sources of work for policy units, the role of politicians in setting a unit's work programme is seen by themselves and others to be limited.

Senior management officials and administrators play a comparatively larger role than elected members in identifying what goes into a unit work programme. Clients for central policy units can include senior officials, such as the permanent secretary and deputy secretaries in central government or chief officers and heads of divisions in local government. These senior officials may be clients either individually or as a group through top policy and management teams which usually meet weekly, and through research and planning steering groups which, in many departments, generally meet only a few times a year.

More frequent clients for units include heads of policy line and administrative divisions and sections at the under secretary and assistant secretary level in central government and the second and third tier level in local government. Work from these clients comes through informal contacts as well as through *ad hoc* and ongoing committees. These contacts and committees can serve several purposes, such as, to formulate requirements and priorities for both the content and work methods of a unit's work programme, to consider the information sources available, reflect departmental and the various division interests, estimate the personnel and financial expenditures, try to accommodate long and shorter term work projects, and review and, if necessary, amend the work programme. Other purposes include assessing the implications of completed work for policy and administrative practice, considering the dissemination of the work, and, perhaps, deciding whether a particular project should be undertaken in a unit's own programme or by an outside agency like a university.[6]

Interdepartmental committees at official levels are also sources of work for some policy units. In central government, the Systems Analysis and Research Unit in the Department of the Environment, the Unit for Manpower Studies in the Department of Employment, the Corporate Planning Unit in the Department of Energy and the CPRS in the Cabinet Office all report to and/or are meant to receive some work from interdepartmental committees. Local government examples include the Central Research Unit at West Glamorgan, the Central Research and Evaluation Unit at Avon and the Information Services Section at Devon. West Glamorgan, for instance, has set up an interdepartmental Research Liaison group chaired by the Deputy County Clerk. The group contains officers representing about eight other departments in the authority and the director of the Central Research Unit. The director is the secretary for the group. The terms of reference of the group are as follows:

1 To co-ordinate and monitor progress on all research projects within the county.
2 To identify areas where further research is needed and where necessary prepare briefs for the research.
3 Arrange for sponsorship of research where necessary.
4 To liaise with outside bodies particularly with University and Area Health Authority with regard to research and research techniques.

Interdepartmental committees usually ensure consistency of work undertaken by departments and various units, integrate priorities of new work, and generally control and approve the work programme of policy units. However, at neither level of government are inter-departmental committees very forthcoming in providing or suggesting work for policy units. Even though units are meant to be available to do work for a number of departments, they are seen as belonging to the department in which they are fomally located. It may also be due, in part, to interdepartmental quarrelling, reticence or a tacit understanding among some departments not to provide the centre with much information.

A significant feature about the work programme of central and departmental policy units is that much of their work is self-initiated. Like other organizations in the policy making process, units not only respond to work requests and preferences, but also initiate preferences and demands themselves. The concept of portfolio aptly describes the initiative taken by policy advisers. Where a stockbroker might regard his or her prime skill as consciously choosing items for inclusion in an investment portfolio in order to achieve such aims as high interest rates or long term capital growth, the policy unit work programme is a research portfolio which can be deliberately manipulated within environmental constraints to achieve aims like survival and high reputation. This thinking is certainly at the level of strategic management, above and beyond that of a research manager, and being proactive rather than reactive seems relatively unusual for an internal government service function.[7]

Some initiative has indeed been given to and assumed by policy units. Policy planners and researchers in British government not only try to find answers to questions, they propose their own questions and query the questions put to them. John Gillespie, a local government officer involved with research and intelligence for many years, has identified several reasons why policy advisers and information providers must take the initiative. While Gillespie is speaking about local government officers his comments also apply to central government:

> In an ideal world the policy maker would specify his information needs and identify his information gaps. Thereafter the information provider would fill these gaps. In local government this has not happened and indeed I wonder whether it has happened anywhere. What takes place is a dialogue with — more often than not — the information provider suggesting questions to which the policy makers might like to find answers.[8]

But why do information providers suggest the questions? Can it be that policy units are expected to explore issues of which other officials are unaware? 'The first difficulty is that policy makers themselves either have not defined their needs or they have despaired of having their needs met since in local government information has been treated as a luxury not as a resource.' The policy maker's second weakness, Gillespie says, has been complacency. 'The attitude "we are doing all right" is all too prevalent. Invariably when pressed as to what the client thinks of the service being dispensed it becomes clear that the client has never been asked. Thus the decision maker is judge and jury in his own case.' However, Gillespie claims the most serious shortcoming on the part of the policy maker has been a fear of better information. 'After all, mistakes in policy could always be blamed on the lack of good information. When this crutch is removed, what then? How often have we come across the senior officer who has been shaken rigid at the thought that performance might be measured by means of better information.[9]

In connection with Gillespie's last point, some administrators are suspicious and hostile toward policy units, reluctant to subject their operations to unit scrutiny. It is very difficult to persuade administrators that it is in their own best interest to raise awkward questions and take on present problems for uncertain future benefits. In addition, administrators and other officials have their own work and day-to-day affairs to do, and suggesting work for policy units often comes low in their list of priorities. A local government corporate planner put it this way: both members and officers have expended considerable effort in achieving the target savings required of the various committees, and there really has not been very much time or opportunity for also considering the assignments which might be performed by a central planning unit. Furthermore, some administrators take the view that suggesting research topics and new areas of policy action is not part of their job. They believe their job is to execute policy, and explain and defend existing programmes, not to make policy.

Besides the attitudes and behaviour of other officials, there are factors related to policy units themselves which help to explain why units suggest work. As staff or advisory organizations, part of the role of policy units is to propose ideas and work topics. Such organizations, with an organic internal structure often emphasize responsiveness and the ability to detect new issues and information needs. As policy units are new organizations with a comparatively novel role, other officials — potential clients — frequently have only a vague idea of the role of a unit and its possible use to them. Therefore, for purposes of organizational survival and effectiveness, policy unit staff must suggest work and ideas to show other officials the uses of the unit and to establish unit credibility.

The arrangements for determining the work programme of policy units can be characterized as an interactive process between the units and their clients. Units receive requests for work from politicians and officials through personalized and structured channels. Units also initiate tasks and generate their own work by suggesting proposals to management committees, planning and research liaison groups, through informal contacts with line officials, and at their own discretion. Policy units also exercise a degree of initiative when they define or interpret a task sponsored by a client.

The head of the Home Office Research Unit has highlighted the importance of the interaction between policy makers (ministers and administrators) and policy advisers (social scientists) to the formulation of a research programme:

> No programme, of course, starts from scratch; previous work will suggest further inquiry, and it is thus inevitable that while a good many of the items in a programme will originate with the social scientist, his initiative will have to be tempered by constraints such as legislative and operational requirements for information, the extent and quality of resources available to carry out the work and, not least, the goodwill of those who will be asked to cooperate in the research by providing information.[10]

The relationship of policy advisers to their clients is like that of MPs to their constituents. Policy unit personnel are not simply the delegate or thinkpiece of a client but have some discretion and independence from the client in terms of choice of topics, definition of problems and selection of work methods. Policy planners and researchers are not always bound by specific instructions from clients, but can initiate and issue their own instructions. Many unit members see one of their roles as educating their clients, in the way that MPs try to keep constituent activists informed. Unit members also generally take account of the interests, opinions and views of clients. As the MP is dependent upon his or her constituency for support through the electoral process, the policy adviser is dependent upon clients for support through the policy process and the market for policy planning and research.

The interaction between policy units and other officials in the formulation of unit work programmes has become closer over the past ten years. In central government the Rothschild report on government sponsored research and development,[11] has had an impact on the work programme and interorganizational relations of policy units, such as the Home Office Research Unit and the Social Research Branch in DHSS. The Rothschild report argued that research needs and priorities should be determined by the customer or actual user of the research, rather than by the contractor or researcher. Although the report was concerned with natural science research, the customer—contractor principle has been adopted by many departments in Whitehall for guiding the relationship between social science research and policy.

Partly as a consequence of the application of the Rothschild customer—contractor principle, some policy units have become more closely integrated with administrative divisions in their departments. This has meant a broader range of projects and policy interests, and a larger number of customers for some units. A senior researcher in the Civil Service has noted that the Rothschild philosophy, 'has placed the responsibility upon administrators to articulate their requirements for research more precisely, and has brought home to researchers the need to justify their efforts in terms of solving the problems facing government'.[12]

Likewise in local government the relationship between policy units and other officials has probably become closer over time. According to Booth, the customer—contractor model of policy advice is 'the dominant standpoint in current thinking about the organization of social services research' in local authorities.[13] Thus, as Leigh notes, since the early 1970s the freedom of social services researchers to decide research priorities 'has in some departments been slightly eroded as research management has been strengthened and as people have begun to be more familiar with the output of research and its possible impact for change'.[14] The relationship between policy units and their clients can be more fully demonstrated through an examination of the criteria used in the identification and selection of work topics.

Choosing topics

Because of the increasing importance and cost of the policy planning, research and statistical functions in government, it is essential to establish criteria providing guidance on the choice of subjects and priorities. Selecting a problem for a policy analyst to work on is both an economic and political decision:

> It is an economic decision because the analyst is a scarce resource whose talents should not be wasted on trivial assignments or on problems that defy even approximate solution. And it is also a political decision. Choosing the right problem has crucial implications for the political efficacy of the analyst, the policy and its sponsors. It is one of the critical steps the analyst takes toward ensuring his own success. In addition, which policies are analyzed and which issues are raised influence who wins and who loses from governmental problems.[15]

Policy planners and researchers express several values in suggesting and accepting work topics. The following criteria represent many of the major factors that policy unit personnel themselves take into account when choosing topics: political implications, administrative feasibility, 'quickies', the unit can do it, avoid cans of worms, anticipate issues and develop a distinct domain.

Political feasibility is a crucial variable in policy analysis. The work topic should have, either directly or indirectly, relevance and acceptability to the governing politicians. The former head of the central research unit at Newcastle City has said: 'It should always be the case that research projects are to an extent conditioned by the priorities for service provision which the council sets itself'. Although it may not always be possible, 'most research projects on-going at any one time will be of topical political importance'.[16] Similarly, in deciding what planning operations should be embarked upon in central government departments one consideration of policy steering groups is whether the topic responds to known ministerial interests or instructions. Paying heed to the political implications of policy and research work involves some awareness of the political environment, constraints, public demands, value judgements underlying the issues and the policy advice and, of course, the commitments and interests of the governing officials. The effective policy adviser, however, does not live by political feasibility alone.

Policy planners and researchers choose work topics that have senior official support, and can be implemented — the resources and skills are available. Unit officials carry out projects that provide a service, give people what they need and want, and do useful and practical things. Other considerations taken into account are that a planning exercise or inquiry must have a foreseeable and useful end-product, can be readily implemented given the resources, and that the resources can be easily obtained in the present economic climate.

Thus, when policy planners and researchers say they pick topics on the basis of whether it is a 'goer' or not, they are referring to considerations of political and administrative feasibility. Whether a problem is worth attempting depends upon whether change is possible, the attitudes and actions of key actors, and the extent to which a consensus exists or can be formulated. As one official expressed it, 'we push at half open doors, there's no use in banging your head against a brick wall'.

The administrative feasibility of policy ideas can be largely discerned from the agency philosophy of client organizations within government. A recent examination of the Treasury by the Ball Committee found that: 'There is at any one time a house view as to what the policy options are, and any new proposals have to run the gauntlet of informed scepticism'. The committee identified constraints which influence the work programme of government economic advisers:

> At times, some options (such as a strict rule for the growth of the money supply) have not attracted much attention, because most of the economists in the Treasury have regarded them as not being of major importance. At other times, no doubt a formal incomes policy, with rigid control of the wage packet by government regulation, has not attracted much effort from the simulators, because it was judged politically impractical to pursuade Ministers of any virtues which such a policy might have.[17]

All public organizations develop a distinctive viewpoint, and a collective outlook on their general mandate and on particular issues. Expressed another way, government agencies are not impartial or neutral on most issues touching on their mission. Hence, certain policy problems and options, especially if new or unconventional, may not readily be selected by policy unit staff or other advisers for examination.

Many clients suggest and many policy unit officials prefer to select short term problems which produce quick results that are helpful to administrators and policy makers. Benjamin expresses this view in discussing the work programme of a new research and intelligence unit:

> Nothing succeeds like success. It will be important for the Unit to achieve a few early successes. If the Unit can select a few tasks that are evident 'quickies' i.e. can be completed in a very short space of time, and which at the same time are of obvious advantage to management, this will help tremendously to generate confidence in the Unit, not only on the part of staff in the various departments, but also on the part of the Unit staff themselves.[18]

Though Benjamin is speaking about the early months of existence of a unit, winning the respect and confidence of other officials is an ongoing challenge. Even units that have been in operation for several years still do quickies to develop and improve relations with other officials and demonstrate an ability to meet deadlines and work on timely issues.

Projects that are obvious quickies include the provision of answers to requests for information and solutions to statistical problems. In the Scottish district council of Kirkcaldy, for instance, the corporate planning and co-ordination unit has concentrated on areas likely to give quick returns, such as the creation of structures to implement decisions, rather than direct efforts to the policy formulation process. Consequently research work has not been a high priority in the unit.[19]

The choice of research topics is normally conditioned by a policy planner's assessment of whether the unit can do a technically effective job. Policy advisers, it seems, try to avoid the apparent trait of experts to assume knowledge and authority in fields in which they have no competence. They accept and select topics with some concern for organizational boundaries and technical capabilities. Lord Rothschild maintains that a reason why planners fail 'is that they are sometimes put into bat on a quite unsuitable wicket'. Planners should not do types of work for which their skills and tools have not been developed. 'Planners, too, have skills and instruments of a specific nature and they must take care that they do not stray, they are not seduced, into incongruous occupations'.[20] Lord Rothschild believes that planners should keep out of futurology because it is concerned with improbable events and discoveries whereas planning involves predictions of probable and reasonable events in the future. This assessment is based on factors such as the size of the unit, the available skills, expertise and resources of unit staff, and whether the unit can get the necessary information and co-operation.

'Survival', as John Le Carré has written, 'is an infinite capacity for suspicion'.[21] This is sound counsel for policy advisers as well as secret agents. Some topics and studies proposed to policy units are what we may call 'cans of worms'. These are subjects which for any number of reasons policy planners and researchers are suspicious about and believe are not cost effective; they have a low probability of unit advice being accepted, and perhaps at the same time, have a greater likelihood of attracting conflict and hostility toward the unit. Morover, some issues in the mainstream of departmental interest and activity may be regarded as too sensitive for study because of timing or because of activities going on elsewhere.[22]

Cans of worms vary from one unit to another but examples include: issues that nobody is interested in; work of immense detail and which is insoluble; topics that will get a unit involved in an ongoing interorganizational dispute; evaluation projects, especially those to determine the relative costs and benefits of a number of programmes designed to meet different objectives; problems in areas of detailed implementation; and tasks already done or capable of being done by operational divisions and sections. While evaluation is a central function of the planning and research process the evaluation of existing activities is a common can of worms though the evaluation of proposals is a less dangerous task for a policy unit to undertake. A frequently noted can of worms for *central* policy units is any issue that is clearly and exclusively the concern of one department, unless, of course, the department asks for help from the central unit. Hence, units may turn down work requests and/or redirect them to more appropriate organizations.

In formulating a work programme, policy unit personnel often try to select topics and issues which may not be a priority problem at the moment but which they expect to be a problem in the future and will require advice to be offered to policy makers and administrators. As one unit head has said: 'Sometimes it will be necessary to carry out research on matters which do not appear to have priority but which, on closer examination of the topic matter, reveal problems which the council when it learns of them is concerned to put to rights'.[23] The work programme of the Systems Analysis Research Unit in the Department of the Environment reflects this concern for anticipation, for seeing possibilities. The recent emphasis in the unit's work has been on food production and the manner in which agriculture is likely to develop in the next thirty-five years. The unit has worked on food production because global trends in population, patterns of trade, dietary preferences and other factors indicate that food production is becoming a problem and also because the United Kingdom imports about half of its agricultural produce.[24]

Policy planners and researchers anticipate issues, work requests and reactions on the basis of a multitude of formal and informal contacts, including parliamentary debates and reports, council and committee minutes, official committees, social and economic trends, interest and client groups and the press.

In choosing topics for their programme of work, policy advisers are clearly influenced by considerations of organizational relationships. Policy units try to establish a distinct area of competence and jurisdiction, and try to avoid duplicating work being done in other divisions, departments or in outside bodies like universities. An assistant secretary who was head of the Crime Policy Planning Unit in the Home Office has described this concern as follows: 'If the planning unit is to succeed, it must be accepted by the Office as having a useful function and as doing something which either the rest of the Office cannot do or cannot do as well because it lacks the time or resources, but which it wants to have done'.[25]

Indeed, many units, especially central units, try to choose inter-departmental issues, extradepartmental issues which lie outside the responsibility of all departments in the government or authority, areas where other organizations lack expertise, and items not regarded as any other organization's responsibility. In this way, units select topics which are not being done elsewhere and develop a distinct domain.

The criteria used in the formulation of unit work programmes show a concern on the part of policy units for feasibility — political and administrative relevance and the ability of unit staff to do a job — and an action orientation. Moreover, the criteria reflect a concern for organizational survival and establishing a domain in the policy process. The policy planner's concern for relevance and doing something meaningful 'pushes him to select problems that can be marketed. He does not wait to be asked to do something. Because he wants his work to be significant, he anticipates the decisions of his clients and estimates the future payoff of his product'.[26]

The setting of a unit's work programme is largely an incremental process operating within a political and administrative market. The main features of this selection process are that planning and research topics are picked not just on their own merits but on tactical considerations; that the process is not comprehensive, not all possible issues are examined; that topics radically different from current activities are usually avoided; that topics not related to client interests tend to be given low priority; and that topics are selected from within the existing framework of values and interests. Furthermore, the selection of topics and the availability of information resources are often intertwined. The mark of a good topic is that clients can be found and that officials generally support the idea of a project. In short, the work selection process can be viewed as a mechanism for reducing environmental complexity and uncertainty, and stabilizing interorganizational relationships.

In selecting topics policy units may, of course, take into account various combinations of the criteria outlined. For example, according to a former member of the CPRS, social policies were an obvious area of interest to that unit for several reasons: they involve several government departments and many other agencies, public and private; their intrinsic importance, and the importance attached to them by governments of all parties; their effectiveness can be affected, intentionally or not, by a wide range of activities; and, policies distributed towards them consume a large share of national resources. Public expenditure on them is equivalent to over a quarter of the Gross Domestic Product.[27]

Conflict may arise between one criterion and another when choosing topics for a work programme. Inconsistencies may arise between attempting to provide advice that is both politically feasible and bureaucratically desirable. A unit that tries to produce quick results is unlikely to collect all the necessary information to do an effective job. Also a unit may find it hard to combine creativity with acceptability.[28] Hence, a critical problem facing any policy unit is deciding the relative priority of the criteria in a given project and in the unit's overall work programme. In this context, the management of every policy planning and research unit involves what Sir Geoffrey Vickers calls the balancing function — a number of criteria have to be kept at levels and within mutually related limits which are necessary to survival.[29]

Operating processes

A central feature of policy units is their advisory role. They acquire, create, study and communicate information, research and advice to policy makers and administrators, using a variety of work processes and methods.[30] Some of the main work processes of policy units can be illustrated from an examination of the experience of the R & I Unit in Cleveland.

The Cleveland R & I Unit became fully operational in April 1974. Its permanent establishment is twenty-five staff with additional administrative support. The director is an economist with many years of experience in local government. The other staff come from a variety of academic, industrial and local government backgrounds. The official goals of the unit are outlined in Chapter 3 of this book.

The unit has a considerable and varied work programme, providing operational research, statistics, information and research services to both the county and four district corporate management teams, elected members and departments. The unit is organized into three sections — research, operational research and statistics. It is a management services unit in the county (as is personnel, computer services, corporate estate, and project management and co-ordination) and is not part of any other department nor allied to any professional specialism. The unit director reports directly to the chief officers' management team and has a close working relationship with the chief executive who does not have any significant departmental responsibilities.

In 1977 two of the unit's research officers carried out a study which attempted to analyze the work processes and methods of the unit over the 1974–77 period. The study examined different types of projects, different stages in projects and reasons for success and failure. The research officers looked at thirty-eight projects that had been done by unit members. The study team discussed all the projects with the unit members concerned, and discussed ten projects with members and officers who had been project clients.[31]

The following classification of projects was formulated, based on the research officers' accounts of their projects: making information available to a client to inform his or her decision making, including data collection, processing and interpretation; giving technical advice; providing technical tools for use by clients in their day-to-day work; devising an optimal or a range of solutions to a finite problem; and, drawing attention to previously unrecognized implications of facts/events/trends in the external world.

The research officers indicated that all completed projects went through several stages, as follows:

1   Problem presentation
2   Problem assessment
3   Negotiation
4   Technical stage
5   Report
6   Outcome

While most clients also recognized that projects went through a number of stages, they often had very different perceptions of what should happen at each stage. From the research officers' and clients' accounts, the study team developed a model of the research officer/client interactions at different stages of projects. Figure 7.1 depicts the relations between researcher and client at various project stages.

The Cleveland R & I Unit, like many other units, initiates some of its own projects and approaches potential clients with work proposals. If clients have an urgent problem they may approach the unit for help and state the problem in their own terms. The researchers feel a responsibility to ensure that the problem is stated critically as a prerequisite for good research. This in turn generates two problems. First, clients often do not understand the need to discuss and possibly reformulate the problem definition. This can be a real problem if researchers are tactless in the way they approach such discussions. Second, the client's original statement of the problem may be inadequate for a variety of reasons — vagueness, over-specificity, surrogate problems and so on. After the first stage of problem presentation, clients are quite willing to have little or no contact with the researcher until the first draft report is produced. This can be because the client expects the researcher to go away and find the answer, the client has no particular interest in methodology and defers to the expertise of the researcher, or, because the client often has not the time to get involved in all the project stages. Therefore, researchers do most of the work during the problem assessment and technical

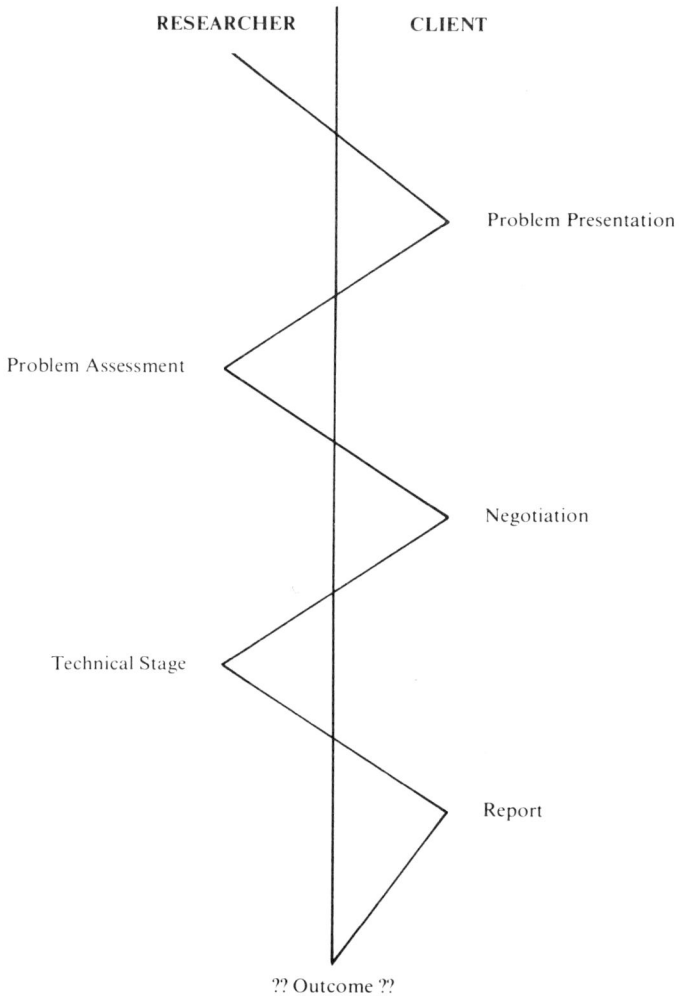

FIGURE 7-1

MODEL OF THE RESEARCH OFFICER-CLIENT INTERACTIONS
IN VARIOUS STAGES OF A PROJECT

RESEARCHER   CLIENT

Problem Presentation

Problem Assessment

Negotiation

Technical Stage

Report

?? Outcome ??

source: R. Fox, "In Retrospect — A Review of Some of
the Work Carried Out In the Research and
Intelligence Unit", diagram 5.

stages on their own and much of the interface work with the client during the negotiation and report stages.

At the second stage of problem assessment the onus usually rests with the unit. This stage involves consideration of a series of questions: such as, what the hypotheses are; what methods to use; how is the problem to be formulated; is it specific to this client or does it have any wider applicability; are there any other potential clients; and, how and where are data to be gathered? Most clients are not involved in what goes on at this stage.

At the third stage of negotiation, the researcher prepares and shows the client a technical specification of the project including information on objectives, methods, intended deadlines and costs. Both sides will have a fairly clear idea as to the technical aspects of the projects, but there is little discussion or negotiation between the researcher and client over all sorts of non-technical aspects and over what happens when the report is given to the client. Clients expect researchers to follow closely the agreed project proposal. However, researchers may wish to change the scope of the project or its emphasis during the technical stage because a change could mean better information for the decision maker or more critical questions to be examined. But most researchers would perceive their role as not to be such that they could, without considerable risk, make changes without discussion with, and agreement by, the client. In the technical stage there is a danger of insufficient contact with the client as the researcher becomes very involved in the back room work of the project. This can be regarded as an irresponsibility on the part of the researcher half of the dialogue.

At the report stage the output can be raw data, tables or a final report. The output may also be oral advice and audio-visual presentations using slides and flip charts. The researcher and client can have different expectations at this stage. The researcher is usually committed to the report and wants to see it seriously considered and more or less implemented. Clients may imply that all they wanted was the report and research to support some preconceived ideas and practices; that this might be the case is usually patently clear to the experienced researcher at a much earlier stage in the project.

Closely related to the report stage is the outcome stage, that is, the actual consequences that derive from the project report. From the client's viewpoint there are a number of possible reactions to a report. Figure 7.2 presents these reactions as a pattern of moves open to clients which may or may not involve the researcher.

Upon receipt of a report the client evaluates not only the report and its content, but also assesses the research officer and unit in terms of trust, track record and whether the research officer should be included in further stages of implementation. The client will also

FIGURE 7-2

THE PATTERN OF OUTCOMES OF
A RESEARCH PROJECT:
THE CLIENTS VIEW?

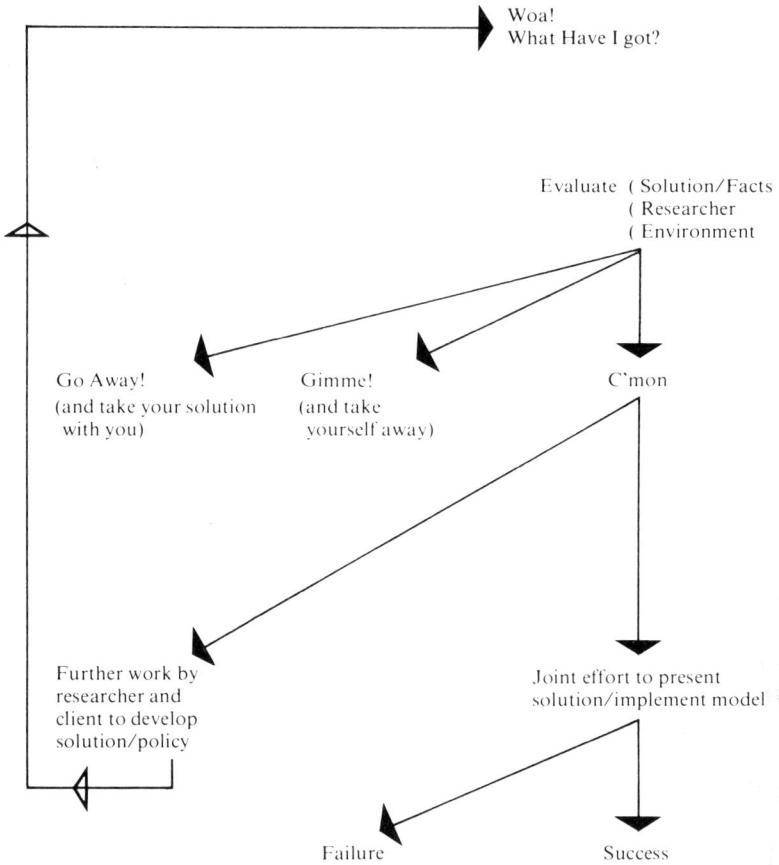

Woa!
What Have I got?

Evaluate (Solution/Facts
(Researcher
(Environment

Go Away!
(and take your solution
 with you)

Gimme!
(and take
 yourself away)

C'mon

Further work by
researcher and
client to develop
solution/policy

Joint effort to present
solution/implement model

Failure

Success

source: R. Fox, "In Retrospect — A Review of Some of
the Work Carried Out in the Research and Intelligence Unit", diagram 6, adapted by the author.

160

evaluate the immediate administrative and political environment to determine the feasibility and appropriateness of the report.

From this evaluation the client may respond in at least three ways. First, the client may reject both the researcher and the solution (go away). This response can take many forms besides an outright rejection of the advice. The client can shelve the solution after gratefully receiving it and thanking the researchers for their efforts. The client may defend the *status quo*, or argue that the solution is ill conceived, or may just avoid meeting the researcher.

Perhaps the most common response is that the client may accept the solution but not involve the researcher and unit in any further steps (gimme). Third, the client may decide to continue the working relationship with the researcher (c'mon) through further work and/or in a joint effort to present the solution to a committee or to implement the solution. On the other hand, the researcher may decide to go along with the client's reaction whatever it is, to make some compromise in the solution to gain some acceptance of it, to meet the client to sell the solution or, in certain cases perhaps, go over the head of the client. On balance, however, clients hold many advantages over policy advisers and researchers.

The experience of Cleveland identifies many of the key elements likely to be found in the work process of policy planning and research units throughout British government.[32] It shows that policy planning and research activities involve a number of different stages and that the researcher and client interaction varies according to the stages of the project. The case also demonstrates the importance of negotiation and client-researcher relations to the possible outcome of the unit's work.

Perhaps the most significant implication of this case concerns the quality of internal government consultancy skills. Management service, research and planning practitioners are not skilful at helping their clients through an experience of change. Since policy advice is basically about achieving change and performance improvements, and since many people are fearful of change, this is an important problem. It is not that officials doing this work are intrinsically incapable of the necessary skills, so much that they and their unit heads frequently do not perceive change agent skills as something relevant.

If only because policy advisers have more experience of research and planning than their clients then they are the experts — and this means not only being expert in technical disciplines but in human relations skills too. The Cleveland researchers concluded that where failures occurred it was their non-technical, human relations skills rather than technical skills that were involved. Indeed, their technical expertise was seldom stretched let alone inadequate. If non-technical concerns are so important why are they so overlooked? Part of the problem is that both clients and advisers have the idea that anything other than a rigidly scientific style is illegitimate for a research function. It is very difficult to generate the more complex but much more useful expectation that one can very usefully advise on the politics of a change situation, that it is possible to do this and provide a rational research input, and that one is not after a slice of power at the client's expense.

The development of a common language between clients and advisers and between advisers themselves is a basic problem in planning and research.[33] Before the study, Cleveland's researchers did not have a common vocabulary or set of organizing concepts. Researchers discussed their work in project specific and/or research technique terms only, so it was very difficult if not impossible to discuss projects at a higher level, learn from experience and get better at the job. A major benefit of the project for the Cleveland unit was that a language did emerge and now they do have discussions to compare their work experience and broaden their range and quality of expertise. The matter of developing a common language for communication is especially significant in the market of policy ideas.

Marketing advice

An important identity question for policy planners and researchers is whether their job is finished when they submit a report, or should they actively promote its acceptance? Should policy analysts and advisers be concerned with the adoption and implementation of their work?

The case against policy analysts being concerned with the marketing of their advice has been stated by Colin Eden and John Harris: 'rational, scientific investigation and analysis cannot take place within the context of dogma, vested interest and institution'.[34] If analysts consciously exclude or favour one alternative as opposed to another for behaviour or institutional reasons, they have abandoned the basic tenets of science. Moreover if the analyst or researcher favours particular alternatives which are consistently ignored by policy makers or are later found to be bad advice, the status of the analyst is jeopardized.

However, as Eden and Harris point out, 'these arguments are relics of the physical sciences that have been virtuously carried forth into the new era of applying science to social systems'. Indeed, to ignore considerations of implementation is to abandon a scientific approach because the policy analyst or adviser 'will not be recognising the acute naivete of social system modelling and our present inability to include that variety in the model which can express the reality of the institutional process, and our knowledge of behavioural science'.[35]

In view of this debate, policy planners and researchers were asked: should a unit simply present the results of their studies, or should a unit actively promote and encourage the acceptance of a study? Do units market or sell their results to other officials?

A large majority of the officials interviewed stated that policy units should encourage the acceptance of their advice, and claimed that they did actively promote their own work. Only a few officials said it would be risky to openly promote their work, and some officials said it depended upon whom they were advising. Sometimes, as the head of one unit put it, 'it's a matter of prayer'.

The need for selling policy advice has been recognized by economists, statisticians, corporate planners and researchers alike, whether in a policy unit or other public organization in British government. Sir Alec Cairncross, former head of the Government Economic Service, has said that economic advisers must take into account administrative procedures and practices, and ministerial and public acceptability:

> Policy takes shape in a climate of opinion; and without the support of public opinion cannot be persevered in. Opinion may be, and frequently is, perverse, ill-informed and confused. But it is largely beyond the reach of economic advisers who are rarely seen or heard and could not, in any event, express views contrary to government policy. They must therefore make what forecasts they can of the acceptability of current policies and frame their advice with some regard to what can be sold, not just to Ministers, but to the public by Ministers. There is a marketing aspect to advising as well as a production aspect.[36]

Concerning proposals for the improvement of data quality or for the generation of new data, Benjamin has said, 'An experienced statistician will know that he will have to accept some bargaining and compromise; his skill is to secure efficiency from less than perfection'.[37] R. Allen has claimed that most corporate planners and researchers in local government do not expect their results to speak for themselves. 'Corporate Planners have sought more traditional local government approaches to bring the benefits of their work'.[38] These approaches include producing reports, ensuring access to committees and chatting up committee chairpersons.

The objectives of marketing policy advice and work are to make known to a client and others the results of a project, to explain technical and complex work to the client, to interest the client in the work done, and to convince clients that decisions taken on the advice can be justified and defended in the bureaucratic and political arena. Ultimately, of course, the aim of marketing advice is to encourage the client to make use of the unit's work.

Policy planners and researchers must market their advice because they are advisory staff. As such, they operate from a comparatively weak power base and their work is subject to approval by other officials. Contrary to classical organizational theorists' conceptions of staff units, not everything policy advisers suggest is referred to superior officials only. Policy units sell their ideas both up and down the hierarchy: up the line to senior officials to get support and legitimacy, and down the line to secure administrators' co-operation to ensure that ideas are viewed as feasible and, if accepted, are properly implemented. Policy units must also sell their ideas because of resistance to change or lack of interest. Line officials may view policy unit staff as intruders and as a threat to their programmes. Politicians may lose interest in a project before it is completed. Hence, marketing policy advice is done for reasons of professionalism and job effectiveness and also for reasons of organizational survival and building co-operative relations with other officials.

Policy unit staff use a number of techniques and tactics for encouraging acceptance of their advice. One is to be sensitive to the political and administrative environment in which they operate. If proposals go against the views of the governing party it's no good going about selling the proposals overtly, say policy advisers. Units also try to be aware of the professional and organizational values of departmental activities they examine. For example, officials in local authorities suggest that any recommendations in the education field that discuss the diminution of the power of headmasters would be very difficult to sell. In a study on the fire brigade in its authority, a central unit recommended that the existing fire trucks not be replaced but be kept in service for several more years. The unit also included a recommendation that an additional allocation be given to keep the trucks maintained and clean. The unit head in charge of this study suggested that the allowance recommendation was inserted in recognition of the prevailing norm in fire brigades that firemen have pride in clean, shiny fire trucks.

Policy unit staff also stress the importance of relating the detail and length of their reports to the type of audience. Benveniste has identified three audiences and how policy advice can be adapted to them:

1   Top policy makers working under time pressures may read only two or three pages and need to be given a highly condensed statement of the nature of the policy being elaborated, the reasons for it, and its potential impact.

2   The staffs of these policy makers have more time to evaluate the report. For these, considerable information has to be presented: the results of research, the nature of the policy

options, and the logical reasoning leading to a particular choice. Data are included but in abbreviated form; as far as possible, it is presented in non-technical terms to facilitate understanding. Where possible, visual material is included, e.g., graphs, tables and photographs.

3   Popularizers — mass media evaluators for whom press releases have to be elaborated — are used to create interest in the exercise.[39]

Thus the marketing process may involve the provision of many kinds of advice including policy, technical, professional, economic and public advice to several different audiences.

Another tactic used by policy units in gaining support for their work is to identify and develop contacts with the centres of power in a department, local authority or government. They look for the key people in the client organization, the good managers and influential officials at the points of decision making, and attempt to develop a working relationship with them. As one programme planner explains: 'you try to be aware of the power structure of the authority, find out where the strengths and weaknesses are, define them, then plan and develop your strategy accordingly'. The director of a local authority unit keeps a card index on members, key officers in the authority, and leading industrialists and other people in the area who have weight, are prepared to talk with the unit, and are on the same wavelength with the policy planners.

Another marketing tactic is consultation and the creation of a coalition of support for ideas. Richard Chapman has discussed this tactic in his case study of the decision to raise the Bank Rate: 'Instead of looking for a consensus, the decision makers, recognising its significance for their authority, set out to create it by consulting and informing as many people as possible'. This procedure seems important for the accumulation of authority. Chapman suggests: 'In this way the importance of consensus may be to confer on the decisions of the administrators a higher degree of authority than they would otherwise have'.[40]

Policy planners and researchers clearly use consultation as a means to create a consensus or at least a basis of support. 'For favourable action on an advisory recommendation to occur, the advisor must normally persuade a large number of people throughout the decision-making organization and foster something of a consensus among the interests affected by the recommendations.'[41] In this sense, the adviser is following a dominant style in British government and public administration. Policy unit staff circulate papers to get comments and views, brief officials and politicians, have informal and formal meetings and chats with various people, and try to keep closely in touch with the grapevine.

Policy units also use a bottom-up approach in building support for their ideas by selling ideas to the officials who would be responsible for implementing them and then go to top management. A seasoned corporate planner in a district council explained the bottom-up approach as follows: 'In theory, when the unit comes up with some research findings and recommendations, such as trends of housing demand, we should go to our boss, the Chief Executive Officer, and sell him on the idea. In turn, he should convey the idea to the appropriate departmental chief officer, either directly or through the Management Team. In practice, what we do is sell the idea to the official in the department who will be responsible for administering the recommendations, and along with him try to sell the idea to his superiors'.

Such an approach would especially be important in the marketing of advice related to technical and professional matters. The bottom-up approach illustrates that giving policy advice is a complex process which does not proceed strictly through hierarchical channels and is much more than the upward flow of ideas and information to senior decision takers. The marketing of advice also suggests that not all power resides at the top of public bureaucracies. To sell ideas and to survive, policy units must take account of authoritative actors throughout the hierarchy.

The marketing process does not just occur at the reporting stage or even at only the later stages of the work process. Rather, the selling of the substantive content of research or advice is closely linked to the reputation of the unit, the formulation of the work programme, the expectations of the client and researcher, and the degree of client participation in the various stages of the project. Selling takes place continuously throughout the whole work process. Effective corporate planners while doing their work will always have one eye on the final product. Indeed, the setting of a unit work programme can be seen in large part as a two way interaction process, with policy units both responding to and forming their work preferences.

The market for policy planning and research is an incremental process guided by notions of political and administrative feasibility and organizational survival. Policy advisers choose topics that have the lowest costs for their clients and themselves. The criteria for the formulation of the work programme shows a reliance upon topics that adapt to rather than radically transform prevailing practices and thinking in the political and administrative systems. Policy units encourage the acceptance of their work, and policy planning and research is marketed to the circumstances in which units are located. This chapter has dealt with how policy advisers obtain and sell their work. The next chapter analyses the impacts of policy units and their advice.

Notes

1   Bruce L.R. Smith, *The RAND Corporation*, p.157.
2   Andrew Leigh, 'Researchers in the Social Services', p.63.
3   Sir Kenneth Berrill, evidence to the (General Sub-Committee) Expenditure Committee, p.606.
4   Sir William Pile, evidence to the Expenditure Committee, Tenth Report, 1975–76 Session, HC 621, p.116.
5   J.A. Hudson, deputy secretary, evidence to the Expenditure Committee, Tenth Report, 1975–76 Session, HC 621, p.458.
6   See John Croft, *Research in Criminal Justice*, pp.8–9, and R. Greenwood et al., *In Pursuit of Corporate Rationality*, p.134.
7   L.J. Sharpe, *Research in Local Government: The Role of the Research and Information Unit of the Greater London Council*, pp.17–18.
8   J.M. Gillespie, 'Policy Information, Provision of Information for Policy Making Problems and Suggested Solutions', p.9.
9   Ibid.
10 John Croft, *Research in Criminal Justice*, pp.1–2.
11 *A Framework for Government Research and Development*, Cmnd. 4814, 1971. See also Lord Rothschild, *Meditations of a Broomstick*, chapter 9.
12 R.V.G. Clarke, 'Penal Policy-Making and Research in the Home Office', p.117.
13 Timothy A. Booth, 'Research and Policy Making in Local Authority Social Services', p.178.
14 Andrew Leigh, 'Researchers in the Social Services', p.64.
15 Arnold J. Meltsner, *Policy Analysts in the Bureaucracy*, p.81.
16 Dr Graham Davies, 'The Central Research Unit of Newcastle City', p.23. See also Arnold J. Meltsner, 'Political Feasibility and Policy Analysis' and W.I. Jenkins, *Policy Analysis*, pp. 231–40.
17 Committee on Policy Optimisation, *Report*, Cmnd. 7148, March 1978, p.31. On the concept of agency philosophy see Peter Self, *Administrative Theories and Politics*.
18 Bernard Benjamin, *Statistics and Research in Urban Administration and Development*, pp.101–2.
19 E.M. Davies, *The Central Research Function in Local Government*, pp.46 and 61.
20 Lord Rothschild, *Meditations of a Broomstick*, p.174.
21 John Le Carré, *Tinker, Tailor, Soldier, Spy*, p.282.
22 C. Wiseman, 'Selection of Major Planning Issues', pp.78–9. See also Albert B. Cherns, 'Negotiating the Contract'.
23 Dr Graham Davies, 'The Central Research Unit of Newcastle City', p.23.

24 *Future World Trends*, pp.19–29, and 'The Systems Analysis Research Unit', p.2.

25 C.J. Train, 'The Development of Crime Policy Planning in the Home Office', p.377.

26 Arnold J. Meltsner, *Policy Analysts in the Bureaucracy*, p.93.

27 W.J.L. Plowden, 'Developing a joint approach to social policy', p.36.

28 Hugh Heclo and Aaron Wildavsky, *The Private Government of Public Money*, p.317.

29 Sir Geoffrey Vickers, *Towards a Sociology of Management*, p.69.

30 For surveys of the work methods that can be used, see E.S. Quade, *Analysis for Public Decisions* and Michael Carley, *Rational Techniques in Policy Analysis*.

31 The following account is based on a presentation by R. Fox, the director of the unit, to a seminar of R & I Heads at IN-LOGOV, 24 October 1977, which the author attended. See 'In Retrospect – a Review of Some of the Work Carried Out in the Research and Intelligence Unit' and a more detailed account by S. Hyde and S. Davey, *'Project Review' (OR Whatever Happened to the Work You Did Last Summer?)*.

32 On the work processes related to other units, see *Report of the Working Group on Energy Strategy*, Energy Commission Paper no.2; Peter Jay, 'PESC, PAR and Politics'; Hugh Heclo and Aaron Wildavsky, *The Private Government of Public Money*; Sir Derek Ezra, 'Long Term Planning for Coal'; Tenth Report, Expenditure Committee, 1975–76 Session, HC 621, Appendix 13; 'The NHS Planning System'; and E.J. Razzell, 'Improving Policy Analysis – the D.H.S.S. Approach'.

33 See J.K. Friend and W.N. Jessop, *Local Government and Strategic Choice* and Peter Kershaw, 'Political realities and local government'.

34 Colin Eden and John Harris, *Management Decision and Decision Analysis*, p.207.

35 Ibid., p.207.

36 Sir Alec Cairncross, 'The Work of an Economic Adviser', p.5.

37 Bernard Benjamin, *Statistics and Research in Urban Administration and Development*, p.24.

38 R. Allen, 'Current Practice Review', p.50.

39 Guy Benveniste, *The Politics of Expertise*, p.165.

40 Richard A. Chapman, *Decision Making*, pp.109–10.

41 Bruce L.R. Smith, *The RAND Corporation*, p.239. For an excellent discussion of how selling research can be an ongoing process, see Robert Pinkham, 'Effective social research for local government'.

8 The impacts of policy units

*Naturally you very often ask yourself whether the
job you are doing is worth while. This is not the kind
of job where you point to scores on a sheet, or a balance
sheet.*

Sir Kenneth Berrill,
formerly Head of the CPRS

And now of course we want to know what difference policy planning
and research units have made to modern government. What impact
has the work of policy advisers had on the structures, processes and
activities of British public administration? What have been their suc-
cesses and achievements, their failures and disappointments? Judgements about the achievements of policy advisers and their organizations are ultimately based on the definition used to determine impact.
The impact of policy units can be usefully considered by identifying
and examining the meaning of success in research and advice as viewed
by policy planners and researchers. It is recognized that the impact
of policy units may have other meanings for other people. A general
discussion of researchers' own criteria for success, however, should
demonstrate many of the possible effects of policy units, and contribute to an understanding of the perceptions of researchers and the
factors related to their job satisfaction.

The conventional view of the impact of research, evaluation and
other forms of policy advice emphasizes a policy making or problem
solving approach. Impact, according to this view, is the immediate
and direct application of research study findings to policy formulation,
programme implementation, or to solve a specific problem.[1] The
standard test for assessing the impact of research and advice is whether
the recommendations from a study are directly applied to a policy
or programme. The general conclusion is that social science research
and evaluation have not had a substantial or significant impact on
government policy makers or programmes. The literature conveys

the picture that major impacts are infrequent and that research is generally not utilized.

The above view of impact is inadequate and misleading. 'Much of the literature', Nancy Brennan notes, 'consists of think pieces and armchair reflections based on the authors' personal experience with evaluation research. There have been few empirical studies'.[2] Furthermore, the literature has adopted a definition of impact taken from the natural and technological sciences. This can be misleading because applications in science and technology are probably more easily identifiable, and also because it overlooks the politics of the policy process. Decisions about public policy emerge from a different sort of process than scientific and technological innovations – a process of continuing debate, to which researchers contribute with many other actors and interests, and in which research findings are seldom applied in a direct technological sense.[3]

The scientific or technological view of impact also contains unrealistic notions of the extent of rationality possible in policy research and advice based on the current state of the social sciences. 'There is no consensus as to what constitutes social science "knowledge" among social scientists, and more important, there is no unquestioned acceptance of this "knowledge" on the part of clients and users.'[4]

The conventional view of impact does not consider that several studies and other inputs on the same issue may lead to policy changes. It also overlooks the gradual impact of research on the attitudes and beliefs of policy makers and administrators, the different kinds of outputs or services of policy research organizations, and other uses of research from the viewpoint of the researcher or client. Indeed, the meaning of advisory impact is a fuzzy term:

> In some cases it may imply the extent to which a research study has been widely disseminated and read, and to others it may mean the attempt to apply research findings to changing the existing policies. Putting knowledge to use though, is not the same as an ultimate result in terms of the way services operate.[5]

Therefore, to judge the impact of research 'requires some agreement about what would be a successful result compared to an unsuccessful one. Simply to have "an impact" has little to recommend it unless one knows whether this means a beneficial or deleterious effect'.[6]

Defining success and assessing impact

Success is not a monolithic concept. To assess the impact of policy units one must appreciate the numerous criteria for success. Policy planners and researchers have many different measure for defining success in their work. In general, the various criteria of success for policy advisers can be grouped according to three broad categories: criteria about the work itself, criteria about the unit as an organization, and criteria that deal with the effect of a unit's work on its environment.

Policy planners and researchers clearly derive some degree of job satisfaction and define success partially in terms of the work they do. One such measure is if the unit produces a report at all and results are made available to the client. Although this may seem a very modest standard of success, it is frequently referred to by officials, and it should be noted that, 'Researchers in all fields of enquiries ... frequently want to extend their project and by going further to seek out more or different explanations for the phenomena they are examining'.[7] A related standard of success is whether the work is produced on time. This is important because it indicates that the unit can meet deadlines and is efficient, and also makes it more likely that the work will be useful to the client.

The methodological rigour and substantive content of work serves as a standard for success. This belief is supported by such comments as: having secured a rigorous piece of thinking; a report that is intellectually sound; taut; with economy of style; a good piece of work in itself; and, high quality work. Some policy advisers refer to doing a complete job as a standard for success, preparing reports and giving advice that is self contained. That is to say, reports that take into account all important facts, recognize disadvantages as well as advantages to options, are clear and are defensible. It should be something the client can use as it is, so the permanent secretary, for example, can read it and put his name to it and have it sent to the minister.

Another criterion for success about the work itself is if the findings in a study contribute to the existing body of knowledge about an issue or programme or improve the methodology. A report may be regarded as a success if it remains relevant and survives critical scrutiny over several years. To some, a successful report is one that cannot be safely ignored and is referred to in subsequent debates and discussions of an issue.

The second category of criteria for success relates to the unit as an organization. Survival — whether a unit maintains itself through time — is obviously an indicator of some success. This is not surprising given that units began with uncertain mandates and often face hostile or apathetic environments. 'The gut measure of success is survival. If you fold, no one will call you successful.'[8] To exist, perchance advise, is success or perhaps more accurately a condition of success. Organizational survival means to obtain basic resource inputs, to achieve structural continuity, to gain credibility, to build support among officials in the political and administrative systems.

Besides survival, development is another measure for success. In one sense this involves the extent to which unit staff enhance their skills and services in particular areas, through training and development, as well as the professional development of unit members through such techniques as team work. In another sense it refers to the development of a sense of unit identity, internal co-ordination and a distinct domain. Finally, development entails the extent to which policy advisers educate administrators and politicians in unit activities so they understand and utilize them. These aspects of organizational development should be a specific concern of the head of a policy unit.

And another measure for success as an organization has to do with adaptiveness. This involves the extent to which the policy unit responds to client requests, adapts to changing demands and clients, and anticipates relevant issues.

The third category deals with the effect of a policy unit's work on its environment. Many policy planners and researchers view their work as having a number of possible impacts on clients, the political and administrative systems and the general public. In short, some things are different as a result of the advice and research of policy units.

Policy planning and research can be viewed as being potentially influential at every stage of the policy process. Here, for example, is a classification of the criteria for success mentioned by the Research and Intelligence Unit in Cleveland County:

1 Results available to client.
2 Report/results considered by client.
3 Report influences policy.
4 Report's recommendation implemented.
5 Recommendations (model, tool) when implemented, are successful.
6 Activity towards which R & I project contributes is successful.
7 Encourage further use of unit's services.[9]

The first two criteria — results available to, and considered by client — deal with the events at the policy formulation stage which lead up to a policy decision. Some policy planners, for example, insist this is the most important standard for judging impact; even if clients do not always accept your ideas, the key question is: do they listen? Once when asked to describe the impact of the CPRS, Lord Rothschild replied, 'I don't know that the government is better run as a result of our work. I think the highest compliment I ever got was from a Cabinet minister who said: "You make us think from time to time". I thought that was a great achievement, considering how much ministers have to do. They don't have much time to think'.[10] Still further, some researchers define success partly by the number of people who complain about their work. At least then they know they are making some impact on others.

Success can be broadened to include not only client satisfaction but also recognition by other officials, citizen groups and the media. Recognition in the local press gives the impression that a unit is having an influence and that helps staff morale. Raising the level of policy debate and discussion and influencing the climate of opinion are common measures for success. While this is difficult if not impossible to measure, it may include the unit offering more or new alternatives at the policy making stage, and having their ideas become part of the agency philosophy or house view within a department. It may also include units instilling in policy makers and administrators a sense of confidence that they are in a better state of control over a situation, having considered some analytical advice or research.

A third criterion for success is that a report influences policy. While a policy is not a single act but a series of actions, one of the more visible aspects of a policy is the official decision selecting one course of action or inaction among various options. A subtle but important distinction exists between a report influencing a policy decision and actually being implemented. The former deals with the policy decision or decision taking stage and the latter deals with the policy implementation stage. Both planners and researchers and other officials make this distinction. One form of organizational resistance policy units face is when officials tell planners they have considered a unit report and agree with it, but then do nothing about implementing the report. Having recommendations transformed into legislation and implemented is, of course, the conventional view of impact in the policy research and evaluation literature.

Policy implementation generally includes the events and activities following a policy decision undertaken to pursue that decision. A programme is normally established to pursue, through a concrete course of action, the policy decision. Policy units may play a role in implementation as well as formulation. In fact, they do more than just provide advisory inputs to decision makers. The policy adviser's concern with political and administrative feasibility provides a connection between policy formation and programme execution. Policy advisers believe that to promote the adoption of their ideas they must pay some regard to implementation and suggest practical guidelines for action. They can be involved in the interpretation of general policy and political decisions and they may sit on administrative committees to help oversee policy implementation and programme design.

Policy outcomes are the actual effects of a policy decision when implemented, whether the effects are intended or not. Some policy planners and researchers divide the concept of policy outcomes into two parts. They distinguish between the consequence of the implementation of unit recommendations, and the performance of the activity towards which the unit recommendations contributed. Thus, one criterion for success is if a unit's recommendations are accomplished when implemented, and a separate and even higher standard of success is when both the unit's recommendations and the activity to which the recommendations have contributed are favourably completed. This distinction suggests that if the activity to which the research project contributed was not successful, a research officer could still claim some success if the research recommendations had been effectively implemented. In other words, researchers could say that they did all they could, and then point to other factors, outside of their control and responsibility, to explain the disappointing performance of a programme.

Finally, success is when a report or project encourages further use of the unit's services. Many policy planners and researchers define success in these terms. Apart from contributing to the continued existence of the unit, policy advisers feel that if a project encouraged further use of the unit's services it indicates client satisfaction and provided the opportunity to establish co-operative relations with other officials. Further use of unit services also indicates an increase in unit credibility in the eyes of policy makers or administrators and a reliance on the unit for certain services. This demonstrates that some work of policy units comes from satisfied customers and from previous projects and impacts. In systems theory terms, the experience of policy implementation and outcomes feeds back to the policy unit. At the same time, the past work of units may generate demands for change in unit activities and even present challenges to its authority.

Impact can therefore be broadly defined as the effects, consequences or results of ideas upon the attitudes and/or actions of people. For present purposes, the primary focus will be on the impact of policy units through their various activities, such as research, information, advice, consultation and analysis, on elected and appointed officials in British government. This definition has certain implications for the study of policy units. Policy units can have multiple uses. Those uses may be direct, tangible and immediate, or indirect, intangible and long term. Moreover, the impact of policy units can be closely linked with many other different elements, making an impact assessment problematic.

Nonetheless, policy units have had some significant impacts upon administrators, politicians and policy, as well as contributing to the state of the art of policy planning and research. At least three general kinds of impacts of policy units can be identified and described. The first deals with the policy planning, research and information capability of British government; the second, with personnel management; and the third, with organizational behaviour and relations. It will become clear that these impacts are all interconnected, and that they are divided here mainly for purposes of clarity.

Advisory capability

There is little doubt that the establishment of policy units has given British government a greater capability for policy planning, research and intelligence. Central government departments and local authorities are placing more emphasis on these functions than in the past, and some policy units have become an important forum for planning, information and research functions. Policy units have introduced particular inputs to government such as statistical advice, for the first time, at an earlier stage, or in a more sophisticated form than had been the case.

From their advisory activities, planning units have also influenced traditional administrative functions in government. In recent decades the combination of a more intensive appraisal of expenditures, programme analysis and review and planning units has created a shift in the role of finance from financial control to financial planning and resource allocation.[11]

Through the formulation of their work programmes, units have to some extent taken the initiative in identifying and suggesting problems and exploring them. One of the contributions of units in this context has been to look at problems that may have received little previous attention, anticipate issues of emerging importance, or promote new perspectives on old issues. Unit work programmes are therefore related to the policy agenda of the British political system, that is, those issues that are of concern to a local authority or the central government at any given time.

To the extent that policy units assist in determining which issues are considered in government through their own work programmes and by drawing certain problems and not others to the attention of officials, they are having an impact on the policy agenda. Thus, policy planners and researchers can add support and possibly improve the chances of a proposal being accepted. 'They also collect, combine and modify suggestions or demands in order to produce packages which may be more readily acceptable to higher authorities. They clearly act both as advocates for some issues and as agents for the regulation and reduction of demands in general.'[12]

In their scanning and analysis of the environment, many units contribute to the identification and articulation of the wants and needs of individuals or groups, and channel these demands to government officials. On the other hand, policy units also perform an information filtering and gatekeeper function by screening and reducing the issues considered by government. These functions are central to politics and policy making. Politics is not only about conflict and power but also uncertainty and learning. Policy making, to quote Hugh Heclo, 'entails both deciding and knowing. It extends beyond deciding what "wants" to accommodate, to include problems of knowing who might want something, what is wanted and how to turn even the most sweet-tempered general agreement into concrete collective action'.[13] Many policy units in Britain have made important contributions in discerning social, economic and physical conditions in their relevant environments. In turn, some units have suggested and formulated possible courses of actions and responses for policy makers from this information. The contribution of units to policy formation and decision making has been varied and is often indirect as well as direct. Units assist in policy making by developing strategy papers, conducting research studies and issuing analyses and participating in departmental or interdepartmental committees. An example from local government can illustrate this role of policy units.

Mid Glamorgan's Intelligence, Research and Development Unit, along with the support of other officers and several outside bodies, has done a study of the industrial structure of Mid Glamorgan.[14] A main objective of the study was to obtain comprehensive information concerning linkages within the key sectors of the county's economy and between these and other sectors. The information obtained included the source of supplies, approaches to firms in Mid Glamorgan, and satisfaction with suppliers. Information was also collected on the size of firms, date of establishment in the county, the locus of decision making, and plans for expansion or diversification.

The study has had a number of impacts and consequences. The Intelligence, Research and Development Unit has established a channel of communication with about 400 area firms. Information has been provided on request to firms wishing to identify a supplier of goods or services in the sectors of the economy covered. It has been possible to identify particular goods and services for which there appears to be an unsatisfied demand. This information can be passed to an existing firm in a related sector, or, if major gaps are identified, specific promotional efforts can be mounted to attract a firm to the county to fill such gaps. One finding from the study was that there was a lack of knowledge, especially on the part of smaller firms, about the various forms of incentives and services available to industry. Consequently, a comprehensive guide to these services and incentives has been included in the Mid Glamorgan industrial directory. Another problem identified was the inadequacy of school leavers and young

176

people, as perceived by industrialists. As a result of this, a meeting has been organized between educationalists and industrialists in the electronics industry to explore this issue. Information generated from the study also provided data for other types of analysis on the county's economy.

Often a significant impact of the work of policy units is upon government information systems. Much of the work of units is dependent on data arising from administrative records available in a suitable form. One impact common to many units has been their ability in getting divisions or departments to set up new data collection procedures and/or modify existing procedures. In addition to providing the unit with necessary information, changes in the data system have helped client organizations by providing, on an ongoing basis, up-to-date data on clients and their environment and thereby enabled the organization to be better aware and better able to respond to needs and issues. An example is housing departments in district councils and improvements to their waiting lists. Payoffs from improvements in data systems also include an increase in the significant information available to the unit and other data users, and a reduction in the time required to obtain data for future work.

In perhaps a majority of local authorities, policy researchers and planners are significantly involved in developing new statistics, storing information and producing regular bulletins for those managing and planning services to keep them in touch with service trends and general issues. The actual impact of the bulletin is its use as a document for general information, as a reference volume, and as a management tool in providing managers with information for general planning and monitoring purposes.[15]

The Fulton Committee called for some central co-ordination of departmental planning units by the Treasury or Cabinet Office to ensure that emerging public problems are tackled systematically, comprehensively and on the basis of common propositions. While no such central co-ordination of policy planning exists in the Civil Service, policy units within individual government departments are contributing to the development of common information bases and frameworks in specific policy sectors such as health, education, criminal justice and penal policy. Likewise in local government, policy unit efforts have contributed to greater consistency in data between organizations and to more comprehensive information which look at issues across organizational lines.

In many cases the policy unit's contribution is to influence perceptions of problems. 'The end product of most planning and research activities is not an agenda of mechanical policy moves for every contingency — plainly an impossible task — but rather a more sophisticated map of reality carried in the minds of the policy makers.'[16] Policy units can have an impact on the map of reality of policy makers and administrators on at least two levels. First, units can make a contribution to thinking in government on a particular policy, programme or problem area. For instance, a senior member of the Home Office Research Unit has described the impact of the unit on penal policy as very like that of the universities. Its contribution to policy has been mostly indirect, 'brought about by adding to knowledge about the penal system and those with whom it deals, by helping to dispel myths about the functioning of the system and its effectiveness, and (to a lesser extent) by analysis and refinement of fundamental concepts'.[17]

Second, at a more fundamental level, policy units can affect root concepts which underlie the entire range of activities of the political or administrative system as a whole. An example is the GLC's R & I Unit which in the late 1960s destroyed the myth that the population of Greater London was growing and could only be held down to eight million through the dispersal of a million people from the area. While the GLC was spending money to encourage people to leave London, demographic work of the R & I Unit found that the population of Greater London was not growing but was in fact declining and would continue to do so. The unit's work caused great initial resentment from politicians, planners and other officials, though it was finally accepted. It highlighted a radical discrepancy between prevailing beliefs and reality, and had a profound effect on the Greater London Development Plan.[18]

Policy advisers have helped to inject basic concepts of economic analysis into the decision making processes of government. In many quarters they have impressed upon administrators and politicians the need for deliberate choices and the ranking of objectives in the face of scarce resources, and that a cost associated with any decision choice is the foregone opportunities of rejected alternatives. Thus, besides having an impact on substantive programmes, policy advisers have contributed to what Yehezkel Dror calls the 'meta-policy process', introducing root concepts and procedures for planning policy, setting priorities and making decisions.

Finally, policy units have reduced some of the uncertainty facing government organizations by expanding the data base on which policy issues are perceived, discussed and formulated. Indeed, it has been argued that the primary function of planning is to reduce uncertainty. In the end, the decisions may not be different from those which would otherwise be made, but they will be less intuitive, perhaps command more confidence, and have other potential benefits.[19] Consider, for example, the Central Research Unit (now Research Section) of Newcastle-upon-Tyne. This unit has done work on providing measures of multiple deprivation, that is, the whole range of economic, social and environmental conditions of the worst off individuals. 'It thus implies not only a concern with poverty in the sense of low levels of income and wealth but in addition a concern with the level of social facilities and opportunities and the level of environmental amenities which together create the individual's living conditions.[20]

Using a set of indicators constructed from 1971 census data, department records and the unit's own 1975 Household Survey data, the wards of the city were ranked according to their degree of multiple deprivation. The unit concluded that the most deprived wards in the city were West City, Benwell, Fawdon and Walker. In its report on this work the unit admitted the conclusions were not surprising: 'For those who know Newcastle there is nothing remarkable in this'. However, the findings and methodology have a number of uses and possible impacts. The work allows a more comprehensive picture of the nature of the problems these areas face and describe Newcastle in terms which relate to the sphere of influence of the council. This provides a background of information for those who draw up the programmes and policies of the council. In the future, the methodology can be used to monitor the effectiveness of policies aimed at these areas by observing changes in the various deprivation indicators for each ward over time. Moreover it could serve as a guide to the differences between areas of the city which can then be related to different resource allocations between areas. In addition to improving the quality of information, a more informed case can be presented when seeking grant aid for urban areas requiring remedial action.

Personnel management

Many of the effects from planning and research units have to do with personnel management in government. We have already examined in previous chapters several areas of personnel management that relate to policy units — recruitment, training, professionalism and staff—line relations. In this section we shall consider how the staffing process of units has influenced the status of specialists, the use of outsiders and secondments, and the careers of policy advisers.

The creation of policy units in British government has resulted in an increased number of permanent positions and full time personnel concerned with policy planning and research activities. The creation of policy units has increased the status of staff in public administration systems. Indeed, one of the arguments for establishing units was to provide new or more attractive career structures for staff specialists and to attract people who would otherwise probably not have an outlet in government service.

In central government, policy units are composed largely of civil servants and therefore have not offered attractive short term opportunities in government to outsiders. A key exception is the CPRS which recruits half of its members from outside central government normally on the basis of two-year secondments. By contrast, policy units in local government are staffed with relatively more outsiders. Local authority units do offer attractive job prospects to specialists who would otherwise have only very restricted opportunities in local government, and also permit local authorities to compete better against other organizations in recruiting specialists like economists and researchers.

For some people in central government and for comparatively more in local authorities, policy units offer career opportunities. In central government, personnel generally remain in a unit for only a few years and are then assigned to an operating division of the department. In these cases, a policy unit is not a career in itself but rather an important training and testing ground in a civil servant's general career. While in a policy unit, civil servants can have an early exposure to the top policy making process and gain diversified experience through job rotation, thinking the unthinkable and working with more experienced policy planners and researchers. In some central government departments, such as Health and Social Security and Employment, the creation of policy units has established and improved the career opportunities of policy oriented staff specialists. This is particularly true for researchers, in line with the suggestions of the Fulton Report. Policy units have contributed to the general improvement in status and career prospects of research officers in the Civil Service over the last decade. As well, but probably to a lesser degree, units have contributed to the status of economists and statisticians in the central government.[21]

The contribution of policy units to the career opportunities of advisory personnel is of more importance in local government. Policy units have created career opportunities for a significant number of research personnel. Since most units are too small to provide a self-contained career ladder, the career pattern of unit personnel in local government is generally through horizontal mobility. Thus, staff move from a unit in one authority to a unit in another. Local authorities benefit from this exchange by obtaining staff with varying backgrounds and experience in other authorities and organizations. The exchange of ideas and information is also facilitated through the emerging professionalism of unit personnel, especially at the local level.

Policy units have an impact on their environment when they recruit part time staff from other divisions and departments or from the general public. Although positions in planning and research units are generally full time, permanent posts, some local authorities supplement the unit's human resources through secondments. Such secondments may be from any local authority department, and indeed there are examples of other public bodies participating in such an arrangement; for instance, in Northamptonshire, the secondment of an officer from the Area Health Authority to the Central Policy and Research Unit. This approach is favoured by a number of policy advisers.

Some local authority policy units recruit part time or temporary staff from the local community. For example, the Central Research and Intelligence Unit at Tyne and Wear conducted a county wide household survey in 1976. With the help of a grant from the Manpower Services Commission under the Job Creation Programme and a budget grant from the county council, the unit was able to hire about 100 unemployed people as enumerators. About 250 unemployed people were interviewed in job centres around the county; 120 were offered jobs and ninety accepted. The enumerators underwent a two-week training programme for interviewers and worked for six months conducting interviews. In the words of the senior official in the Central Research and Intelligence Unit who was closely involved in the project: 'The exercise has shown how fruitful co-operation between officers of both tiers of local government can be. Every one concerned has been rewarded by seeing so many young people previously unemployed given a worthwhile job and worthwhile training'.[22]

Thus, the staffing practices of policy units have encouraged a degree of interdepartmental and intergovernmental co-operation and, in some cases, have provided training for people into the workings of government and of survey research.

The use of secondments has several benefits for the authority and the unit. This approach provides departmental staff with a means of developing their analytical abilities and enables them to assume a different and wider perspective of public services and their own department and activities within this broader scope. It helps to give first hand experience of the work of a policy planning unit and will enable growth of confidence in the ability of such units to be of assistance to departments, and in publicising the units' range of expertise. Secondments, furthermore, provide a means of making resources available for policy planning and research work that may otherwise be extremely limited. Finally, for some advisers the use of secondments recognizes that policy planning is essentially a corporate responsibility and not that of a few élitists.

Organizational politics

'The most significant consequence of setting up a new structure is that it tends to favour some sets of consultative patterns at the expense of others.'[23] Indeed, policy units have had a number of impacts on the relative distribution of influence and authority among actors within government and between actors in government and outside groups.

Some observers argue that efforts to strengthen departmental policy planning have enhanced the power of officials over politicians. For example, Brian Smith contends: 'Ministers will find it even more difficult to resist the choice of policy options pressed on them by their official advisers if they are based on better analysis of the needs of the future, better long-term forecasting and better research carried out by administrators who are better trained in the relevant techniques of analysis'.[24]

Similarly, Phoebe Hall has argued that the move towards more sophisticated planning such as multi-year expenditure projections can 'impose new limits on the extent and speed with which departmental policy can be realigned around Minister's personal or party programmes'.[25] Furthermore, Hall claims that policy research and analysis make it more difficult for politicians to challenge existing policy. 'It takes more political courage for a Minister to risk major change when faced with voluminous and apparently sophisticated scientific data which support an ongoing but unattractive set of policies, than when policies are simply based on hunches or the preferences of the preceding Minister.[26]

However, the power impact of departmental policy planning and research structures has not been simply to reduce the power of ministers. Planning and research can be a double edged sword in the complex relationship between cabinet minister and civil servant. The institutionalization of policy planning and research structures is likely to permit ministers to more easily and regularly scan the policy options being considered by official advisers. These structures and processes may also increase the ability of a minister to sanction and control the policy planning and research work programme of their departments; communicate their ideas of future policy to the administrative system; and have their key policy goals considered and, perhaps, transformed into plans. In some departments in recent years ministerial aides or special advisers have sat on departmental planning steering committees providing an input and a formal link between the planning process and the political process.[27] Moreover the power of knowledge should not be overemphasized. In politics, facts are very often negotiable and there can be legitimate disputes over what is relevant research and analysis.

In local government, policy units have had an impact on the relationship between elected members and officers generally in the direction of strengthening the role of members in the policy process.[28] An important contribution of many units has been to provide the information and opportunities for elected members to become more involved and influential in policy formulation and review. A councillor in Sunderland, for instance, has said that a major benefit to elected members from the work of the Programme Planning Department in Sunderland is that, 'placing the objectives and targets in priority enabled members to have the great advantage of being fully aware of which targets and which objectives would have to be sacrificed when pruning the estimates'.[29]

Units in local authorities have made members better informed about the council's activities by disseminating information to a broader audience than would otherwise receive it, and interpreting existing information for the benefit of members. Moreover, policy units and related processes of corporate management have probably enhanced the ability of members at the centre of the authority — party leaders and the policy committee — to exercise influence over the administrative system. Indeed, backbench councillors in some authorities complain of a decline in their power due to the rise of policy committees, chief officer management teams and corporate management.

Within departments the formation of units has meant an increase in the organizational support for policy advice and new sources of information. This new policy planning, research and information capability is usually located at or near the top of departmental hierarchies. One organizational effect of units has been to contribute to a strengthening of the authority and influence of senior departmental officials in relation to other departmental officials. In some departments units have contributed to greater centralization by highlighting the relation of different departmental programmes to overall objectives and by assisting senior departmental officials in playing a greater role in resource allocation, research, programme planning and design. It is also likely that some units have modestly influenced the sense of confidence senior officials have in directing their programmes toward objectives. On the other hand, the experience of some government agencies, like the giant Department of the Environment, demonstrates the difficulty in bringing together self-contained policy subsystems and obtaining more effective central policy co-ordination.[30] Here, the lessons to be drawn are that there are varying degrees of policy co-ordination possible depending upon the organizational structure, activities and culture; and that a selective approach to policy co-ordination is more realistic than a synoptic approach in complex organizations.

One reason advanced for policy units was that they could act as a means for co-ordinating policy and resource decisions between a set of organizations. Units were seen, in part, as a vehicle for relating departmental policies to a government's or authority's policies as a whole, thereby reinforcing the collective responsibility of policy makers.

In central government, the CPRS was established in 1971 to enable the cabinet to relate individual departmental policies to the government's overall strategy and to help establish the relative priorities to be given to different programme areas. In short, the CPRS was intended to strengthen the centre of government and the development of a strategy. On this criterion, Maurice Wright has concluded, 'the CPRS has concerned itself less with the development of strategy than with the review of specific policies, issues and institutions'.[31] To be sure, the CPRS has not achieved its initial and, arguably, unrealistic mandate of grand strategic co-ordination. 'It would be strange if, on balance, the departments and their ministers did not prevail most of the time. The CPRS is justified not as a replacement for government by department, but as an occasional modifier of it.[32] Nonetheless, the CPRS has encouraged greater interdepartmental co-operation and helped to get into currency the simple notion that problems are not the unique concern of one department. While the CPRS has never attempted to act as a co-ordinator of departmental planning and research units, its staff believe they have 'at a relatively small cost, both helped to improve the machinery for decision taking at the centre and helped departments to relate their individual policies to the Government's strategy as a whole'.[33]

One area in which the CPRS has achieved some success in interdepartmental co-operation has been on particular aspects of social policies such as income maintenance programmes, personal social services, health, housing, education and employment. In 1975, a report by the CPRS, *A Joint Framework for Social Policies*, was published. The report argued that because of resource, legislative programme and institutional constraints, lack of information, and the absence of a mechanism for determining priorities in the field of social policy, a new and more coherent framework was required for the making and execution of social policies. Based on the report, ministers endorsed a work programme consisting of the development of better data presentation and analysis for social policy decisions, and specific studies in several areas related to social policy.

This work programme has had a number of consequences.[34] First, several organizational developments have resulted from the programme. A Social Group of senior statisticians in the Central Statistical Office was set up in 1975. A strategic forum for ministers has been created, providing them with a chance to discuss and reach agreement on a general framework for social policies. An interdepartmental group has

184

been established to examine issues of policy on financial poverty.

Secondly, there have been efforts to improve social policy information systems. The Social Group is attempting to improve the use of existing information on social policies and improve the presentation of data on changes in the social field to ministers and senior officials. A social report has been developed which contains key statistics and a brief commentary on social policy trends. A start has also been made in the monitoring of individual social programmes, and regular forward looks are being produced to anticipate problems beyond the short term.

Thirdly, work in these areas has led to published CPRS reports on the working arrangements between central government and local authorities, and on the longer term implications of population changes for public policies. Moreover, further work is being done on the disabled, and the relationship between housing policy and other social policies. These published reports and internal studies have promoted more open avenues of exchange between government and the public, politicians and officials and between government departments, various policies, and different time frames for policy and decision making.

It has been suggested by some commentators that the introduction of corporate planning and management in local authorities may result in a redistribution of effective power by reducing the ability of individual departments to 'take an independent line which runs counter to generally agreed policy'.[35] While policy units are only one element in the corporate approach in local government, an examination into their role provides some evidence to assess the impact of corporate management and planning on the relative positions of influence of departments. In general, policy units have not caused a major redistribution of power but have, in some situations, contributed to marginal shifts in the relative influence of departments.

The department which probably has benefited most in policy making effectiveness from the establishment of policy units is the chief executive/clerk's department. Some time ago in a study of town clerks in English local government, T.E. Headrick observed, 'As far as developing a body of consistent officer advice on general policy the Town Clerk is largely powerless'.[36] In the 1970s and early 1980s both the role and power of the clerk has expanded in the area of policy formulation and co-ordination. Along with corporate management, policy planning and research units, which are frequently located in the chief executive's department, have provided chief executives and clerks with a new potential power base from which to develop a general strategy for the authority.[37]

Policy units also have consequences for the relative power of departments in the budgetary process of local authorities. Many policy advisers believe their activities have helped to change the rules of the resource allocation game and rationalize the budgetary process of who gets what. Units have provided senior administrators and politicians with better quality data than before and supplied them with a common framework for discussion. One consequence of corporate planning and policy units has been to strengthen the ability of small departments to compete with the large spending departments over the allocation of new resources. To the extent that a policy unit provides information and analysis to small departments that did not have a policy planning or research capacity, and that analysis is acknowledged by other chief officers, a unit can help strengthen the position of such departments in the policy process.

Another effect of units on interdepartmental relations has been to establish a series of formal and informal networks among officials which obviously alters the pattern of their working day. Units have increased and regularized interdepartment contact below chief officer level through providing advice, conducting studies, co-ordinating interdepartmental projects or providing support services to working parties.

The relations between government organizations and non-governmental groups in their environment have changed as a result of policy units. Hall and others contend that the growth of policy planning and research units within government has resulted in 'a major shift in the relative positions of independent and departmental research and planning'.[38] The balance in planning and research capacity has been tipped in favour of government departments, and the opportunity for outside groups to influence policy through policy analysis has been weakened.

According to Hall, departments are less vulnerable now to outside criticisms and are also in a better position to influence the type of research being conducted outside government. For example, the Howard League for Penal Reform, a promotional pressure group, gained much of its strength in the 1950s from being well informed at a time when the Home Office and Prison Commission were undertaking very little research and evaluation. The establishment of the Home Office Research Unit in 1957, giving the government control over more information on penal policy, weakened the League's position. Whether this shift has maintained itself over time or has occurred in other areas, and how much weight should be assigned to information against other sources of power, are difficult questions which require further empirical investigation. In general, over the last decade or so the balance in problem awareness and analysis appears to be shifting from private research institutes to public service researchers. 'This change may make officials more sensitive to outside efforts; but more probably the capacity to influence the policy agenda through independent research will decline as the civil service builds stronger data defences.[39]

A related impact of units has been to provide outside groups with a focal point or input to the government bureaucracy when seeking information or conducting research. Policy units act as a link between departmental policy work and external policy research, making officials aware of research findings. Moreover, some units contribute to the control of external research commissioned by departments by establishing standards and providing the expertise with which to evaluate research findings.

Research exercises undertaken by some units have mobilized non-governmental resources to play a complementary role in the policy process. This work approach is called action research or participative research and refers to 'the involvement of all the organisational actors in a particular area in systematic study of their common problems, so as to arrive at a common answer and implement a common remedy'. Those involved would include service deliverers and consumers, along with some support staff. In effect, the researchers hand over the direction of the project to these actors, involving them at all stages from the inception to implementation. 'The people providing and receiving services are themselves the researchers, evaluating their own efforts and proposing their own solutions to common problems.'[40] The role of the researcher therefore is to support the service providers and receivers in participating in the research process.

An example of a policy unit employing these principles is the Greenwich Programme Planning Unit in its study of lone parents. The study was jointly undertaken by the borough and the local welfare rights group and sought to ascertain the problems of lone parents in Greenwich, the current provision of assistance and what improvements could be made. A project advisory group was set up to direct the project with participants from a variety of local sources. Participants represented general practitioners, churches, Gingerbread (an organization for lone parents), Greenwich Welfare Rights Group, teachers, lone parents, social workers, health visitors, the borough's social services department and the Programme Planning Unit. Help also came from the councillors of the borough, the Greenwich and Bexley Area Health Authority and the Inner London Education Authority. 'The professional researchers acted principally as advisers to the research advisory group, with voices no louder than any other member.'

A research officer from the Programme Planning Unit who was a member of the project advisory group has described the project as operating at three levels: 'it is a conventional research project gathering information and presenting it to decision makers. Then it is a project orientated towards action: helping parents to organise and providing them with help and information. Finally, it provides action learning opportunities to its various participants and improves co-ordination between them'.[41]

The research officer involved has noted the following actions directly generated by the project: 'the growth of local press interest, the provision of an information booklet for lone parents by the borough council and the commitment to work for more help for lone parents. Individual parents have been helped by the forwarding of details of their needs to the relevant authorities by the group. More substantial developments are expected to take place when the report is published. Certainly, the group has been well prepared for change'. If policy units adopt participative research as a working method it will lead to researchers involving themselves more closely with outside people in the area under study. 'The long term role of the researcher in this type of project is difficult to define but it may lie in that of a catalyst for research or merely as a technical advisor'.[42]

Policy units have therefore influenced several authority and consultative relationships in the governmental system. The setting up of planning and research structures has generally tended to favour executive politicians over backbench politicians as well as administrative officials, strengthen senior management in relation to other departmental personnel, support decision making at the centre of central and local government, encourage interdepartmental networks, and, strengthen in-house policy analysis skills relative to external research capabilities.

The general thrust of several of these developments is towards greater centralization of authority and influence in the political and administrative systems. This tendency has been repeatedly noted about many government reforms in Britain, the United States and elsewhere in recent decades. However, these centralist impacts are both relative and modest in nature. Much of the policy and decision making in British government is still done by individual departments and their administrators. At the same time, through corporate strategy processes and participative research methods, policy units are encouraging the decentralization of consultation and involvement in research and planning to other actors inside government as well as clientele and interest groups outside government. As these processes and research methods are increasingly used, new opportunities are provided for demands and supports entering the political system from a wider cross section of actors and groups.

Therefore, policy units do not simply have the centralizing effects usually attributed to administrative reforms predicated on rationality; they can also stimulate decentralized patterns of participation and consultation.

There is no doubt units have enhanced the policy planning and research capacity of British government. Research and planning units have also provided a number of information inputs into the policy process. They are contributing toward defining policy objectives, conducting priority reviews, examining proposed or actual programmes to assess their effectiveness, providing liaison and co-ordination services, performing firefighting duties such as doing rush assignments on immediate issues, and conducting survey research. In addition, it is possible to identify more general political system roles of the policy units.

Policy units perform a public learning function in which they inquire into the nature, causes, and possible resolutions of public problems, and attempt to reduce governmental uncertainty about policy choices. Through the analysis of their environment units identify and measure wants and needs, and channel these inputs to government. Policy units contribute to priority determination through their work programmes. Units contribute to policy making when they assist politicians and senior officials in defining organizational objectives and advise on what policies and programmes should be given priority. With respect to the functioning of the department or authority in which they are located, a number of units perform a corporate function when they provide advice or develop and apply techniques which contribute to a more unified and integrated approach to issues. Many of these impacts of units are not peculiar to them but are potential functions of research in general. This points to the most important potential contribution of policy units; they are an institutional means of building into government policy planning and research personnel and activities on an ongoing basis.

Notes

1   See Nancy Jane Brennan, 'Variations in the Utilization of Evaluation Research in Federal Decision-Making', chapter 2; Michael Q. Patton et al., 'In Search of Impact'; Phoebe Hall et al., *Change, Choice and Conflict in Social Policy*; Yehezkel Dror, *Design for Policy Sciences*; Albert B. Cherns et al., (eds) *Social Science and Government*.

2   Nancy Jane Brennan, op. cit., p.18.

3   See David Donnison, 'Research for Policy'.

4   Karin D. Knorr, 'Policymakers' Use of Social Science Knowledge', p.172.

5   Andrew Leigh, 'The Work of Social Services Researchers and Its Impact on Social Policy', p.105.

6   Ibid., p.104.

7   Andrew Leigh, 'Researchers in the Social Services', p.60.

8   William F. Glueck, *Management Essentials*, p.23.

9   R. Fox, 'In Retrospect — A Review of Some of the Work Carried Out in the Research and Intelligence Unit', diagram 3.

10   Lord Rothschild, 'Thinking about the Think Tank'.

11   Sir Richard Clarke, *New Trends in Government*, p.10.

12   Phoebe Hall et al., *Change, Choice and Conflict in Social Policy*, p.41.

13   Hugh Heclo, *Modern Social Politics*, p.305.

14   Victor Gallant, 'Study of the Industrial Structure of Mid Glamorgan', p.2.

15   Andrew Leigh, 'Management Information Bulletins and Social Services Managers'.

16   B.L.R. Smith, *The RAND Corporation*, p.230.

17   R.V.G. Clarke, 'Penal Policy-Making and Research in the Home Office', p.115.

18   Bernard Benjamin, 'The G.L.C. Research and Intelligence Unit 1966–70 — History'.

19   Guy Benveniste, *The Politics of Expertise* and Bernard Benjamin, *Statistics and Research in Urban Administration and Development*.

20   Central Research Unit, Newcastle-upon-Tyne, 'Multiple Deprivation Indicators for Local Authority Policy Evaluation', p.1.

21   See Civil Service Department, 'The Response to the Fulton Report — Part 3', pp.46–7; and R.G.S. Brown and D.R. Steel, *The Administrative Process in Britain*, second edition, chapter 4.

22   R. Apps, 'Tyne and Wear's Census, Tyne and Wear Household Survey 1976', p.14.

23   R.G.S. Brown, *The Management of Welfare*, p.182.

24   Brian Smith, *Policy Making in British Government*, p.109.

25 Phoebe Hall et al., *Change, Choice and Conflict in Social Policy*, p.80.
26 Ibid., p.79.
27 On the role of ministers in a department's policy planning organization see, for example, C.J. Train, 'The Development of Criminal Policy Planning in the Home Office', pp.380—1. See also J. Bruce-Gardyne, *Whatever Happened to the Quiet Revolution?*; R.K. Alderman and J.A. Cross, 'Ministerial Reshuffles and the Civil Service'; Lord Boyle, 'Ministers and the Administrative Process'; and Bruce Headey, 'Cabinet Ministers and Senior Civil Servants: Mutual Requirements and Expectations'.
28 The strengthened position of elected members in relation to officers is a general trend in local government linked to several developments: younger members, increased attendance allowance, increasing level of organized party politics and stronger political leadership, the introduction of policy committees and related corporate structures and processes. See John Barwicker, 'Member Involvement in Corporate Planning and Management: Some notes on current experiments' and Lord Redcliffe-Maud and Bruce Wood, *English Local Government Reformed*.
29 J.A. Blackburn, 'A Rejoinder: Sunderland and the Elected Member', p.16.
30 Martin J. Painter, 'Policy Co-ordination in the Department of the Environment, 1970—76'.
31 Maurice Wright, 'Public Expenditure, Inflation and PESC', p.16.
32 Hugh Heclo and Aaron Wildavsky, *The Private Government of Public Money*, p.319.
33 'The Role of the Central Policy Review Staff in Whitehall', a note submitted by the CPRS to the Expenditure Committee (General Sub-Committee), p.8.
34 W.J.L. Plowden, 'Developing a joint approach to social policy'.
35 Iain Hill, *Corporate Planning: Revolution Through Evolution*, p.8.
36 T.E. Headrick, *The Town Clerk in English Local Government*, p.183.
37 Michael Honey, 'Corporate Planning and the Chief Executive'.
38 Phoebe Hall et al., *Change, Choice and Conflict in Social Policy*, p.79.
39 Keith G. Banting, *Poverty, Politics and Policy, Britain in the 1960s*, p.149.
40 Robert Pinkham, 'Effective Social Research for Local Government', p.24.

191

41   Ibid., p.25.
42   Ibid., p.26.

9 Beyond survival

Organizations are born in a climate of excitement and hope; they must survive in a world of test and challenge.

Gordon L. Lippitt

The recognition of an explicit policy planning and research function in British government is comparatively recent; indeed, it is completely new to some central government departments and local authorities. As a distinct type of public organization in Britain, policy units are permanent government organizations which provide policy oriented staff services to politicians and public servants. Policy units, furthermore, are developing organizations in the formative years of their existence.

The early years of units have been a period of organizational survival and building. When established, many policy units represented more an act of faith or fashion than a well considered step toward government reform. They have not only attempted to affect public policy formulation and administration, but, as comparatively new organizations and a new organizational type, have tried to establish themselves in the political and administrative systems. The experience of units has been one of recruiting staff, establishing and learning about their place in government, developing relations with other officials, and learning about the types and methods of work suitable for discharging their tasks.

Units at both levels have goals of planning, information and research services, and liaison. Units at both levels have also experienced goal ambiguity, and unit members have played a major role in goal setting. The main difference between units at the two levels, in terms of goals, is that local government units display a relatively greater concern with corporate planning. In terms of personnel, units in central and local government have a number of common features, although more outsiders and specialists are recruited to units in local authorities and more steps toward professionalism have been taken at the local level. All units have generally experienced similar interorganizational relationships. There has been co-operation but there has also been conflict, competition and indifference.

Policy units, like other new government organizations recently introduced in Britain, have tended to adopt an evolutionary approach to developing their role. The emphasis of most units since their inception has been 'on modest beginnings, the low profile, making short term gains, earning respect and building from there'.[1] The functions and activities of policy units at both levels of government are far from fully developed, and units are still working out their roles. Indeed, as Bloomfield has remarked, 'there remains a strong sense that at least until recently British policy planning has been a tender plant growing in an alien environment'.[2]

Planning and research units have not sold out their original goals in order to survive. Instead, most units have managed to stay alive by abridging their mandates and only partially pursue their official goals. Policy advisers have softened their pursuit of comprehensive and long term analysis and concentrated on more specific and short term advice. The pursuit of their mandates has been selective mainly because of political and administrative constraints. Such an abridgement of goals was probably the only feasible course of action for these small and new units operating within an apathetic or hostile environment with their broad objectives. Goal abridgement has therefore been essential for effectiveness and efficiency, and for gaining support and credibility.

The environment has had important effects on policy units. The origins of units, the setting and modification of unit goals, and their work programme, illustrates the importance of interaction between units and their immediate political and administrative environment. Policy planners and researchers have been sales personnel seeking recognition and acceptance from their environment in at least three ways. First, units have had to promote themselves and sell policy makers and officials on the general idea of policy planning and research. Policy units have also tried to sell officials on specific work programme proposals. Finally, units have been engaged in selling their advice both during the work process and at the output stage. There is a potential risk that all this selling will lead to high expectations that policy units cannot meet; the ensuing gap between promise and practice will reinforce the organizational conservatism which initially provoked the marketing of units. Policy advisers should therefore be aware of selling on too grand a scale. The sales strategy of policy units should be a judicious mix of missionary zeal and practicality.

The importance of relating a unit to its environment emerges from an examination of the behaviour and activities of unit heads. As personnel managers, policy planners, research managers, representatives, promoters and protectors, the unit head acts as a crucial link between policy advisers and administrators and politicians, and much of their activities reflect a concern for organization building and survival of the unit. While many of the structural and procedural reforms to British public administration introduced during the late 1960s and early 1970s appear to have withered away, at least policy planning and research units have survived.

Survival has a price. The need to gain organizational support and legitimacy has inhibited the development of policy units, and the application and sophistication of policy planning and advice has been less than that originally hoped. The difficulties encountered by policy units in developing a longer term perspective in government illustrates the trade-off between policy advice and organizational survival. Consideration of the planning goals of units is particularly relevant because numerous government and academic inquiries in the 1960s and 1970s emphasized that an essential role of policy units should be long term planning. Furthermore, policy units represent, in part, a grouping of workers and functions according to the principle of time and an attempt to institutionalize the long term within public administration systems.

Policy planners and researchers were meant to use the future to address the present. They were intended to free administrators and policy makers from the tyranny of the present, by introducing the opportunity of the future. In a real sense, advisers were not to be involved in day-to-day administration, tomorrow was their ticket to today.

Experience indicates, however, that policy units pursue long term planning in only a limited and intermittent fashion. Generally, unit activities are aimed more at the short run than the longer term. At both levels of government efforts toward long term planning and related activities have been significantly less than expected or intended.[3] This situation demonstrates that the politics of advice is the politics of survival.

To a large degree, the limited pursuit of long term planning is a result of influences from the administrative and political context in which policy units are a part. Units operate in the zone of administrative politics, where the higher levels of the political and administrative processes interact.[4] In this zone, policy units are subject to the opposite tendencies of political and administrative behaviour. 'Politics tends towards flux, bureaucracy towards routinisation. The problem of blending these contributions is illustrated by the difficulties of achieving forward planning in government. Located within the bureaucratic structure, planning units may be well-staffed but usually have little policy impact; but politicised, such units or "brain trusts" tend to lack weight and continuity.'[5]

Macdonald and Fry assert that long term policy planning with government departments challenges the central principles of civil servant neutrality and ministerial responsibility:

> It is the long term which is essentially political, and if the planning units are to deal in the long term they cannot escape this. They are impaled in the horns of a dilemma: if they are well-established, are of good repute, and are authoritative in their subjects, they are bound to conflict with the principle of ministerial responsibility; if they are not, they will contradict the principle of their own existence.[6]

Hence the politics of the future pose real problems for the organizational livelihood of planning units.

Some policy advisers believe that not very much long term work is done because on the one hand ministers prefer a good speech to a long term plan, and on the other hand, the value of long term planning is not really appreciated within the Civil Service. Other advisers believe that long term planning takes up too much of unit resources and restricts a unit's ability to do short term work and quickies. Even where adequate resources are allocated to units, long term activities still may not be performed. A long term role is seen to conflict with a policy adviser's need, especially in the first few years, to win the respect and confidence of officials. Thus, operationally oriented short term work has been emphasized by some units at the expense of longer term activities.

This need to be somewhat cautious in order to win support also applies in no small measure, although varying from authority to authority, in gaining the respect and confidence of the politicians. If they are really convinced of the value of such a unit, and this is by no means easy to achieve given the widespread types of individuals that make up elected representatives, then the opportunity to develop will be increased considerably.

In some units the performance of a firefighting role, that is, dealing with emergencies and short term problems, whether intended or not, has dominated and in some cases prevented the development of longer term activities. This situation cannot be simply solved by keeping units separate from the heat of daily concerns. The survival and morale of policy units depends upon doing short term work and not being left out in the cold. On the other hand, however, British experience, at least in central government, demonstrates 'that making resource questions the centrepiece of the work of the policy planning organization, risks the exclusion of wider and longer term issues'. Policy units in central government departments largely concerned with resource allocation and 'establishing what a particular policy or programme needs in terms of manpower or finance, setting it in order of priority among other demands, obtaining authority for the resources required and allocating them accordingly',[7] tend to have little time left for longer term work. This leads us to suggest that people in charge of policy units should be aware of the trade-offs between short term effectiveness and long term planning, and between rational policy advice and organizational survival.

Some, though by no means all, of the failures that policy planning and research units have experienced can be attributed to the units themselves for not recognizing the importance of explaining their role and operating in areas most likely to achieve the respect and support so necessary for success.

The impact of policy planning has also been less than intended because of the nature of the power relationships between units as staff and other line officials:

> In order to accomplish anything, the staff must secure some co-operation from the line. This requires giving in to the line by moderating proposals, overlooking practices that do not correspond to rigid technical standards, and in general playing a rather subservient role in dealing with line. If this is not done, the staff's suggestions would probably go unheeded. This in turn would make their output zero for the time period, and their general relevance for the organization would then be questioned.[8]

This power imbalance is particularly evident in the role of central policy analysts and advisers situated at the senior hierarchical levels. Central analysts, 'will be disenchanted when they find that all power does not reside at the top. Most significantly, they will not know much about the operating programs of the agencies. As outsiders they will have a hard time learning from people at the bottom'.[9]

Thus, analytical staff have not been policy *planners* so much as *policy* planners. They have tended to emphasize identifying and measuring policy goals and focusing on current activities more than emphasizing forecasting and forward planning.

Organizational survival extends beyond simply continued existence to include developing a special identity. Policy units must evolve from the bare survival of staying alive to move toward spiritual survival and developing a distinctive organizational culture. The analysis of policy and research personnel showed that policy units displayed characteristics contributing towards a developing special identity. Unit posts are generally full time and permanent, offering some career opportunities. Unit personnel are comparatively young, have a high level of educational attainment, and undergo some training and sharing of experiences as unit members. In addition, some preliminary efforts toward professionalization have been undertaken. Policy units have improved the status of policy oriented staff roles in government.

The role conceptions of policy planners and researchers and their perceptions of the administrative and political systems are key variables in explaining policy unit behaviour. Unit staff assess the administrative and political feasibility of their work programmes, often trying to anticipate and pursue topics that will make a quick and favourable impact. Whether a policy unit is even established in the first place is influenced by the attitudes and personalities of key policy actors, and by their perceptions of the resources available and needed to carry out planning and research.

The academic study of public administration in Britain has been criticized in recent years as being too heavily concentrated on institutional structures. While that may be proper criticism, we must not ignore the importance of structure in the policy process. As an example of machinery of government reform, policy units have been fitted into the existing political and administrative systems of power and values. A proper understanding of government reform requires an examination of the role conceptions and behaviour of actors within administrative structures and processes. It also requires taking account of the problems of introducing and integrating policy units into the existing machinery and of the interrelationships that arise. The effects of policy planning and research on the distribution of power will lead officials to support or oppose the work of policy units. Hence, questions such as the location and independence of units are of central interest to the bureaucracy and will influence administrators' reactions to the introduction of units and have implications for the success of units. Organizing and conducting policy advice in government is bound to be a political activity.

Examination of the relationship between politicians and the bureaucracy suggests some revisions to current views about the role of politicians. The institutionalization of planning and research activities has provided politicians with a greater capacity to involve themselves in the policy process. Moreover, the introduction of policy units has resulted in a broader advisory and analytic capacity.

The future for policy units

Two fundamental factors will influence the prospects for policy units: the economic situation in which British government finds itself and the political and organizational context in which units operate.

Policy units, along with other government organizations, face a period of economic restraint, no growth and cutbacks. And, as Greenwood and others have argued, 'it seems likely that the necessity of economic restraint will not be a short term phenomenon, but will be with us for some years'.[10]

The present period of restraint within the British system of government has important implications for the prospects of policy planning and research units. The possible consequences of government restraint for policy units can be seen in the following observation about corporate planning in local government:

> Corporate planning developed in a period of financial growth when the future seemed rosy and there was opportunity to examine analytically the complex problems facing local government and to plan to meet them. Certainly 'plans' were basic to the idea of corporate planning — short, medium and long term, multi-disciplinary in preparation, comprehensively tackling a multitude of problems. But the financial experiences of recent years have apparently dealt a blow to such optimism. The tacit assumptions about continued growth have been rudely overturned and planning itself, corporate or otherwise, may seem pointless in a period of such uncertainty and restraint.[11]

Policy advisers assert that their role is as important if not more important in a period of restraint than in a period of growth. This state of the economy argument that policy planning is not needed is a red herring; governments have always had limited resources to some degree. Planning and research ought to be of more use in a period of very limited resources. Although policy units were conceived during a relatively better economic situation than now, there is still an important role for units; advisers just have to play with a different style and method. The current period of government restraints and cutbacks will likely help most policy units because constraints generally make departments examine more closely their priorities and resource commitments, and units can assist in that.

In the context of restraint a number of implications for the future of policy units can be suggested. Bob Fowler and Steve Rogers have identified three consequences for corporate planning units and information in local government. New large scale developments have become less frequent; more partial adjustments to existing information systems appear to be the order of the day. Secondly, the label corporate planning does not appear so frequently, — although similar work may be carried out within service departments or under the heading research and intelligence. Further, control information has had a new lease on life. The need for authorities to tighten their belts has resulted in a renewed interest and determination that the resources available are at least used efficiently, if not effectively.[12]

At the same time, the realities of restraint within government seem to suggest that there can be little or no growth in resources devoted to policy units. Not only are policy units small but they could become smaller. A period of restraint can bring increasing pressure for cuts in policy units resources. Staff functions are often targets for cuts in times of restraint. The fact that policy units are relatively new functions in British government combined with the fact that they have come under some criticism, increases the likelihood that they will be among the targets for cuts. The future of this organizational species is by no means assured. Indeed, in many local authorities and a few central government departments, policy planning and research functions have been cut or not developed during the current period of restraint.

Pressures for cuts in the policy planning and research field must be reconciled with the planning and evaluation demands continually being placed on government. The climate of restraint and the demands on government to respond to new and ongoing problems could lead to policy units performing different functions. Rather than developing new policies and programmes involving significant expenditure, policy units may become more involved in the monitoring of ongoing programmes. The research areas and work methods of policy units may move away from needs oriented research to programme evaluation. The direction any given policy unit develops in a restraint situation is in large part dependent upon the political and organizational context in which it is located.

An analysis of the future of policy units must include the organizational and interpersonal setting in which units operate. Policy units will, of course, continue to perform within certain constraints, some self imposed and other constraints imposed by the external environment. 'The self-imposed constraints' according to Leigh, 'include natural caution, wanting to retain the confidence and good will of colleagues, a need to preserve a customer-oriented approach in which the client says what shall be done with the study, and a natural modesty, not common to all researchers it must be admitted, about blowing one's own trumpet'. External constraints include knowledge and time limits, costs, departmental policy about how to respond to research findings, and the need to handle dissemination in different ways for different levels in the organization and beyond it to other departments, politicians and perhaps the public.[13]

If policy units are to survive and be effective, there are a number of political and organization prerequisites: a strong and influential patron at the official level; senior officials taking policy units seriously and thinking in corporate terms; a high level steering group which ensures representation of the interests of those mainly affected; provision for review of planning and research arrangements on a scheduled basis and under the direction of the steering group, co-operative working relationships between policy planners and researchers and line officials, to ensure effective communication and closer integration; and, experienced staff with fairly senior status.

Policy planning units, like other organizations, go through phases of development. The way in which policy units have developed so far has crucial consequences for their future development. During the 1970s it was possible to pioneer on practically any front and produce useful results. The 1980s, however, are likely to be far more critical for research. As Leigh puts it: 'There is bound to be much more careful questioning of both what is being researched and the subsequent beneficial effects to specific services or methods of social administration. Social services researchers have survived the first challenge, they now face a perhaps less glamorous era of becoming consistently effective'.[14] In short, the future won't be what it used to be.

The continuing challenge facing policy units in British government can be seen in a number of questions around which future dispute is guaranteed. What lies beyond survival? Will planners and researchers become more professionalized? Will staff-line tensions persist? Is longer range planning in government possible? What policy and programme areas should be examined? What criteria should be used for the analysis and evaluation? What is the best way to measure, in a qualitative and quantitative sense, programme objectives and outcomes? What is the meaning of the results? Should they be released? To whom? When? These and other issues are all subjects for bargaining and negotiation between policy unit staff and other actors in the policy process. The use of planning and research techniques is loaded with political, organizational and policy implications.

If there is something to be learned from every effort at administrative reform the lesson from this study is that the pursuit of policy rationality must inevitably deal with organizational reality.

Notes

1 J.M. Gillespie, 'Whither Local Government Research and Intelligence', p.2.
2 Lincoln P. Bloomfield, 'Planning Foreign Policy: Can It Be Done?', p.380.
3 See Tenth Report from the Expenditure Committee, 1975–76 Session; C.J. Train, 'The Development of Crime Policy Planning in the Home Office', pp.382–3; E.J. Razzell, 'Planning Units in Central Government', p.4; R.J. Litschert and E.A. Nicholson, 'Corporate Long-Range Planning Groups — Some Different Approaches'.
4 The zone of administrative politics concept is from Peter Self, *Administrative Theories and Politics*, pp.150–2.
5 Ibid., p.299.
6 James Macdonald and G.K. Fry, 'Policy Planning Units — Ten Years On', p.436.
7 C.J. Train, 'The Development of Crime Policy Planning in the Home Office', pp.384 and 373.
8 Richard H. Hall, *Organizations: Structure and Process*, p.216.
9 Arnold J. Meltsner, *Policy Analysts in the Bureaucracy*, pp. 288–9.
10 Royston Greenwood et al., *In Pursuit of Corporate Rationality*, p.5.
11 B.A. Fowler and S. Rogers, 'Information for Corporate Planning, Introduction', p.1.
12 Ibid., pp.1–2. On how policy units and local authorities have responded to a situation of no growth, see the journal *Corporate Planning*, vol. 3, nos. 1 and 2.
13 Andrew Leigh, 'Researchers in the Social Services', p.67.
14 Andrew Leigh, 'The work of social services researchers and its impact on social policy', p.113.

Appendix

Research sources and methods

Thirty-two policy planning and policy research organizations in British central and local government were selected for study: seventeen units located in twelve central government departments and fifteen units in fifteen local authorities. Those in central government departments were:

Ministry of Agriculture, Fisheries and Food, Departmental Planning Unit

Cabinet Office, Central Policy Review Staff

HM Customs and Excise, Departmental Planning Unit

Department of Education and Science, Departmental Planning Unit

Department of Employment, Research Planning Branch, and Unit for Manpower Studies

Department of Energy, Corporate Planning Unit

Department of the Environment, Central Policy and Planning Unit, Systems Analysis and Research Unit, and Housing Analysis and Monitoring Unit

Foreign and Commonwealth Office, Planning Staff

Department of Health, Central Planning Unit

Home Office, Research Unit, and Crime Policy Planning Unit

Department of Social Security, Social Research Branch, and

HM Treasury, Policy Analysis Division, and Programme Analysis and Review Division.

The policy units examined in local authorities included:

Avon County Council, Central Research and Evaluation Unit

Cleveland County Council, Research and Intelligence Unit

Devon County Council, Central Information Services

Exeter District Council, Corporate Planner

Greenwich London Borough Council, Programme Planning Unit

Harringay London Borough Council, Corporate Planning Unit

Hereford—Worcester County Council, Policy Analysis Leader

Lambeth London Borough Council, Central Intelligence and Monitoring Unit

Mid Glamorgan County Council, Intelligence, Research and Development Unit

Newcastle-upon-Tyne Metropolitan District Council, Research Section (formerly Central Research Unit)

Plymouth District Council, Corporate Planning Unit

Portsmouth District Council, Research Section

Sunderland Metropolitan District Council, Programme Planning Department

Tyne and Wear Metropolitan County Council, Central Research and Intelligence Unit, and

West Glamorgan County Council, Central Research Unit.

While a fully representative sample of the policy planning and research units in British government would be desirable, such a sample cannot be drawn because there is no precisely defined organizational universe of policy units. A range of possible organizations was identified from the published literature, *The Civil Service Year Book* and *The Municipal Year Book*, and a selection made for study on the basis of several considerations.

Policy planning and research units occur at all levels of government in Britain and in different shapes and sizes. Enough had to be chosen to permit comparisons and to suggest some reasonable generalizations based on key elements such as goals, structure and development. A conscious effort was made to include policy units from both central and local government, and from different types of central government departments and local authorities. Of course the amount of resources available for the study — finances, time and personal energy — was of some consequence. Hence, policy planning and research units in public industrial enterprises, and in the Scotland and Northern Ireland systems of local government were not directly surveyed.

Personal interviews with more than eighty people constitute the most important data base for the study; forty-four people in regard to local government and thirty-eight with respect to local government. Some people were interviewed more than once, and a few had worked at both levels of government. The interviews were primarily with officials in each of the units examined for this study, and secondarily with other people who are or have been associated with policy units. The interviews were conducted between February 1977 and June 1978, and were generally one and a half hours in length. All the interviews were face-to-face and were used to collect comparable information and assessments about the origins and roles of the selected policy units, and their development and relationships with other officials from the perspective of policy unit members.

The questions and topics were developed after a review of the relevant literature discussed in the introductory chapter. Especially helpful was the questionnaire contained in Arnold J. Meltsner's book, *Policy Analysts in the Bureaucracy* (University of California Press, London, 1976), pp.295–7. Meltsner's work is a study of policy analysts and advisers in the American federal bureaucracy.

To facilitate gaining access and obtaining meaningful communication with officials, the interviews were confidential in nature and thus the opinions and attitudes of policy advisers expressed in this book are not attributed to specific persons. Conducting confidential interviews was clearly useful in establishing the legitimacy of the study and was compatible with the prevailing norms of British public administration.

A second major source of information for this study was unpublished material, internal working papers, and reports dealing with policy units. Because policy planning and research units are specialist government organizations, little such material has previously been published or made readily available. Evidence drawn from this material complemented the interviews and helped to illustrate something of the work methods and work programmes being pursued by policy units.

Of some additional help was information on policy units published in special studies, and in academic and professional journals. In particular, the *Corporate Planning* and *BURISA* periodicals contain valuable information on the structure and work of policy units and on the opinions of policy planners and researchers in British government. In addition, government reports and documents serve as the basis for information and opinions on the record and can support interview data.

Bibliography

Confidential interviews constituted a primary source of information for this study. Published and unpublished material was also of importance and is presented below in five sections: (a) British Government documents, (b) official documents from local authorities, (c) books, (d) articles, and (e) duplicated and manuscript material.

(A) Central government documents

A framework for Government Research and Development, Cmnd. 4814, 1971.

Cabinet Office, *Future World Trends*, HMSO, London, 1976.

Central Office of Information, *Local Government in Britain*, Reference Pamphlet 1, HMSO, London, 1975.
  The British Civil Service, Reference Pamphlet 122, HMSO, London, 1976.

Central Policy Review Staff, *Energy Conservation*, HMSO, London, 1974.
  A Joint Framework for Social Policies, HMSO, London, 1975.
  The Future of the British Car Industry, HMSO, London, 1975.
  The Future of the United Kingdom Power Plant Manufacturing Industry, HMSO, London, 1976.
  'The Role of the Central Policy Review Staff in Whitehall', a note submitted by the CPRS to the House of Commons Expenditure

Committee (General Sub-Committee) Enquiry into Developments in the Civil Service Since Fulton, 6 December 1976–77.

Sir Kenneth Berrill, Head of the CPRS, Minutes of Evidence on 'Industry and Scientific Research' to the Select Committee on Science and Technology (Science Sub-Committee), 6 July 1976, Session 1975–76.

Population and the Social Services, HMSO, London 1977.

Relations between Central Government and Local Authorities, HMSO, London, 1977.

Review of Overseas Representation, HMSO, London, 1977.

and the Central Statistical Office, *People and Their Families*, HMSO, London, 1980.

Civil Service Commission, 'Government Departments Employing Research Officers', August 1977.

Annual Report, various years, HMSO, London.

'General Information for Candidates', 1976.

Statisticians, Posts in Government Service, HMSO, London, 1976.

Economists, Posts in Government Service, HMSO, London, 1976.

'Home Civil Service – Senior Research Officers and Research Officers', A(2) 652/77, 1977.

Civil Service Department, *CSD Report 1969*, HMSO, London, 1970.

CSD Report 1971–73, HMSO, London, 1974.

'Planning in the Civil Service' by S.D. Walker MS(SA) Seminars: Paper No. 14, March 1974.

Civil Service College Studies 1, *New Trends in Government*, Sir Richard Clarke, HMSO, London, 1971.

'The Response to the Fulton Report – Part 3', part of a memorandum submitted to the Expenditure Committee (General Sub-Comittee), reprinted in *Management Services in Government*, vol. 32, no.1, (February 1977), pp.41–7.

The Civil Service Yearbook, HMSO, London, various years.

Committee on Local Authority and Allied Personal Services, *Report*, Cmnd. 3703, 1968.

Committee on Policy Optimisation, *Report*, Cmnd. 7148, 1978.

Control of Public Expenditure, Cmnd. 1432, 1961.

Department of Education and Science, *Output Budgeting for the Department of Education and Science: Report of a Feasibility Study*, HMSO, London, 1970.

How the DES is Organized, DES Information Division, London, April 1977.

Department of Employment and Manpower Services Commission, *Research 1976–77*, HMSO, London, 1978.

Department of Energy, *Report of the Working Group on Energy Strategy*, Energy Commission Paper, no.2, October 1977.

Department of the Environment, Memorandum to the Expenditure

Committee (General Sub-Committee) 12 July 1976, Session 1975–76.

Circulars 5/73, 104/73, 27/74 and 60/74.

Report on Research and Development, 1976, HMSO, London, 1977.

The Sunderland Study, HMSO, London, 1973.

Department of Health and Social Security, 'DHSS in Relation to the Health and Personal Social Services, Review Team Report – Summary', June 1972.

Annual Report on Departmental Research and Development, HMSO, London, various years.

Circular 35/72.

'Social Security Research Activities of the DHSS', *Journal of Social Policy*, vol. 4, no.4, 1975, pp.349–72.

The N.H.S. Planning System, HMSO, London, June 1976.

Statistics and Research Division, 'Social Research Branch: Research Programme 1977', 1977.

Priorities in the Health and Social Services, The Way Forward, HMSO, London, 1977.

'Joint Care Planning: Health and Local Authorities', HC 77/17, LAC 77/10.

Social Security Research: Papers presented at a DHSS Seminar on 7–9 April 1976, HMSO, London, 1977.

Expenditure Committee (Education, Arts and Home Office Sub-Committee), Tenth Report, 1975–76 Session, HC 621.

Goldman, Sir Samuel, *The Developing System of Public Expenditure Management and Control*, HMSO, London, 1973.

Greater London Act 1963.

Home Office, Research Unit, 'Summary of Research Within the Unit and of Research Supported by Grant', HMSO, London, various years.

Research Bulletin, (Crown Copyright), various issues.

Programme of Research 1977–78, HMSO, London, 1977.

Study No. 44, *Research in Criminal Justice*, by John Croft, HMSO, London 1978.

Home Office Working Paper, *A Review of Criminal Justice Policy 1976*, HMSO, London, 1977.

House of Commons, *Debates*, various volumes.

HM Treasury, Medium Term and Policy Analysis Group, 'Some Effects of Exchange Rate Changes', by John Odling-Smee and Nicholas Hartley, Government Economic Service, Working Paper no. 2, March 1978.

Local Government Act 1973.

Ministry of Health, Circular 2/62.

Ministry of Housing and Local Government, Circular 21/65.

Committee on the Management of Local Government, vol. 1, *Re-*

209

port, HMSO, London, 1967.

Committee on the Staffing of Local Government, *Report*, HMSO, London, 1967.

Report of the Machinery of Government Committee, Cmnd. 9230, 1918.

Report of the Royal Commission on Local Government in Greater London, Cmnd. 1164, 1960.

Report of the Committee on Civil Science, Cmnd. 2171, 1963.

Report of the Committee on Social Studies, Cmnd. 2660, 1965.

Report of the Committee on the Civil Service, Cmnd. 3638, 1968, vols. 1–5.

Report of the Royal Commission on Local Government in England, Cmnd. 4040, 1969, vols. 1–3.

Scottish Office, Central Research Unit Papers, *Evaluation Research in Social Policy*, by Richard Grant and Jim Gallagher, May 1977.

The New Local Authorities: Management and Structure, HMSO, London, 1972.

The New Scottish Local Authorities: Organisation and Management Structures, HMSO, Edinburgh, 1973.

The Reorganisation of Central Government, Cmnd. 4506, 1970.

'The Government's Reply to the HC 621', Cmnd. 1976.

Transport Planning: The Men for the Job, HMSO, London, 1970.

(B) Local authority documents

City of Newcastle-upon-Tyne, Central Research Unit, 'Initial Report of the Central Research Unit', 1974.

'Current Projects', 1974.

Urban Trends 1975.

Survey of the Elderly in Newcastle-upon-Tyne, 1975–76, Social Services Department, 1976.

City of Newcastle-upon-Tyne, Management Services Department, 'Management Services: Initial Report and Objectives 1976/77', July 1976.

Management Services 1977 Annual Report.

City of Portsmouth, Planning Department, *Inner Cities – The Current Position*, September 1977.

Joint Report by the Chief Executive and City Planning Officer, *Policy for the Inner City following The Government White Paper*, 1977.

County of Cleveland, Research and Intelligence Unit, *Annual Report*, 1975 and 1976–77.

County Plan: Objectives and Policies, Resource Planning Committee, 1976.

London Borough of Greenwich, Programme Planning Unit, *Old People's Homes and Sheltered Housing in Greenwich*, Key Issue Report, November 1971.

Domiciliary Services for the Elderly in Greenwich, Key Issue Report no. 6, November 1973.

Services for the Mentally Handicapped in Greenwich, Key Issue Report no. 8, December 1974.

Officers' Management Committee, July 1975, Appendix K, 'The Future of the Programme Planning Unit'.

Lone Parents in Greenwich, Lone Parents Project Advisory Group, Survey Report, 1976.

Community Plan 1977/78 to 1979/80, vol. 6, *Planning and Development Services, Corporate Services, Central Management Services*.

London Borough of Lambeth, Policy Committee, 15 September 1971, 'Chief Executive's Control and Research Functions'.

Community Plan 1978, vols. 1–7, Town Hall, Brixton Hill, London, 1978.

Special Review Committee, *The Organisation and Work of the Council*, April 1979.

Mid Glamorgan County Council, Intelligence, Research and Development Unit, 'Survey of Current Research', February 1975.

West Glamorgan County Council, Central Research Unit, 'Register of Research Conducted by Organisations and Institutions in West Glamorgan Area', March 1975.

'Data Source Inventory', September 1976.

'Socio-Economic Indicator Bulletin', various dates.

West Glamorgan Profile of Social Need, 1976.

(C) Books

Anthony, Robert N., *Planning and Control Systems*, Harvard University Press, Boston, 1965.

Banting, Keith G., *Poverty, Politics and Policy: Britain in the 1960s*, Macmillan, London, 1979.

Bass, Lawrence W., *Management by Task Force*, Lomond Books, Maryland, 1975.

Batley, R. et al., *Going Comprehensive: Educational Policy-Making in Two County Boroughs*, Routledge & Kegan Paul, London, 1970.

Benjamin, Bernard, *Statistics and Research in Urban Administration and Development*, International Association for Regional and Urban Statistics, The Hague, 1976.

Benveniste, Guy, *Bureaucracy and National Planning*, Praeger, New York, 1970.

The Politics of Expertise, Croom Helm, London, 1973.

Blau, Peter M., *The Dynamics of Bureaucracy*, University of Chicago Press, Chicago, 1964.

and Scott, W.R., *Formal Organizations*, Chandler, San Francisco, 1962.

Boaden, Noel, *Urban Policy Making*, Cambridge University Press, Cambridge, 1971.

Bourn, John, *Management in Central and Local Government*, Pitman, London, 1979.

Bovaird, A.G. (ed.), *Register of Research Projects in Research and Intelligence Units*, INLOGOV, University of Birmingham, 1977.

Boyle, E., Crossland, A. and Kogan, M., *The Politics of Education*, Penguin, Harmondsworth, 1971.

Brand, Jack, *Local Government Reform in England 1888–1974*, Croom Helm, London, 1974.

Brannen, P. (ed.), *Entering the World of Work*, HMSO, London, 1975.

Brittan, S., *The Treasury Under the Tories, 1951–1964*, Allen and Unwin, London, 1964.

Steering the Economy: The Role of the Treasury, Allen and Unwin, London, 1970.

Brown, George, *In My Way*, Penguin, Harmondsworth, 1972.

Brown, R.G.S., *The Administrative Process in Britain*, Methuen, London, 1971.

The Management of Welfare, Fontana/Collins, Glasgow, 1975.

and Steel, D.R., *The Administrative Process in Britain*, second edition, Methuen, London, 1979.

Bruce-Gardyne, Jock, *Whatever Happened to the Quiet Revolution? The Story of a Brave Experiment in Government*, Charles Knight, London, 1974.

Bulmer, Martin (ed.), *Social Policy Research*, Macmillan, London, 1978.

Butler, R.A., *Penal Reform and Research*, Eleanor Rathbone Memorial Lecture, Liverpool University Press, 1960.

Caplan, Nathan, et al., *The Use of Social Science Knowledge in Policy Decisions at the National Level*, Institute for Social Research, Ann Arbour, Michigan, 1975.

Carley, Michael, *Rational Techniques in Policy Analysis*, Heinemann, London, 1980.

Cartwright, T.J., *Royal Commissions and Departmental Committees in Britain*, Hodder and Stoughton, London, 1975.

Chapman, Brian, *British Government Observed*, Allen and Unwin, London, 1963.

Chapman, Richard A., *Decision Making*, Routledge and Kegan Paul, London, 1968.

(ed.), *The Role of Commissions in Policy Making*, Allen and Unwin, London, 1973.

Cherns, Albert B., et al., *Social Science and Government*, Tavistock, London, 1972.

Clark, Peter A., *Action Research and Organizational Change*, Harper and Row, London, 1972.

Cockburn, Cynthia, *The Local State*, Pluto Press, London, 1977.

Crawford, E. and Perry, N., (eds), *Demands for Social Knowledge: The Role of Research Organisations*, Sage, London, 1976.

Cross, J.A., *British Public Administration*, University Tutorial Press, London, 1970.

Cyert, R.M. and March, J.G., *A Behavioural Theory of the Firm*, Prentice-Hall, Englewood Cliffs, New Jersey, 1965.

Davies, E.M. (ed.), *Research and Intelligence: Papers delivered at the Annual Conference*, INLOGOV, Birmingham, 1979.

(ed.), *INLOGOV Register of Research Projects — 1979 Update*, INLOGOV, Birmingham, 1979.

The Central Research Function in Local Government, INLOGOV, Birmingham, 1979a.

Davies, J.G., *The Evangelistic Bureaucrat, A Study of a Planning Exercise in Newcastle upon Tyne*, Tavistock, London, 1972.

Dearlove, John, *The Politics of Policy in Local Government*, Cambridge University Press, Cambridge, 1973.

The Reorganisation of British Local Government: Old Orthodoxies and a Political Perspective, Cambridge University Press, Cambridge, 1979.

Denning, B.W. (ed.), *Corporate Planning: Selected Concepts*, McGraw-Hill, London, 1971.

Dickson, Paul, *Think Tanks*, Atheneum, New York, 1971.

Doern, G. Bruce and Wilson, V. Seymour, (eds), *Issues in Canadian Public Policy*, Macmillan, Toronto, 1974.

Downs, Anthony, *Inside Bureaucracy*, Little, Brown, Boston, 1967.

Dror, Yehezkel, *Public Policymaking Reexamined*, Intext, New York, 1968.

Design for Policy Sciences, Elsevier, New York, 1971.

Ventures in Policy Sciences, Elsevier, New York, 1971.

Dunsire, Andrew, *Administration: The Word and the Science*, Martin Robertson, London, 1973.

Easton, David, *A Systems Analysis of Political Life*, Wiley, New York, 1965.

Eden, Colin and Harris, John, *Management Decision and Decision Analysis*, Macmillan, London, 1975.

Eddison, Tony, *Local Government: Management and Corporate Planning*, second edition, Leonard Hill, Bath, 1975.

Etzioni, Amitai, *Modern Organizations*, Prentice-Hall, Englewood Cliffs, New Jersey, 1964.

Evan, William M. (ed.), *Interorganizational Relations*, Penguin, Harmondsworth, 1976.

Ewing, David W. *The Human Side of Planning*, Macmillan, New York, 1960.

Flash, Jr., Edward S., *Economic Advice and Presidential Leadership: The Council of Economic Advisers*, Columbia University Press, New York, 1965.

Friend, J.K. and Jessop, W.N., *Local Government and Strategic Choice*, Tavistock, London, 1969.

Friend, J.K., Yewlett, C.J.L. and Power, J., *Beyond Local Government*, Institute for Operational Research, London, 1971.

Fry, G.K., *The Administrative 'Revolution' in Whitehall*, Croom Helm, London, 1981.

Garrett, John, *The Management of Government*, Penguin, Harmondsworth, 1972.

and Sheldon, Robert, *Administrative Reform: the next step*, Fabian Society, London, November 1973, Fabian Tract 426.

Gladden, E.N., *Central Government Administration*, Staple Press, London, 1972.

Glueck, W.F., *Management Essentials*, Dryden, Hinsdale, Illinois, 1979.

Greaves, H.R.G., *The Civil Service in the Changing State*, Harrap, London, 1947.

Greenwood, Royston (ed.), *Conference Papers on Management and Administration in the Local Government Service 1969–70*, INLOGOV, University of Birmingham, 1970, Occasional Paper no.4.

Greenwood, R. et al., *New Patterns of Local Government Organisation*, INLOGOV, University of Birmingham, 1971, Occasional Paper no.5, series A.

Greenwood, R. and Stewart, J.D. (eds), *Corporate Planning in English Local Government 1967–72*, Charles Knight, London, 1974.

Greenwood, R. et al., *The Organisation of Local Authorities in England and Wales: 1967–75,* INLOGOV, University of Birmingham, 1975, Discussion Paper series L, no.5.

Greenwood, R. et al., *In Pursuit of Corporate Rationality*, INLOGOV, University of Birmingham, 1977.

Greenwood, R. et al., *Patterns of Management in Local Government*, Martin Robertson, Oxford, 1980.

Hall, Phoebe et al., *Change, Choice and Conflict in Social Policy*, Heinemann, London, 1975.

Hall, Richard H., *Organizations: Structure and Process*, second edition, Prentice-Hall, Englewood Cliffs, New Jersey, 1977.

Hambleton, Robin, *Policy Planning and Local Government*, Hutchinson, London, 1978.

Hanson, A.H. and Walles, Malcolm, *Governing Britain*, revised edition, Fontana/Collins, Glasgow, 1975.

Haynes, Robert J., *Organization Theory and Local Government*, Allen and Unwin, London, 1980.

Hayward, Jack and Watson, Michael (eds), *Planning, Politics and Public Policy*, Cambridge University Press, London, 1975.

Headey, Bruce, *British Cabinet Ministers*, Allen and Unwin, London, 1974.

Headrich, T.E., *The Town Clerk in English Local Government*, Allen and Unwin, London, 1962.

Heclo, Hugh, *Modern Social Politics in Britain and Sweden*, Yale University Press, London, 1974.

and Aaron Wildavsky, *The Private Government of Public Money*, Macmillan, London, 1974.

Herman, V. and Alt, J.E. (eds), *Cabinet Studies: A Reader*, Macmillan, London, 1975.

Hill, Iain, *Corporate Planning: Revolution Through Evolution*, Local Government Research Unit, Paisley College of Technology, Occasional Paper, no.2, 1973.

Howell, David, *A New Style of Government*, Conservative Political Centre, London, 1970.

A New Style Emerges, Conservative Political Centre, London, 1971.

Hudson, Keith (ed.), *Research and Intelligence — Current Activities*, INLOGOV, University of Birmingham, Occasional Paper series D, no.1, 1975.

Hussey, David E., *Introducing Corporate Planning*, Pergamon Press, Oxford, 1971.

Corporate Planning: Theory & Practice, Pergamon Press, Oxford, 1974.

(ed.), *Corporate Planner's Yearbook 1974-75*, Pergamon Press, Oxford, 1974.

Hutchinson, George, *Edward Heath*, Longman, London, 1970.

Institute of Local Government Studies and the Programme Management Group, *Corporate Planning Yearbook, Number One*, 1978.

Corporate Planning Handbook, 1979.

Jenkins, W.I., *Policy Analysis: a Political and Organisational Perspective*, Martin Robertson, London, 1978.

Keeling, D., *Management in Government*, Allen and Unwin, London, 1972.

Klein, Rudolf and Lewis, Janet, *The Politics of Consumer Representation*, Centre for Studies in Social Policy, London, 1976.

Kraemer, K.L., *Policy Analysis in Local Government*, International City Management Association, Washington, DC, 1973.

Laswell, Harold S., *A Pre-View of Policy Sciences*, Elsevier, New York, 1971.

Le Breton, P.P. and Henning, D.A., *Planning Theory*, Prentice-Hall, Englewood Cliffs, New Jersey, 1961.

Le Carré, John, *Tinker, Tailor, Soldier, Spy*, Pan Books, London, 1975.

Lee, J.M. et al., *The Scope of Local Initiative: A Study of Cheshire County Council 1961–1974*, Martin Robertson, London, 1974.

Lindblom, C.E., *The Policy Making Process*, Prentice-Hall, New York, 1968.

Marshall, A.H., *Financial Management in Local Government*, Allen and Unwin, London, 1974.

Meltsner, Arnold J., *Policy Analysis in the Bureaucracy*, University of California Press, London, 1976.

Merrington, Simon (ed.), *Current Issues in Corporate Planning*, INLO-GOV, University of Birmingham, Occasional Paper B1, 1974.

Mumford, E. and Pettigrew, A.M., *Implementing Strategic Decisions*, Longman, London, 1975.

OECD, *Educational Development Strategy in England and Wales*, Paris, 1975.

Perrow, Charles, *Organizational Analysis: A Sociological Analysis*, Wadsworth, Belmont, Calif., 1970.

Perry, Norman, *The Organisation of Social Science Research in the U.K.*, Occasional Papers in Survey Research, no.6, SSRC, 1975.

Pettigrew, A.M., *The Politics of Organizational Decision-Making*, Tavistock, London, 1973.

Pitt, D.C. and Smith, B.C., *Government Departments: An Organizational Perspective*, Routledge and Kegan Paul, London 1981.

Quade, E.S., *Analysis for Public Decisions*, Elsevier, New York, 1975.

Redcliffe-Maud, Lord and Wood, Bruce, *English Local Government Reformed*, Oxford University Press, London, 1974.

Richards, Max D., *Organizational Goal Structures*, West Publishing Co., St. Paul, 1978.

Richards, Peter G., *The Reformed Local Government System*, Allen and Unwin, London, 1975.

Ridley, F.F. (ed.), *Specialists and Generalists*, Allen and Unwin, London, 1968.

Ritchie, R.S., *An Institute for Research on Public Policy*, Information Canada, Ottawa, 1971.

Rivlin, Alice, *Systematic Thinking for Social Action*, Brookings, Washington, D.C., 1971.

Robertson, J.H., *Reform of British Central Government*, Chatto and Windus, London, 1971.

Rose, Richard (ed.), *Policy-making in Britain: a Reader in Government*, Free Press, New York, 1969.

People in Politics, Faber, London, 1970.

Rothschild, Lord, *Meditations of a Broomstick*, Collins, London, 1977.

Rowbottom, Ralph et al., *Social Services Departments: Developing Patterns of Work and Organization*, Heinemann, London, 1974.

Schein, Edgar H., *Process Consultation*, Addison-Wesley, Reading, Mass., 1969.

Schon, Donald, *Beyond the Stable State*, Penguin, Harmondsworth, 1971.

Self, Peter, *Administrative Theories and Politics*, Allen and Unwin, London, 1972.

Econocrats and the Policy Process: The Politics and Philosophy of Cost-Benefit Analysis, Macmillan, London, 1975.

Selznick, Philip, *Leadership in Administration*, Row, Peterson and Co., Evanston, Illinois, 1957.

Shanks, Michael, *Planning and Politics: The British Experience 1960–76*, PEP, London, 1977.

Sharpe, L.J., *Research in Local Government: The Role of the Research and Information Unit of the Greater London Council*, London School of Economics, Greater London Papers, no.10, 1965.

Simon, H.A., *Administrative Behavior*, third edition, Collier-Macmillan, New York, 1976.

Smithburg, D.W. and Thompson, V.A., *Public Administration*, Alfred A. Knopf, New York, 1950.

Skitt, John, *Practical Corporate Planning in Local Government*, Intertext, London, 1975.

Slack, Kathleen M., *Social Administration and the Citizen*, Michael Joseph, London, 1966.

Slee Smith, Paul I., *Think Tanks and Problem Solving*, Business Books, London, 1971.

Smith, Brian, *Policy Making in British Government*, Martin Robertson, London, 1976.

and Stanyer, Jeffrey, *Administering Britain*, Fontana/Collins, Glasgow, 1976.

Smith, B.L.R., *The RAND Corporation: Case Study of a Nonprofit Advisory Corporation*, Harvard University Press, Cambridge, Mass., 1966.

Smith, David L. (ed.), *Research and Intelligence in the New Local Authorities*, Centre for Environmental Studies, CES CPII, London, 1974.

Spiers, Maurice, *Techniques and Public Administration*, Fontana/Collins, Glasgow, 1975.

Stacey, Frank, *British Government 1966–1975, Years of Reform*, Oxford University Press, London, 1975.

Stanyer, Jeffrey, *Understanding Local Government*, Fontana/Collins, Glasgow, 1976.

Starbuck, William H. (ed.), *Organizational growth and development*, Penguin, Harmondsworth, 1971.

Stewart, J.D., *Management in Local Government: A Viewpoint*, Charles Knight, London, 1971.

The Responsive Local Authority, Charles Knight, London, 1974.

Thomas, Rosamund M., *The British Philosophy of Administration: A*

Comparison of British and American Ideas 1900–1939, Longman, London, 1978.

Thompson, Victor A., *Bureaucracy and Innovation*, University of Alabama Press, Alabama, 1968.

Tinbergen, Jan, *Development Planning*, Weidenfeld and Nicolson, London, 1967.

Van Loon, Richard J. and Whittington, Michael S., *The Canadian Political System*, Macmillan, Toronto, 1971.

Vickers, Sir Geoffrey, *The Art of Judgement: A Study of Policy Making*, Basic Books, New York, 1965.

Towards a Sociology of Management, Basic Books, New York, 1967.

Weiss, Carol H., *Evaluation Research*, Prentice-Hall, Englewood Cliffs, New Jersey, 1972.

(ed.), *Using Social Research in Public Policy Making*, D.C. Heath, Toronto, 1977.

Wilensky, Harold L., *Organizational Intelligence*, Basic Books, New York, 1967.

Wilson, Harold, *The Labour Government 1964–70*, Penguin, Harmondsworth, 1971.

The Governance of Britain, Weidenfeld and Nicolson, London, 1976.

Wilson, James Q., *Politicial Organizations*, Basic Books, New York, 1973.

Wistrich, E., *Local Government Reorganisation: the First Years of Camden*, London Borough of Camden, 1972.

(D) Articles

Adamson, C., 'The role of the industrial adviser', *Public Administration*, vol. 46, Summer 1968, pp.185–90.

Akinbode, I.A. and Clark, R.C., 'A framework for analyzing inter-organizational relationships', *Human Relations*, vol. 29, 1976, pp.101–14.

Aldermen, R.K. and Cross, J.A., 'Ministerial Reshuffles and the Civil Service', *British Journal of Political Science*, vol. 9, no.1, 1979, pp.41–65.

Allen, R., 'Current practice review', *Corporate Planning*, vol. 2, no.2, 1975, pp.49–50.

Apps, R., 'Tyne and Wear's Census', *BURISA*, no.21, March 1976, pp.13–14.

Archibald, K.A. 'Three views of the expert's role in policymaking', *Policy Sciences*, vol. 1, 1970, pp.73–86.

Armstrong, Sir William, 'The Fulton Report 1. The tasks of the civil service', *Public Administration*, vol. 47, Spring 1969, pp.1–11.

Baldwin, Sir Peter, 'The use of operational research and systems analysis in government decision-making', *Management Services in Government*, vol. 33, 1978, pp.5–19.

Barratt, John and Merrington, Simon, 'Cambridgeshire: an attempt to improve corporate planning without a unit', *Corporate Planning*, vol. 3, no.1, 1976, pp.2–9.

Baumgartel, H., 'Leadership style as a variable in research administration', *Administrative Science Quarterly*, vol. 2, 1957, pp.344–60.

Beloff, M., 'The think tank and foreign affairs', *Public Administration*, vol. 55, Winter 1977, pp.435–44.

Benjamin, B., 'The statistician and the manager', *Omega*, vol. 2, 1974, pp.263–7.

'Research strategies in social service departments of local authorities in Great Britain', *Journal of Social Policy*, vol. 2, January 1973, pp.13–26.

Bennett, Roger, 'The role of research in management decision making', *Management Decision*, vol. 2, 1974, pp.189–98.

Berrill, Sir Kenneth, 'The role of the Central Policy Review Staff in Whitehall', *Management Services in Government*, vol. 32, 1977, pp.121–6.

Blackburn, J.A., 'A rejoinder: Sunderland and the Elected Member', *Corporate Planning*, vol. 2, no.2, 1976, pp.12–16.

Blaydon, S., 'Corporate Planning – can the councillor take control?', *Municipal Review*, July 1974, pp.90–2.

Bloomfield, Lincoln P., 'Policy Planning Redefined: What the planners really think', *International Journal*, vol. 32, Autumn 1977, pp. 813–28.

'Planning Foreign Policy: Can It Be Done?', *Political Science Quarterly*, vol. 92, no.3, 1978, pp.369–91.

Booth, Timothy A., 'Research and Policy Making in Local Authority Social Services', *Public Administration*, vol. 57, Summer 1979, pp.173–86.

'Economics and the Poverty of Social Planning', *Public Administration*, vol.60, Summer 1982, pp.197–214.

Boyle, Sir Edward, 'Who are the policy makers? Minister or Civil Servant? 1. Minister', *Public Administration*, vol. 43, Autumn 1965, pp.251–9.

Boyle, Lord, 'Ministers and the Administrative Process', *Public Administration*, vol. 58, Spring 1980, pp.1–2.

Brody, David, 'An Experiment in the Long-Term Planning of Health Care Services', *Public Administration*, vol. 57, Summer 1979, pp. 159–71.

Brown, R.G.S., 'Organization theory and civil service reform', *Public Administration*, vol. 43, Autumn 1965, pp.313–30.

'Research and policy', *South-Western Review of Public Administration*, no.4, March 1968, pp.11–20.

Butcher, E. and Dawkins, J., 'The corporate approach in local government – an education viewpoint', *Local Government Studies*, vol. 4, no.1, 1978, pp.49–61.

Cairncross, Sir Alec, 'The work of an economic adviser', *Public Administration*, vol. 46, Spring 1968, pp.1–11.

'Economists in Government', *Lloyds Bank Review*, no.95, 1970, pp.1–18.

Camillus, J.C., 'Evaluating the benefits of formal planning systems', *Long Range Planning*, vol. 8, no.3, 1975, pp.33–40.

Caplow, T., 'Organizational Size', *Administrative Science Quarterly*, vol. 1, 1957, pp.484–505.

Carr, D., 'The GLC Research and Intelligence Unit', *Greater London Research Quarterly Bulletin*, no.1, December 1967, pp.5–7.

Cartwright, J., 'Corporate Planning in local government – Implications for the elected member', *Long Range Planning*, vol. 8, no.2, 1975, pp.46–50.

Castle, Barbara, 'Mandarin Power', *The Sunday Times*, 10 June 1973.

Caulcott, T.H., 'Developments in the organisation of government departments', *Management Services in Government*, vol.28, 1973, pp.67–72.

Challis, L., 'The role and development of the social services research group, a discussion paper', *Social Services Research Group Journal*, no.3, April 1978, pp.1–4.

'Components of a model of the utilisation of social science research: the employment of social scientists by organisations', *Papers on Social Science Utilisation*, Monograph 1, CUSSR, Loughborough University of Technology, 1972, pp.152–67.

Chapman, R.A., 'The role of central or departmental policy and planning units: Recent developments in Britain', *Public Administration* (Australia), vol. 34, June 1975, pp.144–55.

Cherns, Albert B., 'Negotiating the Contract', in *Papers on Social Science Utilisation*, Monograph 1, CUSSR, Loughborough University of Technology, 1972, pp.25–35.

Clarke, R.V.G., 'Penal policy-making and research in the Home Office' in Walker, Nigel (ed.), *Penal Policy-Making in England*, Cambridge: Institute of Criminology, University of Cambridge, 1977, pp.115–26.

Collins, C.A., 'Councillors' attitudes: some research findings', *Local Government Studies*, vol. 6, no.2, 1980, pp.35–40.

Cranston, D., 'The case for decentralization', *BURISA*, no.8, December 1973, pp.7–8.

Darlow, G.F., 'Who are the policy makers? Councillor or chief officer? II. Chief Officer', *Public Administration*, vol. 43, Autumn 1965, pp.274–81.

Davies, E.M., 'The Role of Research and Intelligence', *Local Government Studies*, vol. 6, no.2, 1980, pp.70–2.

Davies, Dr Graham, 'The central research unit of Newcastle City', *Corporate Planning*, vol. 2, no.1, 1976, pp.18–26.

Davies, Martin, 'Government and research policy' in Jones, Kathleen (ed.), *The Yearbook of Social Policy in Britain, 1975*, Routledge and Kegan Paul, London, 1976, pp.48–60.

Davies, Michael, 'Can think tank stay free of Whitehall grip?', *The Observer Review*, 16 January 1977, p.30.

Donnison, David, 'Research for policy', *Minerva*, vol. 10, no.4, 1972, pp.519–37.
'The age of innocence is past: Some ideas about urban research and planning', *Urban Studies*, vol. 12, 1975, pp.263–72.

Downs, A. 'A realistic look at the final payoffs from urban data systems', *Public Administration Review*, vol. 27, September 1967, pp.204–10.

Dror, Y., 'Policy analysts: A new professional role in government service', *Public Administration Review*, vol. 27, September 1967, pp.197–203.
'Policy analysis for local government', *Local Government Studies*, vol. 2, no.1, 1976, pp.33–46.

Dunnett, Sir James, 'The Fulton Report 2. Equipping the Civil Service for its tasks', *Public Administration*, vol. 47, Spring 1969, pp. 13–31.

Dunsire, A., 'Administrative doctrine and administrative change', *Public Administration Bulletin*, no.15, December 1973, pp.39–56.

Earwicker, J., 'Member involvement in corporate planning and management: some notes on current experiments', *Corporate Planning*, vol. 2, no.2, 1975, pp.17–20.
'The Birmingham saga', *Corporate Planning*, vol. 4, no.2, 1977, pp.1–6.

East, R.J., 'Comparison of strategic planning in large corporations and government', *Long Range Planning*, vol. 5, June 1972, pp.2–8.
'Improving government expenditure decisions through programme analysis and review', *Long Range Planning*, vol. 6, March 1973, pp.2–9.

Eddison, T., 'Beyond the structures', *Municipal Journal*, 15 November 1974, pp.1439–43.

Ezra, Sir Derek J., 'Strategy in public industrial enterprises', *Journal of General Management*, vol. 1, no.1, 1973, pp.13–15.
'Long term planning for coal', *Long Range Planning*, vol. 7, December 1974, pp.21–3.

Fowler, R.A. and Rogers, S., 'Information for corporate planning, Introduction', *BURISA*, no.27, March 1977, pp.1–2.

Fox, James, 'The brain behind the throne' in Herman, Valentine and Alt, James E. (eds), *Cabinet Studies: A Reader*, Macmillan, London, 1975, pp.277–92.

Fry, Geoffrey K., 'Policy-planning units in British central government departments', *Public Administration*, vol. 50, Summer 1972, pp. 139–55.

Galnoor, I., 'Reforms of public expenditure in Great Britain', *Canadian Public Administration*, vol. 17, Summer 1974, pp.289–320.

Garrett, John, 'Planning government action', *Management Decision*, vol.3, no.3, 1975, pp.50–3.

'Book Review', *Public Administration*, vol. 58, Spring 1980, pp. 105–6.

and Home, Norman, 'A planning system for the British Prison Department', *Long Range Planning*, vol. 5, September 1972, pp. 36–9.

Gillespie, J.M., 'R & I Debate', *BURISA*, no.10, April 1974, pp.9–10.

'A new profession?', *BURISA*, no.12, August 1974, p.8.

'Policy information: provision of information for policy making problems and suggested solutions', *BURISA*, no.14, December 1974, pp.8–12.

Gordon, M.R., 'Civil servants, politicians and parties: shortcomings in British policy process', *Comparative Politics*, vol. 4, October 1971, pp.29–58.

Greenwell, A.J., et al., 'Research and intelligence in the new county councils' in Smith, David L. (ed.), *Research and Intelligence in the New Local Authorities*, Centre for Environmental Studies, CES CP11, London, 1974, pp.17–42.

Greenwood, M., 'Corporate planning units', *Municipal Journal*, 26 April 1974, pp.498–500.

Greenwood, R. et al., 'Contingency theory and the organization of local authorities: Part 1. Differentiation and integration', *Public Administration*, vol. 53, Spring 1975, pp.1–23.

Greenwood, R. and Hinings, C.R., 'The study of local government: Towards an organizational analysis', *Public Administration Bulletin*, no.23, April 1977, pp.2–15.

Grey, A., 'Organizing for corporate planning', *Local Government Studies*, vol. 3, 1972, pp.9–23.

Grey, A. and Simon, A., 'People, Structure and Civil Service Reform', *Journal of Management Studies*, vol. 7, 1970, pp.288–309.

Hall, R.H. et al., 'Organizational Size, Complexity and Formalization', *American Sociological Review*, vol. 32, 1967, pp.903–12.

Hanning, H., 'Our first defence need is better machinery for taking the big decisions', *The Times*, 1 December 1977, p.6.

Hawkins, Kevin and Tarr, Robert J., ' Corporate Planning in Local Government – A Case Study', *Long Range Planning*, vol.13, April 1980, pp.43–51.

Haynes, R.J., 'The rejection of corporate management in Birmingham in theoretical perspective', *Local Government Studies*, vol. 4, no.2, 1978, pp.25–38.

Headey, Bruce, 'Cabinet Ministers and Senior Civil Servants: Mutual Requirements and Expectations' in Herman, V. and Alt, J.E. (eds), *Cabinet Studies: A Reader*, Macmillan, London, 1975, pp.121–39.

Heclo, H., 'The Councillor's Job', *Public Administration*, vol. 47, Summer 1969, pp.185–202.

Hellriegel, D. and Slocum, Jr., J.W., 'Organizational Climate: measures, research and contingencies', *Academy of Management Journal*, vol. 17, 1974, pp.255–80.

Henessy, Peter, 'Rebirth for "think tank" urged', *The Times*, 27 September 1977, p.4.

'Request for background papers fails', *The Times*, 22 March 1978, p.3.

Hickson, D.J. and Thomas, M.W., 'Professionalization in Britain: A preliminary measurement', *Sociology*, vol. 3, no.1, 1969, pp.37–53.

Hill, K.Q. and Coomer, J.C., 'Local politicians and their attitudes to planning', *Long Range Planning*, vol. 10, December 1977, pp. 57–61.

Hinings, C.R. et al., 'The organisation of metropolitan government: the impact of "Bains" ', *Local Government Studies*, no.9, October 1974, pp.47–54.

'Contingency theory and the organization of local authorities: Part II. Contigencies and structure', *Public Administration*, vol. 53, Summer 1975, pp.169–90.

Holtman, C., 'Information systems in local government', *Local Government Studies*, no.6, October 1973, pp.45–58.

Honey, M., 'A systematic approach to setting priorities for corporate planning', *Corporate Planning*, vol. 1, no.2, 1975, pp.13–18.

'Corporate planning and the chief executive', *Local Government Studies*, vol. 5, no.5, 1979, pp.21–34.

Hudson, K., 'R & I at INLOGOV', *BURISA*, no.16, April 1975, pp. 17–18.

Hussey, D.E., 'The role of the corporate planner' in Hussey, D.E. (ed.), *Corporate Planner's Yearbook 1974–75*, Pergamon, Oxford, 1974, pp.81–91.

James, R., 'Is there a case for local authority policy planning?', *Public Administration*, vol.51, Summer 1973, pp.147–63.

Jay, P., 'PESC, PAR and Politics', *The Times*, 31 January 1972, p.19.

'CPRS: Magic Circle or Fifth Wheel?', *The Times*, 21 January 1972, p.19.

Johnson, N., 'Who are the policy makers? Conclusions', *Public Administration*, vol. 43, Autumn 1965, pp.281–7.

'Editorial: Reforming the bureaucracy', *Public Administration*, vol. 46, Winter 1968, pp.367—74.

'Editorial: The reorganisation of central government', *Public Administration*, vol. 49, Spring 1971, pp.1—12.

'Recent administrative reform in Britain' in Leemans, A.F. (ed.), *The Management of Change in Government*, Institute of Social Studies, The Hague, 1977, pp.272—96.

'Editorial: The expenditure committee on the civil service', *Public Administration*, vol. 56, Spring 1978, pp.1—12.

Jones, G.W., 'The functions and organization of Councillors', *Public Administration*, vol. 51, Summer 1973, pp.135—46.

'The prime minister's advisers', *Political Studies*, vol. 21, no.3, 1972, pp.363—75.

'Problems of city government', *Journal of Administration Overseas*, vol. 14, no.4, 1975, pp.216—27.

Jones, Sue et al., 'Subjectivity and Organisational Politics in Policy Analysis', *Policy and Politics*, vol. 7, no.2, 1979, pp.145—63.

James, R., 'Is there a case for local authority policy planning?', *Public Administration*, vol. 51, Summer 1973, pp.147—63.

Judge, David, 'Specialists and Generalists in British Central Government: A Political Debate', *Public Administration*, vol.59, Spring 1981, pp.1—14.

Kakabadse, A.P., 'Corporate management in local government: A case study', *Journal of Management Studies*, vol. 14, no.3, 1977, pp.341—51.

Keast, H., 'Local government research', *Local Government Chronicle*, 27 August 1976, p.794.

Keith-Lucas, B., 'Who are the policy makers? Councillor or chief officer? I. Councillor', *Public Administration*, vol. 43, Autumn 1965, pp.269—74.

Kershaw, P.B., 'Management Information', *BURISA*, no.11, June 1974, pp.17—18.

'Monitoring for management', *BURISA*, no.12, August 1974, pp. 2—4.

'A Sunderland experiment', *Municipal Journal*, 30 August 1974, pp.1037—9.

'Political realities and local government', *Local Government Chronicle*, 21 February 1975, pp.182—3.

'Community analysis', *Municipal Journal*, 7 March 1975, pp.309, 310, 312.

'Community dialogue', *Municipal Journal*, 18 April 1975, pp.507, 508, 510.

'The rationale behind an achievement budget', *Telescope*, April 1975, pp.357—9.

King, R.B.M., 'The planning of the British aid programme', *Journal of Administration Overseas*, vol. 11, no.1., 1972, pp.5—10.

Kingshott, A.L., 'Planning in a Nationalized Industry', *Long Range Planning*, vol. 8, no.5, 1975, pp.58—65.

Klein, R. and Lewis, J., 'Advice and dissent in British government', *Policy and Politics*, vol. 6, no.1, 1978, pp.1—25.

Knorr, K.D., 'Policymakers' use of social science knowledge: Symbolic or instrumental?' in Weiss, Carol H. (ed.)., *Using Social Research in Public Policy Making*, D.C. Heath, Toronto, 1977, pp.165—82.

Kramer, F.A., 'Policy Analysis as ideology', *Public Administration Review*, vol. 35, September/October 1975, pp.509—17.

Kretchmer, B., 'The central unit in Lambeth', *Corporate Planning*, vol. 3, no.1, 1976, pp.27—32.

Leigh, A. and White, M., 'Information needs and planning in social services department', *Policy and Politics*, vol. 2, no.2, 1974, pp. 135—43.

Leigh, A., 'The work of social services researchers and its impact on social policy', *Social and Economic Adminstration*, vol. 11, no.2, 1975, pp.97—116.

'Researchers in the social services', *Local Government Studies*, vol. 3, no.3, 1977, pp.51—70.

'Management information bulletins and social services managers', *Local Government Studies*, vol. 6, no.1, 1980, pp.51—62.

Levine, S. and White, P.E., 'Exchange as a conceptual framework for the study of interorganizational relationships', *Administrative Science Quarterly*, vol. 5, 1961, pp.583—601.

Lister, P., 'Do councillors contribute to corporate management?', *Corporate Planning*, vol. 2, no.2, 1975, pp.1—5.

Litschert, R.J., 'The structure of long-range planning groups', *Academy of Management Journal*, vol.14, March 1971, pp.33—43.

and Nicholson, E.A., 'Formal long-range planning groups: Their evolutionary nature', *Journal of Economics and Business*, vol. 25, no.1, 1972, pp.45—52.

'Corporate long-range planning groups — some different approaches', *Long Range Planning*, vol. 7, August 1974, pp.62—6.

Lodge, T.S., 'The founding of the Home Office Research Unit' in Hood, Roger (ed.), *Crime, Criminology and Public Policy*, Heinemann, London, 1974, pp.11—24.

Lomer, M., 'The chief executive in local government 1974—1976', *Local Government Studies*, vol. 3, no.4, 1977, pp.17—40.

Lukes, J.R., 'Power and policy at the DES: A case study', *Universities Quarterly*, vol. 29, no.2, 1975, pp.133—65.

Macdonald, James and Fry, G.K., 'Policy Planning Units — Ten Years On', *Public Administration*, vol. 58, Winter 1980, pp.421—37.

Mansfield, H., 'Research and information systems in local government', *District Councils Review*, February 1976, pp.34—6.

McLoughlin, B. and Smith, D.L., 'R and I and development plans', in Smith, David L. (ed.), *Research and Intelligence in the New Local Authorities*, Centre for Environmental Studies, CES CP11, London, 1974, pp.47–70.

Meltsner, Arnold J., 'Don't Slight Communication: Some Problems of Analytical Practice', *Policy Analysis*, vol. 5, no.3, 1979, pp. 367–92.

Midwinter, A.F., 'The implementation of the Paterson Report in local government, 1975–77', *Local Government Studies*, vol. 4, no.1, 1978a, pp.23–38.

'Policy planning units in Scottish local government', *Public Administration Bulletin*, no.28, December 1978b, pp.73–90.

Mills, C.E., 'Corporate planning in the British Gas Corporation', *Public Administration*, vol. 52, Spring 1974, pp.27–40.

Mitchell, J.E., 'Special Advisers: A personal view', *Public Administration*, vol. 56, Spring 1978, pp.87–97.

Moriarty, M.J., 'The policy-making process: How it is seen from the Home Office' in Walker, Nigel (ed.), *Penal Policy-Making in England*, University of Cambridge, Cambridge, 1977, pp.129–45.

Moser, Sir Claus, 'Staffing in the Government Statistical Services', *Journal of the Royal Statistical Society*, Series A, vol. 136, 1976, pp.75–88.

Nelson, E.G. and Longbottom, D.A., 'Planning for Effectiveness in the Social Services – An Appraisal of the Corporate Approach', *Local Government Studies*, vol. 4, no.4, 1978, pp.39–52.

Neve, B., 'Bureaucracy and politics in local government: the role of local authority education officers', *Public Administration*, vol. 55, Autumn 1977, pp.291–303.

Nicholson-Lord, D., 'The think tank finally passes the fitness test', *The Times*, 8 March 1978, p.16.

Paine, R.E., 'Corporate planning for a town – a case history', *Long Range Planning*, vol. 8, October 1975, pp.39–54.

Painter, Martin J., 'Policy Co-ordination in the Department of the Environment, 1970–1976', *Public Administration*, vol. 58, Summer 1980, pp.135–54.

Patton, M.Q. et al., 'In search of impact: An analysis of the utilization of federal health evaluation research' in Weiss, Carol H. (ed.), *Using Social Research in Public Policy Making*, D.C. Heath, Toronto, 1977, pp.141–63.

Pennings, J., 'Measures of organizational structure: a methodological note', *American Journal of Sociology*, vol. 79, 1973, pp.686–704.

Peretz, D., 'R & D and corporate planning in government', *Long Range Planning*, vol. 5, December 1972, pp.67–9.

Perrow, C., 'The analysis of goals in complex organizations', *American Sociological Review*, vol. 26, 1961, pp.854–66.

'A Framework for the comparative analysis of organizations', *Ameri-*

can *Sociological Review*, vol. 32, 1967, pp.194–208.

Pettigrew, A.M., 'Towards a political theory of organizational intervention', *Human Relations*, vol. 28, no.3, 1975, pp.191–208.

Pile, Sir William, 'Corporate planning for education in the DES', *Public Administration*, vol. 52, Spring 1974, pp.13–25.

Pinkham, R., 'Effective social research for local government', *Greater London Intelligence Quarterly*, no.36, September 1976, pp.22–6.

Pite, J.C., 'The deployment of staff in the Government Statistical Service', *Statistical News*, vol. 30, 1975, pp.12–16.

Playfair, Sir Edward, 'Who are the policy makers? Minister or civil servant? II. Civil Servant', *Public Administration*, vol. 43, Autumn 1965, pp.260–8.

Pleasance, E.J. and Saldanha, F.G.J., 'The Work Research Unit of the Department of Employment', *Management Services in Government*, vol. 34, no.2, 1979, pp.103–9.

Plowden, W.J.L., 'The role and limits of a central policy staff in government: A note on the Central Policy Review Staff', *Public Administration Bulletin*, no.6, June 1974, pp.22–6.

'Developing a joint approach to social policy' in Jones, Kathleen (ed.), *The Year Book of Social Policy in Britain 1976*, Routledge and Kegan Paul, London, 1977, pp.35–43.

Pollitt, C., 'The Central Policy Review Staff, 1970–1974', *Public Administration*, vol. 52, Winter 1974, pp.375–92.

'Rationalizing the Machinery of Government: The Conservatives, 1970–1974', *Political Studies*, vol. 28, no.1, 1980, pp.84–98.

Prince, Michael J., 'Policy advisory groups in government departments' in Doern, G. Bruce and Aucoin, Peter (eds), *Public Policy in Canada: Organization, Process and Management*, Macmillan, Toronto, 1979, pp.275–300.

and Chenier, John A., 'The rise and fall of policy planning and research units: an organizational perspective', *Canadian Public Administration*, vol. 23, no.4, 1980, pp.519–41.

Ranson, S., 'Notes on a conference – education and corporate management', *Local Government Studies*, vol. 4, no.2, 1978, pp.81–5.

Rayner, B., 'The DHSS research arrangements', *SSRC Newsletter*, no.35, 1977, pp.4–6.

Razzell, E.J., 'Planning in Whitehall – Is it Possible – Will it Survive?', *Long Range Planning*, vol.13, February 1980, pp.34–41.

Regan, D.E., 'The expert and the administrator: recent changes at the Ministry of Transport', *Public Administration*, vol. 44, Summer 1966, pp.149–67.

Rothschild, Lord, 'Power of civil servants', *The Times*, 21 February 1977, p.6.

'Thinking about the Think Tank', *The Listener*, London, 28 December 1972.

Rugman, C.A., 'Corporate planning in local government', *Long Range Planning*, vol. 6, September 1973, pp.17–21.

Russell, C.A.F., 'Organisation of research and intelligence in the Greater London Council', *Local Government Studies*, no.2, 1972, pp.3–12.

Sedgwick, A., 'Keeping it simple: A case study in corporate planning', *Long Range Planning*, vol. 11, February 1978, pp.10–14.

Self, P., 'The Herbert Report and the values of local government', *Political Studies*, vol. 10, no.2, 1961, pp.146–62.
'Is comprehensive planning possible and rational?', *Policy and Politics*, vol. 2, no.3, 1974, pp.193–203.

Shagory, G.E., 'Development of corporate planning staff', *Long Range Planning*, vol. 8, February 1975, pp.70–4.

Sharpe, L.J., 'The social scientist and policy-making: Some cautionary thoughts and transatlantic reflections' in Weiss, Carol H. (ed.), *Using Social Research in Public Policy Making*, D.C. Heath, Toronto, 1977, pp.37–53.
'Government as Clients for Social Science Research' in Bulmer, Martin (ed.), *Social Policy Research*, Macmillan, London, 1978, pp.67–82.

Siddall, J., 'The elected member and corporate planning in Sunderland', *Corporate Planning*, vol. 2, no.2, 1975, pp.6–11.

Skelcher, Chris, 'From Programme Budgeting to Policy Analysis: Corporate Approaches in Local Government', *Public Administration*, vol. 58, Summer 1980, pp.155–72.

Smith, B.C. and Stanyer, J., 'Administrative Developments in 1967: A Survey', *Public Administration*, vol. 46, Autumn 1968, pp.239–79.
'Administrative Developments in 1968: A survey', *Public Administration*, vol. 47, Autumn 1969, pp.329–66.
'Administrative Developments in 1969: A survey', *Public Administration*, vol. 48, Autumn 1970, pp.317–49.
'Administrative Developments in 1970: A survey', *Public Administration*, vol. 49, Winter 1971, pp.403–38.
'Administrative Developments in 1971 and 1972: A Survey', *Public Administration*, vol. 51, Winter 1973, pp.361–410.

Smith, D.L., 'Monitoring and R & I', *BURISA*, no.5, June 1973, p.15.
'R & I at INLOGOV', *BURISA*, no.7, October 1973, pp.5–6.
'Research: further views', *BURISA*, no.8, December 1973, p.6.
'Research and intelligence in the new local authorities', *Local Government Studies*, vol. 7, February 1974, pp.13–25.

Smith, G., 'Some research implications of the Seebohm Report', *British Journal of Sociology*, vol. 22, 1971, pp.295–310.

Smith, T.B., 'Policy Roles: An analysis of policy formulators and policy implementors', *Policy Sciences*, vol. 4, 1973, pp.297–309.

Stanhope, H., 'Defence: adjusting the machinery', *The Times*, 9 April

1978, p.6.

Steel, David R. and Stanyer, J., 'Administrative developments in 1973 and 1974: A survey', *Public Administration*, vol. 53, Autumn 1975, pp.241—86.

'Administrative developments in 1975 and 1976: A survey', *Public Administration*, vol. 55, Winter 1977, pp.385—433.

'Administrative Developments in 1977 and 1978: A survey', *Public Administration,* vol. 57, Winter 1979, pp.407—56.

Stewart, J.D., 'Developments in corporate planning in British local government — the Bains Report and corporate planning', *Local Government Studies*, no.5, June 1973, pp.13—29.

'R and I in the management structure' in Smith, David L. (ed.), *Research and Intelligence in the New Local Authorities*, Centre for Environmental Studies, CES CP11, London, 1974, pp.9—15.

'Policy planning in the new authorities', *Local Government Chronicle*, June 1971, pp.968—9.

Stockfisch, J.A., 'The genesis of systems analysis within the bureaucracy' in Kelleher, Grace J. (ed.), *The Challenge to Systems Analysis*, Wiley, London, 1970, pp.7—20.

Taylor, W.J., 'The member and corporate management', *Local Government Chronicle*, 2 August 1974, pp.761—3.

Terrien, F.W. and Mills, D.L., 'The effect of changing size upon the internal structure of organizations', *American Sociological Review*, vol. 20, 1955, pp.11—14.

The Times, 'Inquiry into role of statistician in policy', 31 May 1977, p.2.

Thompson, James D. and McEwen, W.J., 'Organizational goals and environment: Goal setting as an interaction process', *American Sociological Review*, vol. 22, 1958, pp.22—31.

Tinker, Anthea and Brian, Marion, 'The Dissemination of Research Findings with Particular Reference to Housing', *Journal of Social Policy*, vol. 8, no.1, 1979, pp.61—82.

Train, C.J., 'The development of criminal policy planning in the Home Office', *Public Administration*, vol. 55, Winter 1977, pp.373—84.

Turner, D.W., 'Strategic Planning in the British Airports Authority', *Journal of General Management*, vol. 3, no.3, 1976, pp.12—22.

Vickers, Sir Geoffrey, 'Planning and policy-making', *The Political Quarterly*, vol. 38, no.3, 1967, pp.253—65.

'Policy making in local government', *Local Government Studies*, no.7, February 1974, pp.5—11.

Watson, M., 'A comparative evaluation of planning practice in the liberal democratic state' in Hayward, J. and Watson, M. (eds), *Planning, Politics and Public Policy*, Cambridge University Press, London, 1975, pp.445—83.

Watts, D.C., 'Commentary, the diplomatic service', *The Political Quar-*

terly, vol. 48, no.4, 1977, pp.389—93.

Webb, A. and Falk, N., 'Planning the social services: the local authority ten year plans', *Policy and Politics*, vol. 3, no.2, 1975, pp. 35—54.

Webber, M.M., 'The roles of intelligence systems in urban systems planning', *The Journal of the American Institute of Planners*, vol. 31, November 1965, pp.289—96.

Wedgwood-Oppenheim, A., 'A look at research staff in local authority social services departments', *Clearing House for Local Authority Social Services Research*, no.2, April 1974, pp.95—107.

Weiss, Carol H., 'Research for Policy's Sake: The Enlightenment Function of Social Research', *Policy Analysis*, vol. 3, no.4, 1977, pp. 531—45.

Weiss, Carol H. and Bucuvalas, M.J., 'The challenge of social research to decision making' in Weiss, Carol H. (ed.), *Using Social Research in Public Policy Making*, D.C. Heath, Toronto, 1977, pp.213—33.

Wheatcroft, S.F., 'Integrating British Airways', *Journal of General Management*, vol. 1, no.2, 1974, pp.23—6.

Wildavsky, A., 'The political economy of efficiency', *Public Administration Review*, vol. 26, December 1966, pp.292—310.

'Does planning work?', *The Public Interest*, vol. 24, 1971, pp. 95—104.

'If planning is everything, maybe it's nothing', *Policy Sciences*, vol. 4, 1973, pp.127—53.

Wilding, R.W.L., 'The post-Fulton programme: strategy and tactics', *Public Administration*, vol. 48, Winter 1970, pp.391—403.

Wilson, The Right Hon. Harold, 'Statistics and decision-making in government — Bradshaw revisited', *Journal of the Royal Society*, vol. 136, Part 1, 1973, pp.1—16.

Wotton, Barbara, 'Uses of sociology', *New Society*, vol. 43, 9 March 1978, pp.553—4.

(E) Duplicated and manuscript material

Al-Bazzaz, S.J.M., 'Contextual Variables and Corporate Planning in 48 U.K. Companies', PhD thesis, City University Business School, London, 1977.

Avon County Council, 'Research and Evaluation: Future Pattern of Work', 1977.

Benjamin, B., 'The G.L.C. Research and Intelligence Unit 1966—70 — History', unpublished paper, no date.

Bentley, Ray, 'Housing Strategic Appraisal — Which Method?', paper given at the R & I Conference, sponsored by INLOGOV, 3—4 April

1978, York University.

Bolan, John, 'The Central Research Unit: Its Structure, Skills and Disciplines', draft, West Glamorgan County Council, 1978.

Brennan, N.J., 'Variations in the Utilization of Evaluation Research in Federal Decision-Making', PhD thesis, University of Minnesota, 1976.

Central Research Unit, City of Newcastle upon Tyne, 'Multiple Deprivation Indicators for Local Authority Policy Evaluation', 1976.

Department of the Envrionment, 'The Systems Analysis Research Unit', 1978.

Fox, R., 'In Retrospect — A Review of Some of the Work Carried Out in the Research and Intelligence Unit', paper given at seminar for Heads of Research and Intelligence, INLOGOV, University of Birmingham, 24 October 1977.

Gallant, V., 'Study of the Industrial Structure of Mid Glamorgan', Intelligence, Research and Development Unit, Mid Glamorgan County Council, March 1978.

Gillespie, J.M., 'The Research and Intelligence Unit in Cheshire Post April 1974', note, September 1972.
'Communications For Research and Intelligence — Inside and Outside the Authority', paper presented to seminar of Heads of Research and Intelligence, INLOGOV, University of Birmingham, 24 October 1977.
'Whither Local Government Research and Intelligence', paper given at the R & I Conference, sponsored by INLOGOV, York University, 3–4 April 1978.

Haydon, H.R., Clerk to the Steering Committee, Plymouth Steering Committee, *Local Government Reorganisation, Proposals for the Management of the Plymouth District*, Report C.4, 1974.

Hollingsworth, M., 'The Role of Central Research and Intelligence Units in the Corporate Structure of a County Authority', West Glamorgan County Council, Central Research Unit, 1974.

Hyde, S. and Davey, S. *'Project Review' (OR Whatever Happened to the Work You Did Last Summer?)*, An Account of a Service Performance Evaluation Project Undertaken in the R & I Unit, Cleveland County Research and Intelligence Unit, June 1978.

Institute of Local Government Studies, 'Research and Intelligence in Local Government', seminar proceedings, University of Birmingham, 25 September 1973.

McKinsey and Co., Inc., *A New Planning System for Greenwich*, London Borough of Greenwich, May 1970.

Plowden, W.J.L., 'The Central Policy Review Staff: The First Two Years', paper delivered to Political Studies Association Conference, March 1973.
'The Think Tank: Advising the Cabinet', talk given at the University

of Exeter, Department of Politics, 25 January 1977.

Razzell, E.J., 'Planning Units in Central Government', paper given at INLOGOV, University of Birmingham, 1976.

'Improving Policy Analysis – the DHSS Approach', paper presented at the PAC Conference, York University, 1978.

Society for Long Range Planning, 'Long Range Planning Purpose and Membership', no date.

Taylor, Paul A., 'The Role of Research and Intelligence Units in English Local Authorities', final year project, Enfield College, Middlesex Polytechnic, BA Business Studies, 1975/76.

Walkland, S.A., 'The Committee Structure of the House of Commons and the Relevance of Small Group Theory', June 1970.

Walters, T.V., 'The Work of the Intelligence, Research and Development Unit', paper presented to the Society of Local Authority Chief Executives – Wales Branch, 1975.

Webster, B.A., 'Research and Intelligence Units: Kent County Council', unpublished research project, INLOGOV, 1972.

'Chesire County Council Research and Intelligence Unit', unpublished paper, INLOGOV, 1972.

'Research and Intelligence Units, Sheffield', unpublished paper, INLOGOV, 1972.

West Glamorgan County Council, Clerk's Department, Central Research Unit, 'Some Thoughts on Programming Research', April 1975.

Wilkes, Ken W., 'Planning Units in Whitehall', July 1973.

Wright, Maurice, 'Public Expenditure, Inflation and PESC', paper given at PAC Conference, York University, 5–7 September 1977.

Index

committee 30

Quade, E.S. 131
quantitative analysis 52
Quarterly Bulletin (of the
    GLC) 4
'quickies' 150, 152–3

R & I Steering Group 85–6
Razzell, E.J. 55, 73
Redcliffe-Maud Report
    (Royal Commission on
    Local Government in
    England) 23–4, 34, 39
reform, administrative 5–6,
    22, 29–31, 38–40
Register of Research Projects
    in Research and Intelligence
    Units 84
*Reorganisation of Central
    Government, The* 48, 100
Report of a working party on
    *New Scottish Local authori-
    ties: Organisation and Man-
    agement Structures* (Pater-
    son) 123
*Report of the Committee on
    the Civil Service, see* Fulton
    Report
Report on the Control of
    Public Expenditure (Plow-
    den) 23, 39
Report on the Organisation of
    the Civil Service (Trend) 23
reports, government 3–4
research 10, 12, 14, 25–6,
    28–9
Research and Intelligence
    Group 84–5
'Research and Intelligence in
    the New County Councils'
    47
research and intelligence units,
    Bains Report on 47
DOE, of 7

formation of 3
functions of 5, 77
influenced by reports 53
modish to create 37
nomenclature of 14
objectives of 7, 55
organization of 7
origins of 7
recommended by Society
    of County Clerks 47
social services, for 26
tasks of 47
see also units, policy
    planning and research
Resource and Planning Re-
    search Group 71
Richards, Peter G. 39
Robertson, J.H. 40
Rogers, Steve 199
Rothschild, Lord 56, 76, 103,
    134, 153, 172
Rothschild Report (*Frame-
    work for Government Re-
    search and Development*)
    150
Royal Commission on Local
    Government in England
    (Redcliffe-Maud Report)
    23–4, 34, 39
Royal Commission on Local
    Government in Greater
    London (Herbert Commis-
    sion) 24–5
royal commission 16, 34

SARU (Systems Analysis Re-
    search Unit) 32, 52–3,
    117–18, 146, 154, *see also*
    DOE
SOLACE (Society of Local
    Authority Chief Executives)
    85–6
SSRG (Social Services Research
    Group) 84
Seebohm Committee, (Com-

241

more important than
   growth 104
politics of 2
prerequisites for 200—1
price of 195, 197
priority given to 62—4
relation of size to 104
resources devoted to 138
strategies for 63—4
threats to 63, 200
valuable service essential to
   63, *see also* marketing
Swedish Civil Service 92
systems analysis 128
Systems Analysis Research
   Unit (SARU) 32, 52—3,
   117—18, 146, 154 *see also*
   DOE

'Think Tank', *see* CPRS
transport 30, 33, 127
Treasury, H.M.
   Ball Committee on 152
   co-ordination of units by
      177
   economists in 70
   interdepartmental com-
      mittee membership of
      118
   Plowden Committee and 39
   Policy Analysis Division of
      33, 52, 144
Trend Report (Organisation of
   Civil Science) 23
Tyne & Wear 105, 120, 138,

under secretary 92, 94,
   117—18
United States of America 15,
   73, 188
units, policy planning and research,
      abolition of 137—8
      acceptance of 194
      advantage to councillors

aims of 2, 7
area health authorities,
   in 7
arguments for 40
assessing the work of 3
budgets and 185—6
characteristics of 15—16
choosing topics for 150—6
client expectations of
   132—8
continuity of 16, 189
contributions of 189
co-ordination by 27—8,
   94—5, 183—4
co-ordination of 106
corporate department
   policy 17
corporate management,
   for 24
corporate planning, *see*
   corporate planning
   cost of 2, 200
'created to promote
   accountability' 28
creation of 6
day to day operations
   and 26
defence mechanism for
   government, as 39
definition of 15—16
departmental policy 17
departmental status of
   120
development of 201
evolution of 194
expectations of 56
formalizations of 23
formation of 3, 24, 38—9
Fulton recommendations,,
   see Fulton Report functions of 3, 6, 71, 194
future for 198—201
'goal abridgement' by
   63—4, 194
goals of 45—68 *passim*, 193